The East India Company, 1600–1857

This book employs a wide range of perspectives to demonstrate how the East India Company facilitated cross-cultural interactions between the English and various groups in South Asia between 1600 and 1857 and how these interactions transformed important features of both British and South Asian history. Rather than viewing the company as an organization projecting its authority from London to India, the volume shows how the company's history and its broader historical significance can best be understood by appreciating the myriad ways in which these interactions shaped the company's story and altered the course of history. Bringing together the latest research and several case studies, the work includes examinations of the formulation of economic theory, the development of corporate strategy, the mechanics of state finance, the mapping of maritime jurisdiction, the government and practice of religions, domesticity, travel, diplomacy, state formation, art, gift-giving, incarceration and rebellion. Together, the essays will advance the understanding of the peculiarly corporate features of cross-cultural engagement during a crucial early phase of globalization.

Insightful and lucid, this volume will be useful to scholars and researchers of modern history, South Asian studies, economic history and political studies.

William A. Pettigrew is Reader, School of History at the University of Kent, UK. He was Junior Research Fellow and Tutor in History at Corpus Christi College, Oxford (2007–9). He has authored multiple peer-reviewed articles and a monograph entitled *Freedom's Debt: The Royal African Company and the Politics of the Atlantic Slave Trade, 1672–1752* (2013).

Mahesh Gopalan is Assistant Professor, Department of History at St. Stephen's College, University of Delhi, New Delhi, India. He has published articles in edited volumes on the history of the Indian Ocean and on the Jesuit Missions. He was recipient of the Charles Wallace Research Grant in 2014 and is currently working on a monograph.

The East India Company, 1600–1857

Essays on Anglo-Indian connection

**Edited by
William A. Pettigrew
and Mahesh Gopalan**

Routledge
Taylor & Francis Group
LONDON AND NEW YORK

First South Asia edition 2017

First published 2017
by Routledge
2 Park Square, Milton Park, Abingdon, Oxon OX14 4RN

and by Routledge
711 Third Avenue, New York, NY 10017

Routledge is an imprint of the Taylor & Francis Group, an informa business

British Library Cataloguing in Publication Data
A catalogue record for this book is available from the British Library

Library of Congress Cataloging-in-Publication Data
A catalog record has been requested for this book

ISBN: 978-1-138-21965-6 (hbk)
ISBN: 978-1-315-56346-6 (ebk)

Typeset in Galliard
by Apex CoVantage, LLC

Digitally Printed at Replika Press Pvt. Ltd.

For sale in India, Pakistan, Nepal, Bhutan, Bangladesh and Sri Lanka only.

In memory of
Lieutenant Colonel Dr Bawa Harkishan Singh,
M.C., I.M.S., 1889–1981,
and
Augustus Napoleon Paul and Pamela Paul

Contents

Acknowledgements

This book emerged out of a one-day symposium at the Nehru Memorial Library in New Delhi in January 2015. We are grateful to Dr Mahesh Rangarajan, then director of the Nehru Memorial Museum & Library, and Ms Priyamvada, for their help in organising this event. We thank the Leverhulme Trust for funding this gathering. We also thank those who assisted us in the lead-up to this symposium and our collaboration: especially Mrs Deeksha Bedi, Ms Neha Kohli, Mrs Rita Menon, Mrs Reeta Singh, Mr Sri Krishan Sethi, Mr Bawa Gurmukh Singh, Ms Preeti Gulati, Mr Chandraneev Das and Mr Tathagatha Dutta. We also thank our families for supporting us during periods of absence from home and thank Dr Liam D. Haydon for invaluable editorial support. This book is dedicated to the memory of Lt. Col. Dr Bawa Harkishan Singh, William's wife's great grandfather, who understood so much about Anglo-Indian connection and to Mahesh's grandparents, Augustus Napoleon Paul and Pamela Paul, who lived the Anglo-Indian connection through the transition from British India to independent India.

Abbreviations

BL:	The British Library, London
CSPC:	Calendar of State Papers: Colonial Series
EIC:	East India Company
IOR:	Asian and African Collections (formerly Oriental & India Office Collections), The British Library
NAI:	National Archives of India, New Delhi
TNA:	The National Archives, Kew

Contributors

Aske Laursen Brock is a PhD student at the University of Kent, UK. He researches on the relationship between global commerce and the emergence of the company director.

Sabyasachi Dasgupta is Assistant Professor, Department of History at Visva Bharati University, Santiniketan, West Bengal, India. He specialises in military history in eighteenth- and nineteenth-century colonial India.

Liam D. Haydon is Research Assistant at the University of Kent, UK. His work focuses on the cultural changes brought about by seventeenth-century corporate activity.

Jeena Sarah Jacob is a PhD candidate at the Centre for Historical Studies, Jawaharlal Nehru University, New Delhi, India. Her research looks at processes of state formation in early modern Malabar.

Ruchika Sharma is Assistant Professor, Department of History at Sri Venkateswara College, University of Delhi, India. Her research focuses on the social history of early colonial Bengal.

Rachna Singh is Assistant Professor, Department of History, Hindu College, University of Delhi, India. Her research focuses on carceral regimes and the practices of punishment in colonial South Asia.

Haig Smith is a PhD student at the University of Kent, UK. His work examines the trading corporation as a vehicle for religious governance.

Tristan Stein is Research Associate at the University of Kent, UK. He has published in the *Historical Journal* and the *Journal of British Studies.*

David Veevers completed his PhD at the University of Kent, UK, and has published several works on imperial expansion and the early modern colonial state.

Michael Wagner holds an MBA from Concordia University and a doctorate in History from the University of Oxford, UK. His publications include articles on the Russia, Hudson's Bay and Levant companies.

Introduction

The different East India Companies and the variety of cross-cultural interactions in the corporate setting

William A. Pettigrew and Mahesh Gopalan

The English East India Company remains perhaps the most famous corporation in world history. The company's reach, profits, power and durability make it a stalwart of histories of global trade and empire. Belonging as much to Asian history as to British, in its 257-year history, the East India Company integrated the British and South Asian economies; transformed the financial resources of the British state; altered English fashion, cuisine and economic theory; and transferred massive wealth from Asian to British hands. The company – along with other European competitors – also supplied huge quantities of bullion that helped underpin the workings of the Mughal economy and government throughout the seventeenth and early eighteenth centuries. It also established some of modern India's largest cities: Madras (Chennai), Bombay (Mumbai) and Calcutta (Kolkata). Today, the company has been held up as the best cautionary fable from history about the possibilities of corporate omnipotence in the twenty-first century (Dalrymple, 2015). The East India Company was certainly extractive, but, as the chapters in this book make clear, it also brought India and Britain into close connection prior to the development of the British Empire in Asia in ways that empowered both British and Indian interests: from channelling indigenous finance capital, tincturing debates on sovereignty and shaping processes of state formation and the realms of social and cultural life.

Despite the company's impressive longevity, appreciating the very different incarnations of the East India Company that operated over time, for contrasting purposes and with differing personnel, provides the best way to capture the company's historical significance and meaning. A band of Elizabethan merchants determined to repeat the successes of Portuguese and Dutch spice traders but wisely keen to share the risks of such adventure; a plenipotentiary Stuart 'company state' that managed overseas fiefdoms in Madras, Bombay and Calcutta with a constitutional agility impossible at home; a grand remittance structure for individual 'nabob' fortunes that then came to transform the appearance of Georgian Britain; a transferor of Bengali fiscal revenues to the private and British state's hands; a holding vessel for a vast ethnically diverse Victorian army, the East India Company cut a very different figure to its British stakeholders across its long history.

The company, however, was mostly shaped in response to the rapidly changing South Asian context in which it operated. The seventeenth century represents a period of transformation in the South Asian polity, society and economy. It was marked by the expansion of the Mughal Empire into the peninsula; the rise of the Marathas, the sultanates of Golconda and Bijapur; the growing monetization of the economy and overseas trade and changing patterns of agrarian production (Habib, 1969; Habib and Raychaudhuri, 1982; Gordon, 1992; Habib, 1999; Narayana Rao, Shulman and Subrahmanyam, 2002). The expansion of the Mughal Empire integrated the various distinct regional economic markets and offered a new impetus to trade from port cities like Surat, Masulipatnam and Balasore (Furber, 1976; Dasgupta, 1979, Arasaratanam, 1994; Prakash, 1998; Dasgupta and Pearson, 1999; Pearson, 2005; Subrahmanyam, 2005). This expansion occurred alongside the growing cultivation of cash crops like indigo, opium and cotton. The growing monetization of revenue collection helped increase specie flows around the Mughal economy (Habib and Raychaudhuri, 1982; Habib, 1999).

It was against this backdrop that the English East India Company established its commercial and political operations. The English Company also transformed alongside South Asia's changing socio-political and economic landscape, and by the eighteenth century the company's espoused commercial interests had assumed a distinct political character (Chaudhuri, 1978; Canny, 1998; Marshall, 1998; Armitage, 2004; Stern, 2011). In the early seventeenth century, the company struggled to emerge from out of the shadows of the Dutch East India Company. Having shifted focus from the Indonesian spice islands to the Indian subcontinent and its trading hinterlands in the early decades of the seventeenth century, the company gradually negotiated its way through the pitfalls of seventeenth-century South Asian politics to establish two company ports at Madras and Bombay. It was from these two bases that the English Company negotiated with the Mughal state and its officials in the late seventeenth and early eighteenth centuries. The access that the English Company now had to the Arabian Sea and the Bay of Bengal enabled it to gradually insert itself into elaborate financial and production networks.

The emergence of Calcutta in the eighteenth century as the third English port city offered the company an ideal base from which it could engage with the Mughal Empire. Thus by the eighteenth century, the company moved beyond Gujarat, Bengal and the southern Coromandel to engage with the agrarian producers in central and northern South Asia. The company could thus extend its economic reach beyond the coast and into smaller markets and into the agrarian markets of the subcontinent (Arasaratanam, 1994; Prakash, 1998; Pearson, 2005). This extension allowed the English to expand their commercial basket and move beyond spices and cloth to include commodities like jute and opium. The changing patterns of trade along with the productivity improvements in the English economy transformed Madras, Bombay and Calcutta into new nodal points that connected the expanding English colonial enterprise across South Asia and the Indian Ocean (Chaudhuri, 1978; Marshall, 1998; Chaudhury and Morineau, 1999). Thus, by the end of the eighteenth century, the company presided over growing urban populations supported by English factories, which became footholds for a more complex imperial agenda that inspired the company's vision for the nineteenth century.

The company used the port cities of Madras, Bombay and Calcutta to establish and test various administrative, judicial and other regulatory institutions. The establishment of these institutions alongside the rapidly changing political landscape in South Asia helped build the company's political confidence (Chaudhuri, 1978; Marshall, 1998; Mines, 2001; Brimnes, 2003; Stern, 2011). It was from the centres at Madras, Bombay and Calcutta that the company administrators secured the *Diwani* of Bengal; intervened in the politics of Arcot, Mysore and Hyderabad and enforced the Royatwari System and the Permanent Settlement (Arasaratnam, 1979; Bayly, 1983, Bayly and Subrahmanyam, 1988). These interventions in eighteenth-century South Asian politics enabled the company to imagine itself anew. They encouraged the company to play a more aggressive political role, enabling the establishment of a colonial state apparatus (Bayly, 1987; Benton, 2000; Wilson, 2004). These developments were symbolized by the Regulating Act of 1773 and the St. Helena Act of 1833 that established the office of the governor general of Bengal and governor general of India, respectively.

The engagements of the English East India Company in South Asia also went beyond politics and trade. The company's growing economic and political participation in South Asia was accompanied by an engagement of company employees with local communities. This engagement opened new forms of exchange between England and South Asia, resulting in a two-way dissemination of knowledge, ideas, institutions, social practices, languages, religion and dietary practices (Teltscher, 1995; Bayly, 1996; Brimnes, 1999; Brown and Frykenberg, 2002; Viswanathan, 2002; Fisher, 2004; Wilson, 2004; Mukund, 2005; Oddie, 2006). This was a continuation of an engagement between Europe and South Asia initiated in the fifteenth and sixteenth centuries by the Iberian powers (Rubies, 2000; Zupanov, 2005; Xavier and Zupanov, 2015). In the seventeenth century, the English publicly distanced themselves from being associated with the

Portuguese. But they carefully examined the experiences of the Portuguese and the Dutch East India Company while responding to various situations that confronted them. This knowledge of past European experiences was crucial when English Company representatives embarked on an exercise to understand the local communities they interacted with. This helped generate a corpus of knowledge about South Asia – its various regions, religious and cultural traditions, economic resources and polity. The predominant Eurocentric tenor of such engagements enabled the company state to develop an elaborate imperialist view of the people, polity and culture of South Asia (Bayly, 1983, 1987, 1989, 1996; Edney, 1997).

The changing nature of trade and the growing English commercial participation in the seventeenth century enabled individuals and their families associated with the company to establish new residential establishments in places where the company operated. By the eighteenth century the British diaspora and Anglo-Indian communities in South Asia further enriched the texture of the company's socio-cultural and political engagement. Such engagements introduced a new dimension to these cross-cultural interactions, opening non-official and informal channels of exchange between England and South Asia. The Indo-European households that emerged as a result of this socio-cultural exchange represented the mixed and romanticized image of South Asian princely culture and its English counterpart. This exchange gave birth to a generation of 'English nabobs' and 'Indian memsahibs' (Caplan, 1995; Joseph, 2004; Robb, 2011).

The growing socio-cultural and political engagement and the rapidly changing economic landscape prompted the company to legitimize its presence through the establishment of civil courts and administrative and military institutions. These institutions enabled the company to operate using a new sense of hierarchies based on race, economic status and religious affiliations. The enforcement of new forms of rank, authority and privilege based on the company's understanding of local practices informed through its local agents played an important role in the establishment of the colonial state (Bayly, 1983, 1987, 1996; Brimnes, 1999, 2003; Benton, 2000; Raman, 2012). These interactions also played a crucial role in shaping a growing Anglican Protestant engagement with both European and local communities across South Asia. They enabled the Protestant Anglican Church to review its engagement with the local society and with the company. The church increasingly came to operate at two levels: the first, as an official part of the colonial state, and the second, working alongside various other missionary organizations engaged in the propagation of Christianity including the Jesuits. It was against this backdrop that the church facilitated the establishment of missionary schools and the formulation of a distinct missionary discourse arguing in favour of Western civilizational superiority (Neill, 1985; Teltscher, 1995; Brown and Frykenberg, 2002; Etherington, 2005; Oddie, 2006).

The early colonial state in India had by the mid-eighteenth century altered the nature of English engagement in South Asia. The company was no longer just managing a commercial network; it had also become a colonial military state in South Asia. This meant that the company could now expand its economic and political control through sustained military campaigns across South Asia. The early colonial state also presided over a phase of socio-economic transformation, associated with the growth of the capitalist enterprise, industrialization, the emergence of a working class and the South Asian bourgeoisie.

Throughout its South Asian history, then, the East India Company was a contested and fluid process of integration between the two cultures – British (English prior to 1707) and Indian (which we take to mean all of the cultures of the Indian subcontinent). The company's changing aims helped British and Indian interests to interact in sometimes mutually beneficial processes that spanned politics, economic theory and cultural exchange. Mindful of the multifaceted history of the company, the chapters in this volume offer an insight into the diverse interactions that emerged from the English East India Company's operation in South Asia across three centuries. They offer an insight into the interconnected worlds of the corporation, individuals, families, communities and institutions in gradually transforming cultural, intellectual, political and commercial landscapes.

I

Early historians of the company – some of them writing during the company's existence – divided the company's history into stages that characterized its development (much like the development of the British Empire) as the mutation of an innocent commercial entity into a responsible, patrician and political one around the time of the Battle of Plassey in 1757 (Foster, 1899). These narratives legitimized the British Raj. With the break-up of the British Empire in India around the middle of the twentieth century, histories of the company that stressed its role as a colonizing power gave way to studies that emphasized its significance in the history of Britain (Sutherland, 1952; Sherman, 1976; Horwitz, 1978); mined the company's commercial records to assess its impact on broader economic changes (Chaudhuri, 1964, 1978, 1981, 1986) or began to appreciate the ways in which the company served the interests of cross-cultural 'partnerships' (Furber, 1948, 1976; Lach and Kley, 1965; Kling, Pearson and Furber, 1979; Chaudhuri, 1985; Chandra, 1987; Hasan, 1991, 1992). By the beginning of the twenty-first century, other scholars, led by Philip Stern, have inaugurated a constitutional turn in the study of the company's earlier years to contest the simple trade – empire paradigm of those who focused on the company's eighteenth- and nineteenth-century adulthood (Stern, 2011). To this turn has recently been added a renewed focus on the decentred locations for the changes in the company's story and the ways in which the company's history was compelled less by any sense of corporate strategy and more by the agency of individuals, associations and connections in the company's Asian commercial hinterlands (Veevers, 2013; Erikson, 2014; Pettigrew and Van Cleve, 2014).

The chapters in this book combine the earlier tradition that celebrated the cross-cultural partnerships structured by the East India Company's activities with the more recent emphasis on the decentred, local dynamics that informed and compelled the company's activities. They view the East India Company across its 257-year history as an organization that structured specific kinds of interactions between cultures that reverberated around the spaces and cultures that the East India Company occupied, from London to Madras. This view denies the distinction between metropolitan centre and colonial periphery and integrates cross-cultural dialogue into a global field of reference. It also challenges descriptions of a command-and-control corporate strategy that either succeeded or failed according to local criteria. Instead the corporation is depicted as a transnational, transcultural organization composed of a complex interplay between multiple interests, which succeeded in compelling historical change in ways that individual actors within the vast corporate structure could not have planned.

At the heart of our view of the company there exists a paradox. Historians have long noted how the metropolitan constituencies of the company depicted its non-European suppliers in culturally condescending terms. This superciliousness about Asian peoples was in proportion to the special privileges – and especially the monopoly – which the English investors in the company were so fixated upon. Monopolistic power was deemed to be critical to ensure that commercial activity conducted with what the English investment community regarded as the 'heathen' nations of South Asia could be managed in ways that would benefit the English nation. But as scholars are once again appreciating, by the middle of the company's first century, the company was far more than the haughty expectations of its Leadenhall Street directors (Erikson, 2014). Instead, the corporations' real power lay in the way in which it used its constitutional structure to capture the competing interests of multiple constituencies: the private trade of company employees; the interloping merchants; the directors and, most important, as the chapters in this volume make clear, the company's Asian interlocutors themselves. In short, the requirements of a successful transnational trade dictated that European corporations learn to operate with (and sometimes for) their non-European hosts.

II

The chapters in this volume highlight the distinctive institutional processes at work in the trading corporation – in this case, the English East India Company – in structuring cross-cultural interaction. This distinctiveness often emerged from the ways in which the trading corporation used constitutional means – charters, treaties, bye-laws – to secure and perpetuate commercial gains. As commercial entities, trading corporations necessarily accommodated the interests of their non-European partners. As constitutional entities, they formalized the integration of global and local spaces, domesticating the fruits of global exchange into their local domiciles and structuring transcultural interactions and exchanges in distinctive corporate spaces in their international commercial settings. These global corporate spaces integrated English, European and non-European interests and ideas. In the case of the English East India Company, as the chapters in this volume show, the corporate form allowed for an especially durable and versatile mechanism for Anglo-Indian negotiation that proved to be particularly responsive to South Asian influence and accommodative of diverse commercial, social and political relationships.

The chapters analyse a wide variety of vehicles for cross-cultural interaction: religious practices, sexual union, prisons, art and ships' passes. But in each case, it is possible to detect how East India Company officials and interests in Asia understood the importance of respecting local custom and practice to uphold commercial ambitions and how this understanding was born of local experience and, for the most part, went beyond orders from London. Conversely, the wealth and power of cross-cultural brokers, men like Kasi Viranna of Madras, supplied the monopolistic control over local economies that the company hoped to achieve for itself in settings presided over by cross-cultural political alliances of company and local leaders who were neither solely English nor Indian in character, but hybrid. Despite these broad similarities in how cross-cultural interactions occurred in this corporate context, the overall ambition of this group of chapters is to communicate the variety of forms these interactions took. The East India Company meant differing things to different people in different places at different times, and its fluid structure could be used by each interest for his or her own ends, whether in London or in the subcontinent. The chapters in this book therefore analyse a varied set of changes that reflect the wide variety of historiographic sub-fields that have been used to understand the company's history in India and in England: from alterations to economic theory that derived directly from commercial needs to changes to the loyalty of the Bengal army that derived from a compromise between British and Indian cultures on the issue of caste hierarchy.

III

The chapters in this book are organized to emphasize the very different perspectives on the complex dynamics of the East India Company across the diverse settings of the company's operations and over two and a half centuries that historians have devised. This book is organized into three parts, each of which takes a chronological view of a separate category of Anglo-Indian interaction during the East India Company's career. Part I explores the regulatory worlds of the East India Company across the seventeenth and early eighteenth centuries. Trading corporations have often been viewed as vehicles of national – and therefore mercantilist – regulation. These chapters explore how the East India Company was itself regulated by broader, transnational forces that derived from cross-cultural interactions. In his opening chapter, 'The failure of the cloth trade to Surat and the internationalisation of English mercantilist thought, 1614–1621', William A. Pettigrew assesses the company's early commercial strategy in Surat in the second decade of the seventeenth century and argues that the trading relationships the company's Surat factors developed with local merchants helped to ensure that the prevailing English mercantilist suspicion of bullion exporting would be challenged by the economic realities that forced the English to feed the Mughal state's hunger for silver. The impressive commercial benefits of a multipolar trading system connecting European bullion markets with Surat, the Persian Gulf and the Southern Spice Islands convinced the English Company to ally with Gujarati and Mughal interests to recast mercantilist theory through the famous agency of the company's director and promoter, Thomas Mun. Anglo-Indian commerce propelled changes to mercantilist doctrine with implications for European and Asian economies.

At times change was indirect, as in Pettigrew's account. At other times, it was rather more direct. Aske Laursen Brock's chapter 'Asian influences on the commercial strategies of the English East India Company' shows the ways in which the famous directorial alliances of the East India Company's metropolitan headquarters reflected the power struggles and shifts developed in the company's Asian trading worlds during the second half of the seventeenth century. Through a forensic analysis of the company's directorial networks, Brock demonstrates the nodal point for Anglo-Indian interaction in the company's Madras trade: the renowned broker and financier of English trade in eastern India during the escalation of its trade there – Kasi Viranna. Brock's chapter argues that English officials like William Langhorne, Jeremy Sambrooke, Streynsham Master and Gerald Aungier let their interests in private trade influence decisions on changes in the commercial strategy of the company. The picture that Brock paints is one in which the local pressures faced by company officials in places like Bombay and Madras because of the power of men like Viranna compelled alterations to commercial strategies emanating from London in ways that the company tried and failed to challenge. In the great irony of Brock's analysis, the brokering of Anglo-Indian interactions through Viranna helped convince London to propose a more aggressive stance towards the subcontinent in general, which set into motion the disastrous war against the Mughal state, which led the English public and state to rein in the company's corporate power at home and overseas. Both Pettigrew and Brock offer us an insight into how Asian realities shaped the boardroom decisions taken by the company.

Anglo-Indian interaction could lead as in Brock's case to a growing divergence of interests between the cultures but could also produce a convergence of institutional practices as commerce integrated economic systems across state and cultural barriers. In his chapter 'The East India Company and the shift in Anglo-Indian commercial relations in the 1680s', Michael Wagner describes this process with reference to the growing financial entanglements of the English and Mughal economies in the crucial decade of the 1680s. For Wagner, the principal interaction between the two economies came in the form of state finance. Just as the Mughal state depended upon the imports of European bullion, so too the company's continued operation depended upon its ability to help finance the English state. Wagner concentrates on the financial pillars of the company's operations in the late seventeenth century: its debt financing and its ability to source bullion for export to Mughal territories. The English began to develop new financial instruments in the Asian setting: contracts, joint stock companies, mints, insurance and banks, to buttress their commercial relationships in ways that helped to improve the sustainability of their trade. While at home, the success of these institutional underpinnings for Anglo-Indian interaction helped to ensure a steady supply of state loans and nurtured the establishment of a business press. These institutional means to steady trade became the more durable and more impersonal means to continue interaction across the cultures as brokers like Viranna became less common.

In the final chapter of Part I, Tristan Stein's 'Indian merchants, company protection and the development of the Bombay shipping pass regime, c. 1680–1740' takes the discussion of the mechanics of commercial interaction into the eighteenth century by focusing on a fascinating medium for cross-cultural interaction: the ship's pass. Rather than only representing the

Europeans' favoured means of imposing sovereignty on maritime space, the pass also records the durability of South Asian commercial control into the eighteenth century. Focusing on the Bombay presidency, Stein suggests that the ship's pass shows historians how the English and South Asian merchants collaborated using this instrument of corporate jurisdiction and identification in ways that satisfied both interests: for the Asians, the pass conferred protection; for the English it drew the Asian merchants to their service and interests. The use of the pass was subject to cross-cultural political and commercial negotiation that depended 'as much on the commercial strategies of merchants and shipowners as on the will and orders of the Company'. In this sense, the pass regime was a system of European maritime control that was subject to the influence of Asian powers and that some Asian merchants used successfully to their commercial advantage.

Part II broadens the setting for cross-cultural interaction between the English and the subcontinental population from regulation and political economy to culture. These chapters examine how cross-cultural interactions involved religion, society, domesticity and travel and how these connections changed the societies involved. Beginning Part II, Haig Smith's chapter '"God shall enlarge Japheth, and he shall dwell in the tents of Shem": the changing face of religious governance and religious sufferance in the East India Company, 1610–1701' helps us understand the world of the Protestant Church and its influence within the company establishment over the course of the seventeenth century. Here we see the company back in responsive mode: trying to digest the lessons derived from marvelling at the often-pluralist approach to religion within the Mughal state, while also wishing to use the Protestantism of its English domicile to help order the lives of its corporate employees. The pluralist societies that the company structured in places like Bombay ultimately generated hybrid systems of religious governance unlike those within either the Mughal or the English states. Again, these pluralized fruits of Anglo-Indian interaction were the results of agency from both sides.

Mahesh Gopalan develops the notion of the 'company state' in his chapter 'Maritime society in an early modern port city: negotiating family, religion and the English Company in Madras' by analysing the 'multi-layered engagement between the Company officials, their superiors in London, the local political elites operating within the region, and the diverse residents of Madras' in producing the distinctive social mechanics of the port city of Madras over the course of the company's seventeenth-century engagement with the city. Gopalan examines the role of the Anglican church and company chaplains in influencing the company establishment at Madras. He draws our attention to the changing patterns of family life and the ways in which the company attempted to regulate the social world of the residents of Madras. For Gopalan, these social mechanics can be traced through two interrelated categories of interaction: the family and the moral economy of the town. Gopalan demonstrates that the jurisdictional claims of the company state relied upon the distinctive textured and layered social mechanics of cross-cultural engagement. Again, we see in Gopalan's chapter the ways in which fleeting social connections gave way to the escalation of disequilibrium and the onset of political subjection by the company.

Ruchika Sharma's chapter '"Domesticity" in early colonial Bengal' provides a focused analysis of cross-cultural interactions in the domestic sphere in the late eighteenth century and offers a new means to understand the ways in which company servants and officials participated in 'reverse acculturation' through the most direct form of interaction – sexual contact and reproduction. Through her examination of wills left behind by deceased Britons, Sharma reconstructs the nature of interpersonal relations between the former and native women. Delving into the British social worlds, Sharma shows how company law influenced the native women in their domestic spaces. This chapter explores cross-cultural interaction through the vessel of the individual body, as structured by domesticity and recorded and appropriated through the provisions of the law and inheritance. Sharma uses probate records of company officials to document how Indian women and mixed-race children record the sexual roots of English understanding of the Indian contexts.

In the last chapter 'The travellers' tales: the travel writings of Itesamuddin and Abu Taleb Khan' of Part II, Jeena Sarah Jacob continues Sharma's concentration on the self as a vessel for cross-cultural interaction. For Jacob, the travelogue, across corporate settings, records the internalizing of different spaces. This chapter uses the travel writings of two Mughal officials, Itesamuddin and Abu Taleb Khan, through Georgian Britain to illustrate the interested gaze of Indians in the London of East India House. These journeys offer a view of the South Asian perceptions of English society at the time of the company's political ascendancy. The two authors' prioritization of particular features of British society from government, society, gender and religion orders their engagement with British life but also internalizes this connection into a hybrid form exhibiting their own cultural priorities in a foreign space. The chapters in Part II therefore break away from the dominant commercial and political narrative associated with the histories of the English East India Company. Through their exploration of religion, society, domesticity and travel, they offer us a glimpse of the depth of the English Company's engagement in South Asia, which went far beyond trade and politics.

Part III focuses on the role of cross-cultural interaction in the viability of corporate power. Liam D. Haydon's chapter on 'Jahangir's paintings' offers a rare glimpse of early diplomatic negotiations involving the English and the Mughals' examination of the paintings gifted by the company to the Mughal emperor, Jahangir, at the beginning of the company's involvement with the Mughal Empire in the second decade of the seventeenth century. Through this examination we see the 'variety, and variability, of political strategies and positionings employed by the Company and its servants' as part of their attempts to ingratiate the company before the emperor. Gifts served political and commercial ends. But for Haydon, a painting was – in particular – 'a site of conflict over representation' where we see the ways in which the company improved its engagement with the Mughal state via a 'slow process of intercultural translation'. The company learned to accommodate Mughal taste when selecting the visual media of its gifts as part of its realization of the roots to influence on the subcontinent.

For David Veevers, in his chapter 'The contested state: political authority and the decentred foundations of the early modern colonial state in Asia', corporate power was actualized through cross-cultural interaction via a process that was decentred to Indian contexts rather than operating centrifugally from London. For Veevers, this 'colonial state evolved around a shifting nexus of interpersonal relationships forged between Europeans and non-Europeans in the service of the Company'. As with Gopalan's examination of Madras, for Veevers, the history of this port city in the last decades of the seventeenth century shows to what extent English and Indian power was derived from mutual engagement through the vehicle of the company. As Veevers explains, 'Whether through financial opportunity, social elevation or political influence, Europeans and Asians joined together to determine the development of the Company for their own advantage.' By analysing the family, the business partnership and political factions, Veevers offers a bracing insight into the importance of Anglo-Indian interaction in the development of state apparatus in Madras – an interaction that Indian elites used the company to control.

Rachna Singh's richly researched chapter 'Messing, caste and resistance: the production of "jail-scapes" and penal regimes in the early 1840s' examines the unrest within general population and prisoners during the imposition of messing in the Bihar jails under the company's rule during the early 1840s. Singh attempts a contrast-reading of a violent uprising in the Chuprah jail of Sarun district, simmering discontent in the Gyah jail and the relatively peaceful imposition of messing in the Bhaugulpore jail to examine the different registers in which colonial power/knowledge came to be constituted, how practices of governance were shaped as much by the ruled as rulers and how policy decisions by the company regime were shaped as much by abstract ideas as by lived experience. Singh argues that there emerged, in the process of the imposition, resistance towards, and reimposition of messing, various colonial constructions of caste centred particularly on the norms of commensality, divergent from one another in substance and deployment within colonial policy. Singh shows how one can map the shifts in the philosophy and practices of punishment and the ways in which corporate contexts shaped transcultural interaction about punishment and incarceration in the company's twilight years. Singh argues that the ways in which prisoners chose to inhabit messes, the spatial practices of an entire range of actors within jail scapes and the ways in which messing was 'lived out' gave meaning to the system itself. In other words, these distinctive spatial practices produced the space of the jail in the early 1840s.

Sabyasachi Dasgupta's final chapter 'A case of multiple existences: the loyal Bombay Purbaiya and his rebellious cousin in Bengal' brings the story of Anglo-Indian interaction within the structures of rule determined by the East India Company to a close. In Dasgupta's analysis of the company's army, we have an examination of the seeds of the company's final demise in the 1850s. Dasgupta offers a means of appreciating the most potent component of the later East India Company's state apparatus in India and a productive site of cross-cultural interaction: the army. By comparing the Purbaiya soldiers in the Bengal and Bombay armies (and the particular role of the former in the 'Mutiny' of 1857), Dasgupta is able to demonstrate the perils of Anglo-Indian interaction for the exclusively state prerogatives of the mid-nineteenth-century East India Company. Unlike the Bombay army, the Bengal army functioned with great sensitivity to caste sentiments. It hybridized English military structures with Indian customs at the insistence of Indian participants and despite the frustration of the English leadership. The long-established contours of Anglo-Indian interaction in Bengal (described by Gopalan and Veevers), which one British official after the rebellion described as akin to Europeans becoming 'half Hindoo', led in the nineteenth century to the ending of East India Company's power and its substitution with the direct controls of the British state, heralding a different era of Anglo-Indian cross-cultural interaction under the British Raj. Dasgupta argues that under company rule there emerged a dialogue between alternative social hierarchies. These chapters in Part III offer us an insight into the complex negotiations that engaged the company state, influencing the attitude to art, the development of institutions, notions of punishment and military organization.

The chapters in this volume do not, of course, cover every aspect of Anglo-Indian interaction during the period of the East India Company's existence. Overall, these chapters illustrate the variety of ways in which the English East India Company structured and was structured by the interactions between cultures that calibrated and channelled various interests into historical change of many forms and several settings.

References

Arasaratanam, S., 1979, 'Trade and Political Dominion in South India, 1750–1790: Changing British-Indian Relationships', *Modern Asian Studies*, 13(1): 19–40.

———, 1994, *Maritime India in the 17th Century*, New Delhi: Oxford University Press.

Armitage, David, 2004, *The Ideological Origins of the British Empire*, Cambridge: Cambridge University Press.

Bayly, C. A. and Subrahmanyam Sanjay, 1988, 'Portfolio Capitalists and the Political Economy of Early Modern India', *Indian Economic and Social History Review*, 25(4): 401–24.

Bayly, Christopher, 1983, *Rulers, Townsmen and Bazaars: North Indian Society in the Age of British Expansion, 1770–1870*, Cambridge: Cambridge University Press.

———, 1987, *Indian Society and the Making of the British Empire*, Cambridge: Cambridge University Press.

———, 1989, *Imperial Meridian: The British Empire and the World, 1780–1830*, London: Longman.

———, 1996, *Empire and Information: Intelligence Gathering and Social Communication in India, 1780–1870*, Cambridge: Cambridge University Press.

Benton, Lauren, 2000, 'Colonial Law and Cultural Difference: Jurisdictional Politics and the Formation of the Colonial State', *Comparative Studies in Society and History*, 41(3): 563–88.

Brimnes, Niels, 1999, *Constructing the Colonial Encounter: Right and Left Hand Castes in South India*, London: Curzon Press.

———, 2003, 'Beyond Colonial Law: Indigenous Litigation and the Contestation of Property in the Mayors Court in Late Eighteenth Century Madras', *Modern Asian Studies*, 37(3): 513–50.

Brown, Judith M. and Robert Eric Frykenberg, eds., 2002, *Christians, Cultural Interactions and India's Religious Traditions*, London: Routledge Curzon.

Canny, Nicholas, eds., 1998, *The Origins of Empire: British Overseas Enterprise to the Close of the Seventeenth Century, Oxford History of the British Empire*, Oxford: Oxford University Press.

Caplan, Lionel, 1995, 'Creole World, Purist Rhetoric: Anglo-Indian Cultural Debates in Colonial and Contemporary Madras', *Journal of the Royal Anthropological Institute*, 1(4): 743–62.

Chandra, Satish, ed., 1987, *The Indian Ocean: Explorations in History, Commerce, and Politics*, New Delhi: Sage.

Chaudhuri, K. N., 1964, *The East India Company: The Study of an Early Joint-Stock Company, 1600–1640*, London: Frank Cass & Co.

———, 1978, *The Trading World of Asia and the English East India Company, 1660–1760*, Cambridge: Cambridge University Press.

———, 1985, *Trade and Civilisation in the Indian Ocean: An Economic History from the Rise of Islam to 1750*, Cambridge: Cambridge University Press.

Dalrymple, William, 2015, 'The East India Company: The Original Corporate Raiders', *The Guardian*, London, 4 March.

Das Gupta, A., 1979, *Indian Merchants and the Decline of Surat, c. 1700–1750*, New Delhi: Manohar.

Das Gupta, A. and M. N. Pearson, 1999, *India and the Indian Ocean, 1500–1800*, New Delhi: Oxford University Press.

Edney, Mathew, 1997, *Mapping an Empire: The Geographical Construction of British India, 1765–1843*, Chicago: University of Chicago Press.

Erikson, Emily, 2014, *Between Monopoly and Free Trade: The English East India Company, 1600–1757*, Princeton: Princeton University Press.

Etherington, Norman, ed., 2005, *Missions and Empire, Oxford History of the British Empire*, Oxford: Oxford University Press.

Fisher, Michael H., 2004, *Counterflows to Colonialism: Indian Travellers and Settlers in Britain 1600–1857*, New Delhi: Permanent Black.

Foster, William, ed., 1899, *The Embassy of Sir Thomas Roe to the Court of the Great Mogul, 1615–1619*, London: Hakluyt.

Furber, Holden, 1948, *John Company at Work: A Study of European Expansion in Indian in the Late Eighteenth Century*, Cambridge, MA: Harvard University Press.

———, 1976, *Rival Empires of Trade in the Orient 1600–1800*, Minneapolis: University of Minnesota Press.

Gordon, Stewart, 1992, *The Marathas 1600–1818*, New Delhi: Cambridge University Press.

Habib, Irfan, 1969, 'Potentialities of Capitalistic Development in Mughal India', *The Indian Economic and Social History Review*, II(3): 32–79.

———, 1999, *The Agrarian System of Mughal India 1556–170*, New Delhi: Oxford University Press.

Habib, Irfan and Tapan Raychaudhuri, 1982, *The Cambridge Economic History of India Vol. I c. 1200–c.1750*, New Delhi: Orient Longman.

Hasan, Farhat, 1991, 'Conflict and Cooperation in Anglo-Mughal Trade Relations during the Reign of Aurangzeb', *Journal of the Economic and Social History of the Orient*, 34(4): 351–60.

———, 1992, 'Indigenous Cooperation and the Birth of a Colonial City: Calcutta' c. 1698–1750', *Modern Asian Studies*, 26(1): 65–82.

Horwitz, Henry, 1978, 'The East India Trade, the Politicians, and the Constitution: 1689–1792', *Journal of British Studies*, 17(2): 1–18.

Joseph, Betty, 2004, *Reading the East India Company 1720–1840: Colonial Currencies of Gender*, New Delhi: Orient Longman.

Kling, Blair B., M. N. Pearson, and Holden Furber, eds., 1979, *The Age of Partnership: Europeans in Asia before Dominion*. Honolulu: University of Hawaii Press.

Lach, Donald F. and Edwin J. Wan Kley, 1965, *Asia in the Making of Europe*. Chicago: University of Chicago Press.

———, 1998, 'The English in Asia to 1700,' in Nicholas Canny (ed.), *The Oxford History of the British Empire, vol. 1: The Origins of Empire*. Oxford: Oxford University Press, pp. 264–85.

Mines, Mattison, 2001, 'Courts of Law and Styles of Self in Eighteenth Century Madras: From Hybrid to Colonial Self', *Modern Asian Studies*, 35(1): 33–74.

Mukund, Kanakalatha, 2005, *The View from Below: Indigenous Society, Temples and the Early Colonial State in Tamil Nadu 1700–1835*, New Delhi: Orient Longman.

Narayana Rao, Velcheru, David Shulman, and Sanjay Subrahmanyam, 1985, *History of Christianity in India: 1707–1858*, New Delhi: Cambridge University Press and New Delhi: Sage.

———, 2002, *Textures of Time*, New Delhi: Oxford University Press.

Oddie, Geoffrey A., 2006, *Imagined Hinduism: British Protestant Missionary Constructions of Hinduism, 1793–1900*, New Delhi: Sage.

Pearson, M. N., 2005, *The World of the Indian Ocean, 1500–1800: Studies in Economic, Social and Cultural History*, Hampshire: Ashgate Variorum.

Pettigrew, William A. and George Van Cleve, 2014, 'Parting Companies: The Glorious Revolution, Company Power, and Imperial Mercantilism', *The Historical Journal*, 57(3): 617–38.

Prakash, Om, 1998, *New Cambridge History of India, European Commercial Enterprise in Pre Colonial India, II.5*, Cambridge: Cambridge University Press.

Raman, Bhavani, 2012, *Document Raj: Writing and Scribes in Early Colonial South India*, New Delhi: Permanent Black.

Robb, Peter, 2011, *Sentiment and Self: Richard Blechynden's Calcutta Diaries, 1791–1822*, New Delhi: Oxford University Press.

Rubies, Joan-Pau, 2000, *Travel and Ethnology in the Renaissance: South India through European Eyes, 1250–1625*, Cambridge: Cambridge University Press.

Sherman, Arnold, 1976, 'Pressure from Leadenhall: The East India Company Lobby, 1660–1678,' *Business History Review*, 50(3): 329–55.

Stern, Philip J., 2011, *The Company-State: Corporate Sovereignty and the Early Modern Foundations of the British Empire in India*, New York: Oxford University Press.

Subrahmanyam, Sanjay, 1997, 'Connected Histories: Notes Towards a Reconfiguration of Early Modern Eurasia', *Modern Asian Studies*, 31(3): 735–62.

———, 2005, *Explorations in Connected History: From the Tagus to the Ganges*, New Delhi: Oxford University Press.

Sutherland, Lucy, 1952, *The East India Company in Eighteenth-Century Politics*, Oxford: Oxford University Press.

Teltscher, Kate, 1995, *India Inscribed: European and British Writing on India, 1600–1800*, New Delhi: Oxford University Press.

Veevers, David, 2013, '"The Company as Their Lords and the Deputy as a Great Rajah": Imperial Expansion and the English East India Company on the West Coast of Sumatra, 1685–1730', *The Journal of Imperial and Commonwealth History*, 41(5): 687–709.

Viswanathan, Gauri, 2002, *Masks of Conquest: Literary Study and British Rule in India*, New Delhi: Oxford University Press.

Wilson, Kathleen, ed., 2004, *A New Imperial History: Culture, Identity and Modernity in Britain and the Empire, 1660–1840*, New York: Cambridge University Press.

Xavier, Angela Barreto and Ines G. Zupanov, 2015, *Catholic Orientalism: Portuguese Empire, Indian Knowledge (16th–18th Centuries)*, New Delhi: Oxford University Press.

Zupanov, Ines G., 2005, *Missionary Tropics: Jesuit Frontier in India (16th–17th Century)*, Ann Arbor: University of Michigan Press.

Part I

The regulatory worlds of the East India Company

1 The failure of the cloth trade to Surat and the internationalisation of English mercantilist thought, 1614–1621

William A. Pettigrew

Historians of early modern commerce and political economy remain pessimistic about the conceptual utility and explanatory power of the term 'mercantilism'. Recent authors have either echoed the long-established frustration with formulating a coherent definition of the term or have conceded that mercantilism provides a 'weak conceptual hand' (Hoppit 2014: 23). While the traditional view that mercantilism is fixated above all else on the balance of trade theory has received some challenge, the other (and related) pillar of mercantilist doctrine – that international trade should be conducted in ways that benefitted the nation state – remains strident (Stern and Wennerlind 2013). This view has inadvertently led historians of mercantilism to sustain the 'Eurocentricism' of some of their historical actors when seeking to explain the intensification of global trade in the seventeenth century. According to this view, mercantilism was a pan-European belief system. Conspicuous differences in how separate European nations managed their empires beyond Europe reflected 'epistemic' ideological fissures within the 'metropole', rather than the profound influence of local non-European agency (Pincus 2012: 4). As such, ideological debate about mercantilist policy – although it often developed across national borders within Europe – was as rigidly nationalist in its generation as it was in its ambition (Kafadar 1991; Subrahmanyam 1995; Van Ittersum 2005; Reinert 2011).

This chapter contests this view by arguing that non-European contexts and actors played an important role in stimulating and reorienting ideological debate about mercantilism. Historians of the Atlantic world have succeeded in demonstrating the centrality of non-European peoples and contexts in structuring early modern European empires in the Americas and the belief systems that sustained them (Cronon 2003; Richter 2003; Koot 2012). This chapter examines the relationship between English commercial interactions and the formulation of economic theory by analysing the East India Company's operations in the Persian Gulf and the Indian Ocean and especially in the Mughal port city of Surat in the second decade of the seventeenth century and the way corporate committees in London and in Surat reflected on the development of this trade. It argues that the profound shifts in mercantilist doctrine that writers like Thomas Mun produced derived much of their inspiration and impetus from an appreciation born of the specific corporate setting for a multipolar international trading system that developed from Surat in the years 1614 to 1619. This corporate setting necessitated the simultaneous integration of multiple perspectives on this trading system that the East India Company enjoyed: from London; from the bullion markets of Europe; from Surat, Persia, the Red Sea and Indonesian trades. Out of this integration came Mun's new theory of a multipolar commercial system that disabused earlier writers of a conception of England's international trade that relied on separate balances with individual (rather than integrated) overseas markets (Thomas 1926: 12). Mun famously clarified the doctrine of the balance of trade. But careful reading of the discursive context of Mun's writing shows how his more important conceptual innovation involved the description of this multipolar international market. This description also enabled Mun to demonstrate that money was a commodity like any other, as Mun realised that the Surat trade was profitable because it integrated a complex, multipolar commercial structure in which European bullion could be transformed into Asian commodities at prices that would then yield still greater quantities of money once those goods were shipped back to Europe. By broadening and complicating the perspective on bullion arbitrage, Mun could challenge the long-standing prejudice against bullion exporting that viewed international trade solely in terms of outflows rather than in terms of the international and profit-multiplying exchanges of bullion into commodities and back again.

This chapter suggests that the corporate structure provided by the East India Company was central to the formulation of this doctrine. The company's London committees could measure the success of the Surat trade using accounts. But they could also digest the perspectives on this trading system from the outside; they absorbed some of the insights of their factors, especially the chief factor at Surat, Thomas Kerridge. Kerridge's view of the benefits of exchanging European silver for Indian textiles and then for Indonesian spices to be converted back into far greater quantities of European bullion pre-empted much of Mun's argument. Kerridge himself acutely appreciated how English trade in Surat depended – almost entirely – on the willingness of the English to export bullion to the Mughal Empire. Attempts to move the commercial initiative of the English from Surat to the Persian Gulf in this period to ensure greater vending of English cloth (and therefore lessen the company's reliance on European bullion dealers) and the Mughal and local Gujarati merchants' refusal to permit this move in the short term suggest that Kerridge's (and therefore Mun's) argument in defence of bullion trading voiced the commercial interests of those Gujarati merchants. In this way, Mun's influential theory of money commodification channelled the interests of these Asian merchants, the East India Company's factors (like Kerridge) and the ways in which the company's directors (like Mun) digested the experience of those factors at home to uphold their interests with the English state and public (Muchmore 1970).

In Eurocentric accounts of mercantilism, the overseas trading corporation is the primary executor of mercantilist doctrine because corporations proposed to channel international exchanges in ways that ensured their domicile economy would benefit at the expense of both European trading rivals and the international customers and suppliers of the corporations in places like Surat, Batavia, Cape Coast and Aleppo. But the example of the Surat bullion trade shows to what extent the seventeenth-century English corporation structured transnational commerce and succeeded by accommodating (rather than 'bridling') the commercial interests of non-Europeans. Corporations regularly justified their monopolies and juridical power overseas with reference to the need to 'awe' the non-European barbarians they traded with, but international experience – from the outset – challenged these stereotypes and compelled corporations to seek trades that would produce mutual benefit for English and non-European merchants. As one East India Company minute recorded, profits provided the best means to 'bind' the 'honestie' of non-Europeans (IOR B/6: 447). The East India Company's trade, as K. N. Chaudhuri pointed out long ago, could not have operated without the support of continental European bullion traders and survived because of the extent of demand for its products in Europe (Chaudhuri 1963: 27). Nor could its commercial future have been secured without appreciating the critical importance of accommodating the commercial interests of Indian merchants who tolerated European merchants because they brought precious metals into the Mughal domain. The trade in European bullion by the English Company to the Indian subcontinent offers the clearest evidence of this commercial accommodation.

I

The third decade of the seventeenth century has been a regular port of call for historians of economic thought. These scholars have most often concentrated on the parliamentary debate about the causes of the commercial crisis of the early 1620s and have focused on the printed writings of Thomas Mun who started the debate with *A Discourse of Trade, from England unto the East Indies* (1621). Gerald Malynes then took up the debate with *The Maintenance of Free Trade, According to the Three Essential Parts of Traffique* and then Edward Misselden with *Free Trade, or, the Means to Make Trade Flourish* in 1622. Mun often emerges from such accounts as a maverick theorist who pioneered an integrated understanding of exchange rates and trade deficits with Malynes in particular depicted as a conservative thinker who sustained a mediaeval conception of the substantial and inherent values of precious metals rather than their exchange or commodity values. For many historians of economic thought, this debate pushed and then advertised conceptual sophistication and progress (Appleby 1978; Finkelstein 2000).

Scholars have not devoted careful attention to the preface to these debates and in particular the context for the opening salvo from Mun himself. Mun wrote to deflect the charges that the East India Company's bullion exports aggravated the domestic economic crisis by creating a shortage of coin. But the conceptual innovations of Mun's treatment of the mechanics of international trade cannot be understood without appreciating an additional and related contextual shift during the second decade of the seventeenth century: the growing importance to public commercial debate of direct experience of non-European trade. The domestic economic crisis partly derived from an efflux of bullion to continental Europe. Mun's argument is perhaps best understood as an attempt to distract attention away from that cause and towards an international solution. For that reason, any attempt to appreciate Mun's theoretical achievement must contextualise his writings into an understanding of the relationship between domestic crisis and the escalation of English trade beyond Europe in this period as well as into the pre-existing printed perceptions of how the international economy functioned.

Mun's challenge to the bullionist position went against the grain of centuries-old economic thinking. Although the sixteenth century saw greater integration of the English into European money markets and the beginnings of sustained extra-European trade via the Muscovy Company, mediaeval precepts of state economic policy remained: that international conspirators used exchange rates to defraud the English economy and that the depletion of precious metal supplies undermined the power and wealth of the kingdom. To combat the efflux of bullion, policymakers in the sixteenth and seventeenth centuries sought to resurrect the fourteenth-century remedy – the statute of employment – to compel foreign merchants to purchase English commodities with imported goods – thus preventing the outflow of English bullion (De Roover 1949: 11).

Two things changed in the seventeenth century. First, as constitutional debate intensified under King James I, the royal prerogative's means of raising money without the Parliament became more controversial, and a devaluation of the currency, though it might have helped gather revenue for the Crown, was increasingly regarded by councillors as a dangerous last resort (Malynes 1610). Second, the extent of extra-European trade greatly increased in the first decades of the seventeenth century – and largely under the auspices of another branch of the prerogative – the chartered corporation. These trades – to Virginia, to India, to the Levant and to Russia – complicated mediaeval narratives of bilateral trade in which a domestic market could be undermined by international financial conspirators. The companies, as exclusive bodies in a charged constitutional climate, also provided focal points for public anger and fear during the periods of economic crisis. As such, by the seventeenth century, corporations, and especially the East India Company, often shouldered the accusation traditionally levelled at foreigners – that they depleted the nation's wealth to enrich impersonal and transnational interests.

Despite the large expansion in overseas trade from England during the opening decade of the seventeenth century, England was plunged into a period of economic hardship in the second decade. The crisis had two related dimensions: one was the shortage of coin; the other was the failure of the cloth trade – England's traditional export monoculture. The shortage of coin limited the liquidity of the domestic economy and therefore restricted trade, but it also posed problems for the state because the royal mint generated funds for the monarchy. The shortage of coin was blamed on various factors. The most plausible explanation argued that silver had been undervalued by an erroneous alteration, in 1611, to the bimetallic ratio of silver to gold (Supple 1964: 167). This mistake motivated money dealers on the continent to purchase English silver, drawing it out of the kingdom in the process. King James I proposed to solve the problem with an abortive attempt to substitute brass coinage for silver in the same year (TNA: SP14/67, 72). Merchants were also forbidden from purchasing silver at prices higher than those stipulated by the royal mint (TNA: SP14/73, 139). Throughout the period, advisers to the king proposed to enhance (or devalue) the currency. But this was persistently rejected on the grounds that the inflationary consequences would hurt those on fixed incomes, rich and poor (Supple 1964: 169). More popular solutions included halting silver exports or stimulating cloth exports.

If coin provided the seventeenth-century English economy with liquidity, unfinished cloth was its principal commodity and export good. In the second decade of the seventeenth century, economic projectors – chief among them Sir William Cockayne – questioned whether England could benefit more from finished wool exports rather than exporting the unfinished raw material to Europe where it would be manufactured. In 1614, in what became known as Cockayne's project, King James approved a large-scale experiment to see if this could be achieved. The result confirmed the supremacy of weavers on the continent and badly affected the scale of exports in England's monoculture trade in wool. From 1614 to 1616, the scale of English wool exports reduced by 20 per cent. This failure aggravated the commercial crisis (Wilson 1960). King James's financial woes continued alongside the national economic depression and added to the pressures for merchants to provide a solution to both. In the so-called Addled Parliament of 1614, James tried and failed to extract revenue from the Parliament and then decided to suspend the legislature for several years. With continental Europe descending into religious war and the Parliament recalcitrant about financing the monarchy, merchant and royal eyes turned to extra-European trade with a more determined gaze. This naturally led to a focus on overseas trading corporations.

This focus integrated parallel discussions about the concurrence of Dutch commercial supremacy with English economic crisis. It concentrated on explaining the success of the Dutch in the spice trade, their closer-to-home herring fisheries as well as ongoing theoretical deliberations between the Dutch and the English about the dominion of the seas (Khan 1923: 24). As initial hopes of discovering precious metals in these new corporate settings faded, several English writers began to promote the local fish trade off the British Isles over the distant markets that corporations concentrated on, especially when it was understood that these corporations enriched the heathen by exporting English bullion. This genre had begun with John Keymer's 1601 tract 'Observations on Dutch Fishing' and continued through similar writings such as Tobias Gentleman's *England's Way to Winn Wealth* (1614), which described fish as the Hollanders' 'principal Gold-mine' and proposed it as a means for the English to improve their specie pile and a principal way for the English – if not addressed – to be depleted of their bullion by the Dutch (Gentleman 1614: 8, 10, 15). Although local in its focus, Gentleman's anti-corporate argument also echoed through the shift of policy articulated by the Virginia Company propagandist John Smith (1614), in his blueprint for successful colonising, the *Description of New England*, written in the same year, in which he saw the future of English commercial interests in fish and timber trading rather than in precious metals. This writing helped to establish the false binary between commodities and bullion that Mun and others challenged.

No such initial hopes of solving the specie drain surrounded the foundation of the East India Company in 1600. From the beginning of its trade, the company had understood – from Dutch experience – that specie would be required to trade in Asia. The privileges to export bullion that the company enjoyed represented one of the most important arguments for the company's corporate sovereignty. In the company's first charter of 1600, it received the right to export up to £30,000 of bullion, with £6,000 of that to be minted at the Tower of London. The company, however, was under strict instructions to bring in as much bullion to England as it exported and that exports of bullion should not be made to those countries at war with England (Birdwood and Foster 1893: 180–8). As K. N. Chaudhuri pointed out, the undervaluation of sterling within Europe in relation to Asia (and to a lesser extent in England within Europe) provided the company with the opportunity to buy the goods of an economy where the merchant's currency was stronger and to sell such goods in their home markets where demands (and prices) were high (Chaudhuri 1963: 27). Although the East India Company enjoyed the right to export bullion, it was in constant dialogue with the providers of that constitutional privilege: the monarch, the Privy Council and the Parliament. These bodies did not merit its core commercial strategy of bullion arbitrage. The company understood the importance of depicting itself to these audiences as a commercial entity that upheld the national interests of the English economy. The company had to balance the commercial imperative to export bullion with a public profile that depicted its trade as beneficial for the nation as a whole. The company therefore proposed a diversified trade that exported some bullion but also shipped English commodities – especially wool (Birdwood and Foster 1893: 197–8).

II

As early as 1613, with the economic crisis escalating, the East India Company's Asian trade appeared to offer the perfect solution. This came in the form of a dramatic shift in the company's geographical focus from the South East Asian spice islands to the western ports of the Mughal Empire and the Persian Gulf. The company officials heralded trade with the Mughal port town of Surat, in particular, as the potential saviour of the English economy. Early in 1613, an East India Company factor at Surat, Thomas Aldworth, wrote back to the company's management in London. Aldworth appreciated both the need to find an outlet for the cloth and to placate those domestic interests who objected to the company's exporting of 'money'.

> [T]hrough the whole Indies there cannot be any place more beneficial for our country than this, being the only key to open all the rich and best trade of the Indies, and for sale of our commodities, especially our cloth, it exceeds all others, insomuch our hope is you shall not need to send any more money hither, for here and in the neighbour cities, will

> be yearly sold above a thousand broad cloths and five hundred pieces of Devon kerseys for ready moneis, and being sorted according to our advice herewith sent you, will double itself.
>
> (Danvers and Foster 1896–1902: 1.238)

Aldworth's optimism about the commercial prospects of Surat stemmed from the declining influence of the Portuguese in the Persian Gulf and the perceived likelihood of some kind of Anglo-Dutch Protestant commercial alliance in West India (CPSC 1862: 314). Aldworth's hopes appeared to have been shared by officials in the English state as well. Expectations of a profitable trade with Surat entered official circles, with the first minister, Henry Howard, the earl of Northampton, expressing hope of a successful foundation for the trade with the 'Great Mogul' (Green 1858: 214).

In a pattern that became familiar, the East India Company made reference to these international operations to help improve its political profile at home. The company hoped to translate Aldworth's optimism and Howard's hope into continued political influence at home by noting the dire financial circumstances of the monarch during the botched parliamentary negotiations over the king's finances in 1614. At this time, the company attempted to alter its charter's expectation that it imported as much specie as it exported, presumably as coin became more difficult to procure in Europe (CPSC 1862: 270). But the public deliberations about the economy during the Addled Parliament again saw the East India Company scapegoated as the large-scale exporter of bullion. Pressure on the company appears to have been most severe in late March and early April 1614, with the company's governor, Sir Thomas Smith, having to attend the Parliament on a daily basis to 'answer any imputations that may be cast upon the Company' (CPSC 1862: 288, 290).

But Smith proved to be able to turn these pressures into commercial opportunities. By April 1614, noting the severity of the king's financial shortcomings and the unlikelihood of the Parliament providing the king with money, the company gifted £600 of gold plate to the king's broker, Robert Carr, Lord Somerset, and then, in June, recorded its intention to secretly remit funds directly to the king in exchange for help in halting the barrage of opposition it experienced in the Parliament over the previous few months (Green 1858: 239, 299). These transactions became notorious throughout the company's Asian network, with one factor overhearing a company servant interpret Smith's control over the monarchy as evidence that Smith and the company 'for their private benefits will overthrow the state of the commonwealth of England' (Danvers and Foster 1896–1902: 2.245). Smith's gift appears to have quieted the opposition in public, though the company noted a 'scandal cast upon' it by the goldsmiths, who, as active money changers across international boundaries, had perhaps the most to gain from the undervaluing of English silver and wished to divert blame away from themselves to the politically vulnerable East India Corporation (Green 1858: 372). These deliberations continued into September 1615 when Governor Smith pleaded with the king to support the company's patent for bullion exports with reference to the amount of custom the last two ships had brought into the king's hands (some £14,999, according to Smith) (CPSC 1862: 428). In this way, the company succeeded in achieving exemption from a royal proclamation banning the export of bullion (TNA: SP14/141, 86).

The East India Company's campaign to maintain its constitutional support and its bullion privileges was jeopardised by constant opposition in the Parliament and was also aggravated by printed attacks. Tobias Gentleman's vision of an English economy built on locally accessible raw materials was turned on the trade of the East India Company in 1614 in a pamphlet called *The Trades Increase* (1614) by Robert Kayll. Kayll criticised the far-flung focus of the East India Company's trade and championed the fisheries as gold mines close at hand. Kayll reserved special opprobrium for the East India Company whose trade defied all expectations in bringing the English into contact with 'greedy Rauens, and deuouring Crowes', which depleted English timber supplies at home and English mariners overseas, inflated the price of victuals at home, lessened the exports of domestically produced commodities and, of course, exported bullion to enrich the heathen and impoverish Christendom. Kayll instead sought to promote fishing as a trade that was close at hand rather than 'remote' trade that led to 'cost of purse, and losse of people' (Kayll 1614: 6, 14, 20, 32, 40–41).

Highly sensitive to its public profile in 1614, the East India Company had Kayll arrested at the intercession of Maurice Abbott – an East India Company director, who appealed to his brother, the archbishop of Canterbury, to have Kayll detained (Foster 1934; Ogborn 2007: 107). Having watched the failure of the parliamentary supply, the East India Company cosied up to the monarchy with gifts and could therefore expect some protection in prosecuting those who targeted its privileges in print. Not content with this course, however, the company also resorted to the eloquence of one of its own. The following year (1615), Dudley Digges, a company director, responded with a foundational argument about the importance of specie trading to the generation of profits at home in the *Defence of Trade*. Digges defended the international ambitions of the East India Company's commerce from Kayll's assault. Digges took the opposing view to Kayll about the domestic utility of far-flung trades and the East India Company who was like a hive of 'laborious bees' who brought honey 'from furthest parts abroad' to 'clothe and feede the poore, and give the willing man imployment' while the 'idel Drone and greedie Catterpillars prey upon the substance of the Subject here at home, with eating usurie and harmefull arts, while such a Spider in a corner spends his fruitlesse dayes perhaps in weaving weake objections against them'. Digges disputed Kayll's autarkic view of England's commercial future by arguing that it was one thing to have the resources to subsist within your realm, but the root to national wealth was in finding markets to sell the surplus.

> The truth is, in strict tearmes of need, our Land that flowes with foode and rayment may Bee, without all other Nations, but to Bee Well, to flourish and grow rich, wee must find vent for our abundance, and seeke to adorne vs out of others superfluities.
>
> (Digges 1615: 2–3, 31)

Digges also challenged Kayll's inconsistent but traditional depiction of intra-European competition and conspiracy alongside the solidarity of Christendom. While Keymer and Kayll based their arguments on England's commercial jealousy with Holland, Digges wished to show that England's interests were allied with the Dutch whom Digges described as 'in reason of state, and through band of Religion, best assured friends'. Digges tested the logic and sincerity of Kayll's concern about European competition by showing how Kayll's version of the East India Trade would necessitate the English purchasing the goods of the East from their Iberian competitors, a situation that would put England 'vnder the Lee, in awe and subiect to much inconuenience, rather then make double the profit to our selues and to the Common-wealth by fetching fro the wel-head, from the Indies, rather then weaken them'. Digges lampooned Kayll's argument about the depletion of treasure and scorned the continued influence of this argument 'before the King, before the Parliament, at the Councell Table; nay, almost every Table'. He listed the speciousness of this criticism of the company because of the amount of silver the company brought in and the amount of cloth it now intended to export, as well as the possible source of additional trading silver from its factors at Japan (Digges 1615: 47–48; CPSC 1862: 48).

In addition to Digges reaction to Kayll, the East India Company continued to propose and publicly promote a commodity trade to Surat to deflect constant public and official pressure. To further develop the idea of India as a vent for English cloth, the East India Company appointed an ambassador, Sir Thomas Roe, to liaise with the Mughal court. Although Roe would be a representative of the state, his brief remained subordinate to the commercial interests of the company's factors at Surat. The initiative was promoted by the chief factor in Surat, Thomas Kerridge, sometime during the summer of 1614, who was to retain control over all commercial issues (CSPC 1862: 327; Danvers and Foster 1896–1902: 2,108). With demand for cloth buoyant in Surat and Agra, and with supply abundant due to the failure of the Cockayne experiment and public will acute, the East India Company began to increase the proportion of goods it shipped and decrease its commercial reliance on bullion exports. In 1603 the percentage of goods was 9 per cent. By 1612 it had increased to 34 per cent. It then reached a peak of 62 per cent in 1614 (Chaudhuri 1963).

III

The company's hopes of using Surat as an outlet for English cloth were, however, rapidly corrected. By August 1614, Thomas Aldworth wrote to the company explaining how 'we were much all deceived' by the initial craze for purchasing English cloth by 'great men, in regard of the novelty, to cover some of their elephants and to make some saddles for their horses'. Aldworth added that 'for garments they use none in these parts, neither in rainy nor cold weather . . . for certainly this place is not for cloth, as we first expected'. Later correspondents of the company explained that local Lahore cloth was a quarter of the price of the English variant, which was, in any case, prone to consumption by a local worm (Danvers and Foster 1896–1902: 6, 182, 200–201). Factors later described how the only serious consumer of English cloth was the Mughal state, which sought to use its buying power to impose prices on the company (Danvers and Foster 1896–1902: 6, 251).

Rather than promote the exporting of bullion, however, Aldworth proposed to direct the company's trade away from Surat and the Indian subcontinent entirely and into trade with Persia. Aldworth sought to placate the London committees and notified them

> 'we have now made full enquiry concerning the state of Persia, where we are certainly informed of the vent of much cloth in regard their country is cold and that men, women and children are clothed therewith some five months in the year, and is very well sold and at a better rate than here, and what they have is brought overland from Aleppo with great charge'.
>
> (Danvers and Foster 1896–1902: 2.97)

Such was the factors' appreciation of the commercial difficulties of selling English cloth in Surat and the political problems of a continued supply of bullion from Europe that they proposed to shift England's Asian company once more, this time from India to Persia.

For the next several years, the English East India Company's officials in India upheld the directors' expectations of a fruitful cloth trade on the possibility of identifying and establishing a trading post in the Persian Gulf. The Persian scheme was promoted by factors with reference to a future time when 'less moneys may be transported out of our land' (Danvers and Foster 1896–1902: 3.84). The scheme's supporters also made reference to the Ottomans' war with Persia and how this had restricted the supply of cloth to the Ottoman Empire. The English quickly fixed on a position known as Jask to the east of the Portuguese island stronghold of Ormuz. The English adventurer, Robert Steele, who promoted the venture, boasted that the Persian markets would vend 'six times the amount of English cloth that the Surat markets could consume' (Danvers and Foster 1896–1902: 3.177).

While East India Company merchants and directors discussed the logistics of this Persian adventure, the Surat factory's trade began to settle down and mature as more bullion flowed in from 1615 onwards. The Surat factors began to promote the commercial advantages of having precious metals to trade in. Factors mentioned that coinage was in short supply in the western parts of the Mughal Empire. They explained that this would mean that imported European silver would have significant purchasing power and would help, overall, to ingratiate the English with the local traders. A Surat factor, William Edwards, mentioned how local indigo cultivators were being imposed upon by local monopolists and could therefore be cultivated as long-term commercial partners for the English if the English merchants could purchase indigo with specie (Danvers and Foster 1896–1902: 3.153). This situation was made still more favourable by the continued absence of Portuguese competition at this time. William Edwards, summarised in the early months of 1615: 'As there is great hope of a profitable trade in these parts, so it calls upon a continual open hand with these people, . . . and so we are to buy their loves with our moneys' (Danvers and Foster 1896–1902: 3.17). The English in India began to use their specie imports to improve their profile with the Mughal authorities, citing how their specie imports enriched the emperor's kingdoms with silver (much as Governor Smith had done at home with King James) (Danvers and Foster 1896–1902: 4.101). Factors also explained how specie provided liquidity that enabled factors to wait for prices to fall after the arrival of European ships (Danvers and Foster 1896–1902: 3.84).

Responding to these descriptions and presumably seeking to profit from the gifts disbursed to King James and his entourage, the company sought and achieved in July 1616 a new letters patent increasing its permitted bullion exports (Birdwood and Foster 1893: 479). By late 1616, factors had begun to celebrate the commercial model that became the chief engine of the East India Company's profits (and which Thomas Mun later described): purchasing silver in continental Europe, exchanging that for textiles or indigo in India, exchanging those for spices in South East Asia and shipping those to continental Europe to be exchanged for more silver (Danvers and Foster 1896–1902: 4.279).

IV

Against this backdrop of commercial success built on disbursing coin from London (but with a residual concern about bullion exporting) emerged an epistolary dispute about the mechanics of international trade that saw the Surat factor, Thomas Kerridge, pre-empt many of Mun's most important arguments in response to the English ambassador's, Sir Thomas Roe's, 'substantialist' view. In Roe's view, we have a perfect emblem for the entrenched view of trade as a bilateral conflict between nations and – moreover – between religions. Trade, for Roe, also had important constitutional connotations with the control of the money supply, in particular, highlighted by Roe (as with Malynes) as a crucial buttress for the royal prerogative. Roe was a notoriously unreliable witness, but his views on trade exhibit impressive consistency throughout his correspondence (Mishra 2014). Kerridge is a more obscure figure. His dedication to the commercial fortunes of the Surat factory at a time of considerable instability and high mortality is impressive, however. Kerridge stayed at Surat for several years (from 1612 to 1620 and returned for two years in the 1620s) and argued forcefully for the factory's interests throughout that time. In the dispute between the two men, we see rival conceptions of the commercial possibilities of Surat that shed light on their respective attitudes to social hierarchy, the constitutional determinants of state regulation, England's place within the European economy (and its place in Christendom) and – most important – differing conceptions of international trade.

The tensions between Roe and Kerridge began to escalate in the summer of 1616. Roe had been appointed to promote and develop the cloth trade but quickly grew pessimistic about the future of this trade. Resenting the dominance of the factors, Roe appears to have resisted all of their proposals while the factors refused to countenance his view that if the trade to India could not be conducted with English commodities then it ought to be abandoned entirely. Roe proposed to abandon the Indian trade if vent could not be found for English cloth because 'our state cannot beare the exportation of mony' (Foster 1899: 165). Kerridge – as a more experienced operator in India – alternated between frustration at having to subordinate the interests of the English to local merchant preferences and a more optimistic, multilateral view of the East India Company's trade in which Kerridge began to understand how such subordination provided a path to durable and profitable trade. Kerridge did not reject the possibilities of the cloth trade, but instead prioritised the trade to the South in spices to be shipped to Europe and exchanged for silver (Foster 1899: 166). Kerridge did not allow silver to be seen as a nationalist product whose shipment out of the realm into a unitary, foreign, rival commercial space was understood to be deleterious to the Kingdom's resources. Instead he viewed silver, as

Mun later did, as a commodity that flowed and mutated through international channels and could be procured if goods with sufficient demand were shipped. Rather than thinking of the East India Company as an exporter of silver, Kerridge structured international trade so that the company could use its Asian trades to procure silver as part of an international system.

Roe responded to this view by arguing that Christendom was a separate economic space that England's economic vitality depended upon. As far as Roe was concerned, using silver sourced from Europe made little difference to the argument because 'wee are as well members of Europe as Citizens of England, which is but one lymme and if the whole growe poore wee beare our proportion'. Roe upheld his statist credentials by following with a straightforward defence of the prerogative and concern about the lack of specie at the king's mint (BL: Add MSS 6115: 104). Kerridge replied to this with a more dynamic picture of exchange rather than imbalance. For Kerridge, the profits of shipping South East Asian commodities to Europe would bring 'Double Custom' because 'the proceede whereof by reemployment bringeth Continuall profit both to the state and Commonwealth'. Kerridge disputed the integrity of economic interests across European nations within Christendom and expounded how the Dutch would seek their 'own benefit, weigh not our loss'. In a manner again pre-emptive of Mun, Kerridge described if the monies were not sent to India then more would need to be sent through Turkey to procure the same amount of Indian goods brokered by the Ottomans (IOR G/36/84: 56).

To this, Roe responded by contrasting Kerridge's view with his own experiences of the prejudices of those in the Addled Parliament in 1614 (in which Roe was the member for Tamworth) who set more value in 'mony' than they did in 'China dishes, silks, spices, dyes and trash . . . the fuell of yearely pride and gluttony; for . . . none of these will sett out a fleete to sea nor pay an army'. Roe added to this policy argument his witnessing of the Parliament's determination to 'limit' both the East India and the Levant Company's corporate privileges during the Addled Parliament 'supposing the Crye of the Kings mynt to be as mournfull a hearing as if the liver, the fountayne of blood, should complayne in a natural body'. In this observation, Roe was at pains to point out that the Parliament (rather, one assumes, than he) believed that the minted monies would privilege the good of the commonwealth because they are 'the property of divers men, being enfranchised and naturalized by the Kings stampe and impression' (BL: Add MSS 6115: 114).

V

What explains the important differences between Roe and Kerridge's respective positions? Ironically for Roe, who often overstepped his brief in commenting on commercial matters, his intervention appears to support the agenda of the corporation as a whole. In espousing a bullionist position and in shunning material gain, Roe sought to posture self-consciously as someone outside the merchants' fraternity – learning from experience that merchants would receive little respect at the Mughal court (Danvers and Foster 1896–1902: 2.131). Roe sought to elevate the position of the English in the Mughal Empire by asserting the interests of the English from a position of equality. His refusal to ape local custom and his determination to be seen as a state (rather than a company or mercantile) official record his determination to place the interests of the English ahead of local commercial concerns. Although he often suggested that the Portuguese and Dutch were too heavy handed with the Gujaratis, Roe proposed that local merchants ought to be stood up to (Foster 1906–1927: 3). In this he followed his brief. For Roe, espousing the statist, bullionist position was part and parcel of a stubborn refusal to sustain his patrician and gentlemanly persona in the face of the substantial cultural challenges posed by an unfamiliar environment.

But for Kerridge the situation was different. Kerridge, in privileging the interests of the factors, therefore favoured the interests of the local Indian merchants. He had to account for his actions against financial criteria and as a mere merchant was far more exposed to the day-to-day commercial challenges of a trading life in Surat. He better understood the local merchants' concerns and understood what it felt like to be at the mercy of capricious and often-threatening local officials (Danvers and Foster 1896–1902: 4.343). Life was much easier for Kerridge if he could secure a constant and substantial supply of ready money to trade with the local Indian merchants and the Mughal state. Kerridge may have often complained about the 'insolent and insupportable' merchants of Surat, but he fully understood their upper hand (CSPC 1870: 2.258).

In this way, Thomas Kerridge's view offers an observation of commercial realities that were partly dictated by local Indian merchants. Mughal officials had always proposed to interfere and disrupt English trade since the factory at Surat had begun. One of Roe's first achievements was to report such activity to the emperor and achieve some relief. But the merchants 'on the spot' like Kerridge were at best commercially impotent or at worst powerless to stop the drain of the company's resources if a trade in cloth was to be insisted upon by London. Once the English had secured a sustainable export trade to Indonesia from Surat, they began to make money. This trade generated mutually beneficial commercial partnerships with local Indian merchants. This enduring trading model posed a threat to the commercial successes of the Gujarati merchants in Surat because the English began to eclipse the Indian merchants in that trade (Foster 1899: 161).

But the value of silver supplies from Europe meant that the loss of the 'southern' trade to Indonesia was a price worth paying for the Gujarati merchants and the Mughal state. Faced with the prospect of the English either buying their way into the trade in Indonesian spices by using silver to purchase Indian textiles or spices or abandoning the Surat trade altogether to trade in English cloth or coral to the Persian Gulf and, from 1618, to the Red Sea, the local Indian merchants strongly favoured the former. Gujarati merchants refused to purchase English cloth. They worked hard to limit the ease with which English merchants shifted from Surat to the Persian Gulf – especially the Gujarati merchants' valuable trade routes between Surat and Mocha and from there to the pilgrimage routes of Arabia in the Red Sea. Kerridge channelled the opposition of local merchants by seeking to undermine the attempts of the English to develop their commercial interests in the Red Sea and in Persia.

English factors noted the official resistance to their attempts to eclipse the Indian merchants in the Persian Gulf in 1619. Is-haq Beg, the governor of Surat, informed the English merchants that he rejected their plans to develop an English-carrying trade to Persia for fear of incurring the 'general exclamations of all the people' and reminded them that they should be grateful for the privileges they enjoyed already – especially the opportunity to trade to the Spice Islands. Company factor, William Biddulph, pushed the point further and appealed to the Mughal prince, Prince Khurram, at Lahore that the English be allowed to develop their commercial interests in the Red Sea. The prince declined this plan on the grounds that he would 'not begger his people for us' (Foster 1906–1927: 176). Not put off, Biddulph lobbied the emperor himself at Agra, but the Indian merchants beat him to it. Again, Biddulph received the news that the Surat merchants would not permit the development of the interests of the English in the Persian Gulf and Red Sea because they believed that the English had enough commercial opportunity in the South.

These requests of the Indians that the English prioritise their trade to the Spice Islands record the Gujarati merchants' concern about being eclipsed by the English in their Red Sea trades. But they are also statements of the Indians' enthusiasm and need for English bullion. At no point did Mughal officials or local merchants propose that the English be excluded from Mughal markets. Instead, the Indians wished to sustain trade with the English. Their enthusiasm reflected state policy. Edward Terry, Roe's chaplain, and a regular at the Mughal court from 1616 to 1619 described how 'the People of any Nation being there [are] very welcome [if they] bring in their Bull[i]on, and carry away the others Merchandizes' (Terry 1655: 119). The Mughal state was acutely short of coin throughout this period. The supply of silver through the Persian Gulf from the Ottoman

Empire was in decline from 1610. By 1611 (the same year the ratio of gold to silver was adjusted in England), Emperor Jahangir devalued the rupee. The Mughal state always maintained a higher mint price for silver than the market price to ensure that foreign bullion could be used for state purposes. Much like the situation of the English, the Mughal state and economy depended upon the liquid supplies of coin. Taxes were paid in coin, and revenues from trade could be more easily gathered by the state if the supply of coin was effective. In 1618, the Mughal state was forced to close one of its mints at Ahmadabad perhaps in response to dwindling supplies from overseas merchants including the English (Haider 1996: 298–364). As such, when the English appeared to switch their silver import trade to either a Persian trade in cloth or a coral export trade from Mocha, which directly challenged the livelihood of local Surat merchants, the emperor steadfastly resisted. In this way, the Indian thirst for coin encouraged first Kerridge's and then Mun's theoretical disabusal of the English state's need to prevent the export of coin.

VI

Sir Thomas Roe returned to England in September 1619 with his papers and possessions. He received a warm welcome from the company. The digesting of information from overseas factories was a central task for the East India Company's ruling committees. Roe was privileged enough to embellish his correspondence in person. Roe attended the Court of Committees on 6 October 1619. He explained how his embassy had transformed the commercial fortunes of the company. Roe made no secret of his ill feeling for Thomas Kerridge. Roe mentioned how developing the English trade in the Red Sea, which Roe mentioned the Surat factors had resisted, would advance the commercial prospects of the English. The minute books then record how

> having made this general relation, (which gave very good content and satisfaction,) the Company inten[d]ed to meet at some special times with him [Roe] to view all his notes and writings, sort them, endorse them, and put them to be kep[t] in their several places, where they may be found hereafter upon an occasion to use them.
>
> (CPSC 1870: 2.xxxiv–xxxvi)

This ruling would have placed all of Roe's correspondence, including (one assumes) the letters from Kerridge, at the disposal of the Court of Committees (Danvers and Foster 1896–1902: 5.332). The court then proposed that Roe be honoured by appointment as a director. Although Roe continued to join the Court of Committee meetings for the coming weeks and to brief the court about the prospects of the cloth-based Persian trade, Roe declined the offer of formal membership of the court.

Thomas Mun was present for much of Roe's testimony about the Surat trade. Roe's evidence, along with the discussion of a commercial alliance with the Dutch company that would have involved the sharing of convoys to western India, appears to have provoked an audit of the Surat trade. Along with Alderman Hugh Hamersley, Mun completed this task. The results were impressive. Mun calculated that the five ships sent to Surat since the establishment of trade there almost seven years earlier produced a total profit for the company of £210,860 (Foster 1906–1927: 313). Mun then declared as part of his summary that 'no place proveth so good, so sure, nor any trade to profitable' as that to Surat (Foster 1906–1927: 318). Munn's depiction of the values of the Surat trade was one in which Surat was at the centre of a multipolar trading system. While Mun shared Kerridge's view of the commodification of money, he also appreciated how Surat could be 'the life of' other trades to Persia and the Red Sea that Roe (who was present for the presentation of Mun's findings on 9 November) also celebrated (IOR B/6: 447). The corporate committees in London provided the best place to integrate the interests of factors, accountants and ambassadors into a cohesive view of the full possibilities of the Surat trade, which placed Surat at the centre of a transnational web of commerce that connected Bantam, Jask, Mocha and London and blended the interests of the company, its factors, the Gujarati merchants as well as the English, Mughal and Persian states. The failure of the cloth trade to Surat had forced the search for new markets for cloth that helped to create a multipolar market, which altered perspectives and perceptions of the international trade in bullion.

In early 1621, the company printed Mun's famous *Discourse of Trade* as part of its defence of its privileges against parliamentary assault. Although it did not mention Surat explicitly (describing instead the Indian trade as a whole), this work distilled the committee's appreciations of the huge commercial value of the multipolar commercial network focused on Surat. Mun's central concern was in robustly contradicting the now-clichéd and somewhat unreasonable criticism that the East India trade drained the Kingdom of specie (Mun 1621: 1). Although Mun frequently sustained the traditional bifurcation of the world economy into Christendom and the 'infidel' countries at the surface of his analysis, his depiction of the precise mechanics of the global economy fractured these monoliths up. He voiced his own experience of Mediterranean trade and finance to compare the English expectation of a trade in domestically produced commodities with those of Venice, France and the Netherlands, who freely exported bullion to Turkey rather than their own domestic commodities and were able to increase their inflow of bullion by doing so. Mun also demonstrated the huge scale of the specie trade between Turkey, Persia and India and stressed how such movements between sworn enemies were part of the properly functioning international commercial system. Mun used these 'infidel' case studies to support his argument that international trade in precious metals was not a transaction that helped to empower a nation's rivals. Instead, such commodification of specie and its integration into a multifaceted international system would enrich that nation. These international examples that would be most instructive for those 'perhaps not hauing the knowledge of occurrents in forren partes' were designed by Mun to demonstrate that the international economy was multitransactional and could not be stymied by the mistaken belief that viewed international trade solely from a domestic national perspective – as a series of outflows. With the international perspective provided by Mun, the international economy became discernable as a series of entrepôts for arbitrage in 'superfluities' of many kinds including bullion, the fruits of which would be translated into tropical commodities 'from Port to Porte in the Indies' and then again back in Europe into more bullion (Mun 1621: 16, 21).

Mun hoped to make his own argument compelling by citing the data he had been asked to digest on Roe's return from India. This information not only demonstrated the recent buoyancy of the trade in English exports to India since 1617 and the potential of the Persian trade in silk as a consumer of English commodities but also placed the export of bullion into the context of the legal limits established by the English state and the large quantities of bullion that the trade brought in (again, as dictated by the charter). This juxtaposition of the commodity exports and bullion exports led Mun to the climax of his theoretical insight: 'For let no man doubt, but that money doth attend Merchandize, for money is the prize of wares, and wares are the proper vse of money; so that their Coherence is vnseparable.' This insight was, of course, designed to pave the way for a justification for the East India trade that did not judge the trade according to how many English commodities it vended, but how much specie it brought back into the English economy due to the re-export of Indian 'wares' to the rest of Christendom. England ought to be a nation that traded in bullion as a commodity like any other rather than a nation that fetishised and engrossed specie in a manner that it rendered the Abyssinian's 'dull, lazy, and without artes' (Mun 1621: 16, 26, 56–57).

Mun's pamphlet pushed Dudley Digges's argument about the national benefits of distant trades and disputed Kayl's traditional fixation with national autarky. This emphasis reflects Mun's biography. Earlier in his career, Mun had worked throughout the Mediterranean trade (Gauci 2008). Edward

Misselden extolled Mun's international outlook, enthusing that 'his diligence at home, his experience abroad, have adorned him with such endowments, as are rather to be wisht in all, then easie to be found in many merchants of these times'. Throughout his defence of the East India Company, Mun also attached great importance to the experience of international situations for merchants who might serve the nation: 'This mysterie of Merchandising might be left only to them, [Note: Merchants by education are onely fit to trade in forren parts.] who haue had an education thereunto' (Mun 1621: 55). Gone were the classical allusions of Dudley Digges and in was the clarity of international experience of men like Thomas Kerridge. But Mun, implicitly observing the importance of the commercial agency of Mughal officials and Gujarati merchants, went one step further by suggesting that those Englishmen who objected to the export of bullion to Asia were the real authors of national decline for failing to accommodate the interests of foreigners in mutually beneficial trading relationships. For Mun it was embarrassing that a trade that depended upon the countenance of 'the pollicie and strength of Strangers' might be 'subverted by ourselves' (Mun 1621: 3–4).

Conclusion

Assembling the discursive, political and commercial context of Mun's early mercantilist writing helps to explain much about his early challenge to the 'bullionist' position. In the writings of Dudley Digges, and especially the correspondence of Thomas Kerridge, we are provided with a dress rehearsal for Mun's argument that international trade is inherently beneficial for the Kingdom and that money ought to be understood as a commodity like any other. The emergent global perspective on trade helped challenge the mediaeval conception of national accounts and proposed a more complex and advantageous commercial world where the value of national commodities could be multiplied exponentially as they followed the channels of international trade and exploited price differentials. Mun's determination to celebrate international experience and 'the pollicie and strength of Strangers' connects his earlier writings to the clearly acknowledged appreciation by mercantile actors like Kerridge that the East India Company would succeed only if it placed the commercial ambitions of its Indian customers ahead of the deeply ingrained opposition to bullion exporting that Digges found at 'every Table' in 1615. The need to accommodate the commercial interests of the infidel was perhaps what Mun had in mind when he described the 'necessity beyond resistance' of the international movement of commodities.

In these prefaces and contexts to Mun's writings, we see in clearer relief an acknowledgement of the importance of non-European contexts and people to the development of mercantilist doctrine than in Mun's pamphlet. The challenge to the bullionist doctrine would have lost much of its rationale were it not for the insistence in Surat that the English trade in silver not cloth. Sure enough, the English would go on to abandon their Persian experiment at Jask. They would destroy the Portuguese base at Ormuz and then encroach further into the Gujarati control over trading routes in the Red Sea, but at a critical 'knife edge' juncture from 1614 to 1619, local Indian merchants compelled the English to fixate on a bullion trade for Indian textiles and then for Indonesian spices. This compulsion and this fixation proved to have a lasting influence – via Mun – on how the English conceptualised the root causes of economic gain from international trade. As the institution that gathered the capital and personnel and constitutional privileges to establish trade in Surat and as the organisation that collected the information and funded the printing of new theory, the East India Company integrated, channelled and then publicised the international experience of cross-cultural commercial relations into new economic thought that challenged domestic prejudices.

Experience generated in international markets helped to alter the precepts of economic theory at home in such a way that the mediaeval view of national wealth deriving from static supplies of precious metal would be challenged by those who had observed the multifaceted and diversified exchanges of a complex global market. But how could paternalist views of non-European civilisation permit this alteration? The notion of an abstract, impersonal and mechanical market that Mun developed in some of his later writings provided one way to attribute commercial agency to one's cultural enemies (Mun 1664). Out of this tacit acknowledgement of corporate subordination to non-European markets came the willingness to abstract and depersonalise markets from their social and political contexts and to render them automatic. Here was a politically neutral means of describing the commercial realities of early modern international trade that captured the commercial power of non-Europeans. The corporation provided the international framework and the commercial imperative and constitutional agility to integrate these perspectives and the concentrated political will at home to formulate them into new theoretical perspectives.

References

Manuscript

Correspondence of Thomas Roe. BL Add MSS 6115.
EIC Factory Records, Surat. IOR G/36.
EIC Minute Books: 1617–20. IOR B/6.
State Papers Series: various years. TNA: SP14/67–73.

Print

Appleby, Joyce. 1978. *Economic Thought and Ideology in Seventeenth Century England*. Princeton: Princeton University Press.

Birdwood, Sir George and William Foster (eds.). 1893. *The First Letter Book of the East India Company, 1600–1619*. London: Quaritch.

Chaudhuri, K. N. 1963. 'The English East India Company and the Export of Treasure in the Early Seventeenth Century', *Economic History Review*, 16(1): 23–38.

Cronon, William. 2003. *Changes in the Land: Indians, Colonists, and the Ecology of New England*. New York: Hill and Wang.

Danvers, F. C. and William Foster (eds.). *Letters Received by the East India Company from Its Servants in the East (London, 1896–1902)*. Oxford: Oxford University Press.

Digges, Dudley. 1615. *Defense of Trade*. London.

Finkelstein, Andrea. 2000. *Harmony and Balance: An Intellectual History of Seventeenth Century English Economic Thought*. Ann Arbor: University of Michigan Press.

Foster, William (ed.). 1899. *The Embassy of Sir Thomas Roe to the Court of the Great Mogul, 1615–1619*. London: Hakluyt.

———, 1906–1927. (ed.). *The English Factories in India, 1618–1669*. Oxford: Oxford University Press.

———. 1934. 'The Author of the Trades Increase', *Times Literary Supplement*, March 29.

Gauci, Perry. 2008. 'Mun, Thomas (*bap.* 1571, *d.* 1641)', *Oxford Dictionary of National Biography*. Oxford: Oxford University Press.

Gentleman, Tobias. 1614. *England's Way to Winn Wealth*. London.

Green, Mary F. (ed.). 1858. *Calendar of State Papers: Domestic Series, James I 1611–1618*. London: HMSO.

Haider, Najaf. 1996. 'Precious Metal Flows and Currency Circulation in the Mughal Empire', *Journal of the Economic and Social History of the Orient*, 39(3): 298–364.

Hoppit, Julian. 2014. 'Mercantilism: Just a Label', *Times Literary Supplement*, August.

Kafadar, Cemal. 1991. 'Les Troubles Monetaires de la fin du XVIe Siecle et la Prise de Conscience Ottomane du Declin', *Annales*, 46(2): 381–400.

Kayll, Robert. 1614. *The Trade's Increase*. London.

Khan, Shafaat Ahmad. 1923. *The East India Trade in the 17th Century in Its Political and Economic Aspects*. London: Oxford University Press.

Koot, Christian J. 2012. '"Balancing Center and Periphery", in the Forum: "Rethinking Mercantilism"', *William and Mary Quarterly*, 69(2): 41–46.

Malynes, Gerald. 1610. *A Treatise of the Royal Merchant of Great Brittayne*. London.

Mishra, Rupali. 2014. 'Diplomacy at the Edge: Split Interests in the Roe Embassy to the Mughal Court', *Journal of British Studies*, 53(1): 5–28.

Muchmore, Lynn. 1970. 'A Note on Thomas Mun's 'England's Treasure by Forraign Trade', *Economic History Review*, 23(3): 498–503.

Mun, Thomas. 1621. *A DISCOVRSE of Trade, from England vnto the East-Indies: Answering to Diuerse Obiections Which Are Visually Made Against the Same*. London.

———. 1664. *England's Treasure by Forraign Trade*. London.

Ogborn, Miles. 2007. *Indian Ink: Script and Print in the Making of the East India Company*. Chicago: University of Chicago Press.

Pincus, Steven. 2012. 'Rethinking Mercantilism: Political Economy, the British Empire, and the Atlantic World in the Seventeenth and Eighteenth Centuries', *William and Mary Quarterly*, 69(1): 3–34.

Reinert, Sophus. 2011. *Translating Empire: Emulation and the Origins of Political Economy*. Cambridge, MA: Harvard University Press.

Richter, Daniel K. 2003. *Facing East from Indian Country: A Native History of Early America*. Cambridge, MA: Harvard University Press.

Roover, Raymond de. 1949. *Gresham on Foreign Exchange: An Essay on Early English Mercantilism with the Text of Sir Thomas Gresham's Memorandum for the Understanding of the Exchange*. Cambridge, MA: Harvard University Press.

Sainsbury, W. Noel (ed.). 1862. *Calendar of State Papers: Colonial: East Indies, 1513–1616*. London: HMSO.

———. 1870. *Calendar of State Papers: East Indies, China and Japan, 1617–1621*. London: HMSO.

Smith, John. 1614. *A Description of New England: Or the Obseruations, and Discoueries, of Captain Iohn Smith (Admirall of That Country) in the North of America, in the Year of Our Lord 1614*. London.

Stern, Philip J. and Carl Wennerlind (eds.). 2013. *Mercantilism Reimagined: Political Economy in Early Modern Britain and Its Empire*. New York: Oxford University Press.

Subrahmanyam, Sanjay. 1995. 'Of Imarat and Tijarat: Asian Merchants and State Power in the Western Indian Ocean, 1400 to 1750', *Comparative Studies in Society and History*, 37(4): 750–80.

Supple, Barry. 1964. *Commercial Crisis and Change in England, 1600–1642*. Cambridge: Cambridge University Press.

Terry, Edward. 1655. *A Voyage to East-India*. London.

Thomas, P. J. 1926. *Mercantilism and the East India Trade: An Early Phase of the Protection v. Free Trade Controversy*. London: P. S. King.

Van Ittersum, Martine. 2005. *Profit and Principle: Hugo Grotius, Natural Rights Theories, and the Rise of Dutch Power in the East Indies, 1595–1615*. Leiden: Brill.

Wilson, Charles. 1960. 'Cloth Production and International Competition in the Seventeenth Century', *The Economic History Review*, 13(2): 209–21.

2 Asian influences on the commercial strategies of the English East India Company

Aske Laursen Brock

When Sir Jeremy Sambrooke, a former member of the East India Company's (EIC) committee, made his last will in 1703, two years before his death, he made a special mention of a gold ring that he wanted to bequeath to his son Samuel Sambrooke. He wanted to give his son the 'Table diamond ring which I commonly weare on my finger and was given to me in India by Cassa Verona as a remembrance of him' (TNA: PROB 11/481/374). Jeremy Sambrooke had been a factor in Madras in his youth, and there he had encountered the influential Indian merchant Kasi Viranna, referred to as Verona by the Europeans. Viranna embodied the powerful Indian merchant who fused political suave with commercial success, and he facilitated connections between the English factors and the southeastern Indian world. While Sambrooke was in India, he experienced how the success of trade was dependent on cooperation with the most influential of the Indian merchants, and they formed close commercial ties. This meant, indirectly, that through Viranna and his network of European and Asian partners in Madras the Court of Committees of the EIC in London was connected closely with the commercial and political world of India. The Court of Committees in London needed powerful local allies in India to ply its trade, but the relationship was not without problems. The company in London was not interested in too great a reliance on the powerful local merchants, but for the English factors on the ground, cooperation with Indian merchants was of special importance during the conflicts in India in the 1670s.

The aim of this chapter is to investigate how political and commercial developments in India in the 1670s and 1680s were disseminated within the EIC's Court of Committees in London and how these exchanges resulted in new commercial strategies for the company. The seventeenth century saw the English and other European companies in a much weaker position than in the century to come, and changes in both Europe and Asia created a situation in which cooperation between Europeans and Indians was essential. The English in India were wholly dependent on cooperation with their Indian hosts. They needed Indian partners to obtain the cargo they wanted to send home, and they needed partners to navigate the complex political landscape. However, as the relationship developed it became more of a mutual relationship. The settlements grew in Bombay, Madras and later Calcutta, and more of the influential and powerful local merchants saw closer cooperation with the English as a way of maximizing their profit (Marshall 1976: 261; Hasan 1991: 356; 1992: 69). Not infrequently, the company's Court of Committees as well as factors complained about this dependency as, for instance, expressed when the company court in London required cheaper indigo. The company factors complained that they 'are forced to trust Banians or Cattarees who buy at the market price as Armanians, Persians & other merchants doe' (IOR G/3/7: 4). Even with this disharmony, the EIC was reliant on the good will of, in particular, the large portfolio capitalists – local merchant grandees.

First, this chapter will seek to emphasise the influence of the Indian political context on the development of trade in India between the different Indian principalities and the European – in this case, English – trading companies in the latter part of the seventeenth century. Second, it will investigate the relationship between powerful local merchants in India and the English company. In conclusion, the chapter aims to demonstrate how political developments in India, the cooperation with Indian merchants and differing interpretations of the same influenced changes to the existing commercial policy of the EIC in London. The internal changes in India and the networks created through these changes were as important to the forming of commercial policy as domestic changes in England. The organizational latitude of the EIC necessitated a significant amount of agency by the servants overseas and created a situation where the overseas was reacting before the company in London, and not always in accordance with the wishes of the Court of Committees in London (Veevers 2013: 690–1). The chapter will also discuss how the development of new English commercial strategies was tightly connected to the cooperation with foreign merchants – in this case, Indian merchants – and the encounters with powerful polities abroad such as the Mogul Empire, the Kingdom of Golconda and the rising power of the Marathas.

In 1673, the third governor of Bombay, Gerald Aungier, wrote back to the EIC's Court of Committees with the positive message that it had come to an agreement with the Maratha leader Shivaji (IOR G/3/6). Company factors had been caught in the fighting between the Moghul and the Marathas; the already-weak position of the EIC in India became even more exposed. The letter to the company in London illustrates the reality of the overseas servants of the company. Even though factors in India were meant to trade, they also had to concern themselves with the conflicts and political tensions of India. Aungier expressed that he understood the peace treaty with Shivaji to be concluded, but simultaneously he indicated that it was uncertain exactly when it would be confirmed. The company factors were more or less completely at the mercy of the different rulers of India – primarily the Mughal emperor Aurangzeb and his nawabs – but with the rise of the Marathas during the latter part of the seventeenth century, the existing equilibrium was upset. As a result, the company servants were relying more and more on the relationship with local merchants and officials to acquire the commodities requested by the court in London, or as requested by the people and syndicates in England backing the factors' private trade. The Mughal Empire was dependent on conquest from the earliest conception to keep the generals and nobles within the empire satisfied. Rebellions against the Mughals followed in the wake of these conquests; therefore, the struggle between the Mughal sovereign and the Maratha insurgents in the later part of the seventeenth century was not a new phenomenon; the area had experienced multiple minor and major struggles. Dr H. K. Naqvi calculated 144 revolts against Emperor Akbar in the late sixteenth and early seventeenth centuries alone. Shivaji's uprising was likewise described as that of an unruly zamindar or aristocrat (Pearson 1976: 223–6; Gordon 1993: 78).

The Maratha raids of the countryside and Mughal reprisals stunted trade and cultivation of crops by driving the peasants off the land. In the wake of the raiding, groups of bandits added to the disintegration of public order. This in turn meant it was more difficult for *jagirs* – the tax collectors – to collect their revenues, and this scarcity led to internal squabbles between the Mughal officers (Richards 1990: 637). For the European trading companies, this power struggle had become evident when Shivaji sacked Surat in 1663 and again in 1670 when he continued to Bombay to harass the English; the political situation in India and the relative weakness of the English had become a danger to the East India trade as a whole. The European traders in Surat were not looted but fought back from within walled encampments; however, the local merchants lost most of their belongings (Fryer 1698: 87; Richards 1993: 209). Gerald Aungier confessed his hopes of a future booming trade in Bombay, but commercial success was possible only if the English traders were 'not disturbed by the warr with the Dutch & more by continuous dissention betweene the Mogull & Shivaji'. Aungier had to concede that until some sort of agreement was reached 'all trade is in a manner obstructed, both by sea & Land by reason of the Armys & fleets a Broad on both sides' (IOR G/3/6: 38; Fryer 1698: 87; Richards 1993: 209). Between the Dutch naval strength, the expanding Shivaji and the struggling Mughals, the English trade suffered. The movements of Shivaji had become increasingly important for the servants in the EIC factories, and the letters they sent back to England during the 1670s expressed a renewed urgency regarding internal Indian politics. The previous sack of Surat convinced the company servants in Bombay that 'Shivaji intends nothing lesse then to attempt Surrat', and as a result 'the trade in Surrat will not be so Currt this year as the Last, for the People were then so affrighted by Shivaji' (IOR G/3/6: 38). The tense political situation forced other Europeans to react and 'both Dutch and French are keeping Armed men for defence of their houses in case of his approach to assault the Towne'. The English Company servants in Bombay also acknowledged the need for increasing a military presence in the affected areas, and they 'sent from hence [Bombay] 40 souldiers to secure the Companies Estate there' (IOR G/3/6: 11). The EIC servants on the ground wrote to the company and urged them to invest more heavily in forts and soldiers, but received disheartening answers from London who viewed the extra costs for soldiers as 'unnecessary charges' (IOR G/3/7: 7). Instead, the company in London reminded its servants in India that peace was the best business for them (Stern 2011: 62–63).

European trading corporations in India did illustrate some level of understanding of the political situation on the subcontinent, and Jeremy Sambrooke was not the only person on the Court of Committees who had practical experience from the overseas during the 1670s and 1680s. Fifteen per cent of the members on the Court of Committees who served the company during the 1670s had lived overseas for longer or shorter period and had a practical understanding of the overseas as well as experience of cooperation with local agents. Overseas influence on the court can be explained through the participation of these people, but even the committees who had not been in India themselves often had intimate connection with the subcontinent by proxy of their factors in India handling the private trade of the committees. The court in London and the powerful merchants and rulers in India were not separated by six degrees, but merely two. From Kasi Viranna in Madras to the four different governors of the EIC during the 1670s, Sir Andrew Riccard, Sir Nathaniel Herne, Sir William Thomson and Sir John Banks, there were either two or three links. During the last decades, no fewer than three committee members had worked alongside Viranna in Madras. Even in a socially structured society, and in spite of linguistic issues, the possibility to communicate with, and thereby affect, one another was there (de Sola Pool and Kochen 1978). Moreover, the notion of India was introduced to the wider audience in England during the period in plays and the popularization of travel literature and atlases. In his *Atlas of Asia* from 1673, publisher John Ogilby described – among many other things – the internal political relationships of Mughal India. In his description, he explained, 'The Army which the *Mogol* is oblig'd to keep constantly in *Decan* only, to curb the mighty King of *Golconda*, and the

King of *Visiapour*, with all their Assistants, is seldom less than about 25000 Horse' (Ogilby 1673: 159). The atlas was a part of a larger project, which brought the entire world to London and connected commerce with the restored monarchy (Batchelor 2014: 78, 173). In the same years as Ogilby published his atlas, John Fryer travelled to India and Persia on the bidding of the EIC. His work was not published until 1698, but, in the meantime, he had been requested at least 400 times to publish his narrative, according to himself. The demand for the knowledge on India was in other words palpable. In his narrative, Fryer describes how the English attempted to navigate the complex political situation between Aurangzeb and Shivaji in their embassy to the latter (Fryer 1698: Chapter IV). Fryer was employed by the EIC and must have briefed the company regarding the situation in India upon his return. Even if it took time for news to travel between the two continents, the connection between the two spheres was relatively close.

However, even with a certain understanding of developments in India due to Englishmen who travelled the subcontinent, the need for local trading partners who could navigate the internal conflicts became increasingly evident and, in particular, native merchants who fused commercial power with political contacts within the Mughal Empire or one of the other rulers. Sanjay Subrahmanyam and C. A. Bayly have integrated commerce further into the understanding of early modern Mughal society and of a Mughal political economy. They demonstrated that merchant princes, referred to by the authors as 'portfolio capitalists' (1990: 250–2), who yielded both political power and commercial clout had an important position in the Mughal system. They illustrated that who had previously been understood as warrior-princes with minor mercantile interests were really important merchants with political means: they were traders first and politicians and warriors second. The portfolio capitalists were frequently tax farmers in the areas where the European companies settled, and as the struggle between Aurangzeb and Shivaji disrupted the zamindars' business, it meant a change in the relationship between them and the Europeans. The Mughal officials therefore had an increasing interest in encouraging English trade, even when it meant bending imperial rules slightly (Hasan 1991: 356). The letter books of the EIC illustrate dealings with both smaller Indian merchants and portfolio capitalists: the merchants were of smaller scale and of the *Banian* caste, whereas the portfolio capitalists seemingly transcended caste and religious division. They came from a varied background, although they were, for the most part, Muslims. The different merchant groups – both the smaller *Banian* merchant and the larger portfolio capitalist – were dependent on the continuance of trade, but unlike the incorporated European companies they lacked the common organization, and the organization of trade remained social in character – with friction between different groups as a natural outcome enhanced by cooperation with the Europeans in the area (Das Gupta 2004: 14, 64).

Kasi Viranna was one of the most important of these commercial entrepreneurs in the 1670s. He rose to prominence through his business in Madras, which was located south of the immediate fighting between the Mughals and Marathas. As a result, Madras went through a period of relative prosperity: between 1668 and 1678, the settlement doubled in size to 50,000 people (Master and Temple 1911: 388–9). With this prosperity followed Viranna's wealth as he was – in the words of the company in both London and Madras – the chief merchant and leader of commerce in the city (Watson 1980b: 202). The wealth became obvious when a company servant wrote back to the EIC to complain about Viranna's success: 'Sir William [Langhorne] governs within the Fort and Verrona [Viranna] without' (Ogborn 2008: 89–90). Sir William Langhorne's relationship with Viranna facilitated his own downfall in the end. Langhorne went to India to investigate large discrepancies in the Madras functioning governor's accounting but did not eventually fare much better himself. The company in London was not entirely satisfied with the private trade he conducted, and the auditor Major Puckle found that Langhorne had received large sums of money from Viranna. In 1676 the company decided to replace William Langhorne with Streynsham Master who had extensive experience from India. Not long after had he arrived in India James Oxenden wrote to Master to inform him that his connections in England had had troubles keeping Master as the agent of Madras even before he had begun his tenure. The opposition against Master was so powerful that Charles II became involved. The EIC governor and deputy governor, the brothers William and Robert Thomson, were summoned to Whitehall and were told that 'his Majesty desired Sir William Langhorne's continuance att the Fort for two years longer' (IOR Ms EUR/E210/1). However, as Master had already been sent out, it was pointless to call him back again, so in the end the change was not effectuated. The Court of Committee in London had different informal agents in India. For instance, some backed Langhorne, some Master and others again Gerald Aungier. Frequently leading members of the company's committee pursued larger-scale private trade in India through the contact with factors (Coleman 1963: 79). Streynsham Master was likewise dependent on Kasi Viranna, and again the company in London was critical of the relationship between its servant and the influential merchant. In the company's dismissal of Streynsham Master in the end of 1680, it specified that the company had hoped for other merchants to be encouraged to trade with English. 'Wee observe that Impertinent and thredbare excuse you give for the merchants by which we suppose you meane Verona and his partners making their cloth soe bad' (IOR

Ms EUR/E210/2: 239). Kasi Viranna died suddenly in 1680, but before his demise, he had outlived a number of English governors of Madras who all had relied on his skills. However, some of Viranna's former English trading partners later became successful in English boardrooms. Both William Langhorne and Jeremy Sambrooke went on to serve on the Court of Committee of the EIC and the Royal African Company, and Streynsham Master became one of the driving forces behind the New EIC in 1698. He worked with the English and the French and farmed the customs for Golconda. His connections and his skilful navigation of the commercial and political landscape became a necessity for the Europeans in India (Watson 1980b: 207; Sharm 1998; Ogborn 2008: 92). Viranna's very young son Muddu Viranna and former business partners replaced him. In response to this, the company brought together new and old merchants in Madras by organizing them in a variation of a joint stock company. Eventually, the Indian merchants ended in the company's debt, and the EIC could exploit the markets in a way more beneficial to them.

In London and the EIC's headquarter in Leadenhall Street, the 1670s was tumultuous in a different way than the conflicts in India. In the 1670s only fifty-two different individuals held the positions as governor, deputy or committee member. In the following decade, the number increased with 44 per cent to seventy-five individuals and rose even further in the 1690s to eighty-one, before settling on fifty-five different individuals in the first decade of the eighteenth century. The average number of individuals who served on the Court of Committee of the EIC 1600–1709 is sixty-six, so arguably the 1670s and the 1700s were rather calm and tranquil periods whereas the other periods were periods of more extreme fluctuation (first multinationals). Nonetheless, what these fluctuations generally point to is a company in upheaval, which, considering the period's general societal upheaval, might not be altogether surprising. However, in all likelihood, they point to internal struggles and changes within the company. They therefore illustrate the 1670s as a decade of relative peace at the company's headquarters, but they also point to the 1670s as being a decade that furthered differences within the EIC. This in turn led to upheaval and major changes in personnel and policy within the EIC in the 1670s.

The prevailing explanation for the policy changes to the commercial strategies of the EIC in the historiography has been Josiah Child's rise to power. However, Child's 'faction', a term used loosely throughout the existing literature to explain the changes (Scott 1910: 321; Chaudhuri 1978: 116; De Krey 1985: 24; Lawson 1993: 51; Pincus 2009: 372), is rarely developed much further than to state that it existed and supported Child in his endeavours. What is more, the focus on factionalism within the company as a causal explanation overlooks the influence and effect of Indian politics on these developments. The contemporary pamphlets pointing out the existence of a faction led by Josiah Child were written by stark opponents to him and his control of the company and should be understood in that light. One of the contemporary critics mentions that Child had given the trade over to very ignorant people, thereby probably referring to the nobles who found their way onto the EIC's board in those years (Anon 1691: 3–4). The nobles in question were Henry, Duke of Beaufort, George, Lord Berkeley, Charles, Lord Worcester (Child's son-in-law), James, Lord Chandos (first multinationals).

Other important board members in the EIC distanced themselves from Child after the Mughal war and claimed that they were strongly opposed to Josiah Child and his policies. Sir Henry Johnson, the brother of a former EIC servant in Bengal, became involved in the parliamentary proceedings against the company (BL Add Mss 22185), and Thomas Rawlinson likewise claimed to have been at odds with Child, albeit not until after Child's death (Bodl. Mss Rawl. Lett 63). It is too simplistic to view the changes to the commercial strategy as a result of Josiah Child's influence in the company. However, it is possible to detect changes to the company policy in Child's writings from the period, in particular, when juxtaposed with his former trading partner Thomas Papillon, as well as from criticism by people outside the company. Child and Papillon are relevant points of departure when examining the development of the company's commercial strategy. During the 1670s Child and Papillon were both important members of the Court of Committees and stood for election as governor and deputy governor, respectively, in 1676. However, after the votes had been cast, they were both excluded from holding posts in the company, by the request of Charles II. It is unclear why Charles II felt it necessary to interfere in internal EIC business and exclude the two. Some have argued that Thomas Papillon was a dissenter and later a Whig, and Child was guilty by association. A final explanation given for Charles II's distaste for the pair of them is their role in collecting evidence for the impeachment of Sir Thomas Osborne, Lord Danby, alongside Sir Thomas Littleton (Letwin 1959; Bond 1976: 78–79). Moreover, they had both traded privately in Indian diamonds together in a partnership with the first governor of Bombay, George Oxenden, and in 1677 they went into business with Streynsham Master and his kinsman James Oxenden and Humphrey Edwin, another future EIC committee members (CKS U1015/O15/1; BL Add Mss 40698). In other words, both Child and Papillon were embedded into the Indian trading world – through the company itself, and the trading arrangement with Oxenden and Master – though they never spent time in India themselves. They previously had a close partnership, but their interpretation of the Indian political situation and how the company should proceed commercially differed. They present an interesting case of how Indian developments were understood and interpreted in England. The crux between the two was the understanding of force in the trading relations between the EIC and the powerful Indian merchants and the Mogul Empire.

The use of force in the trading relations between European companies and Asian merchants and principalities was an important question already from the foundation of the English EIC. The first English ambassador to India, Sir Thomas Roe, did not recommend the use of fortresses to secure Anglo-Indian relations. In his descriptions of his Indian adventure, 1615–1619, he noted how the forts were too expensive and provided little if any real protection for the British. However, this did not mean that Roe believed in peaceful relations with the Moghul Empire. Instead of fortresses, the ambassador was in favour of using England's maritime power to secure the East Indian trade and continued presence in India. A show of power was – in the opinion of Roe – essential in trade both towards the Moghul Empire and towards the other Europeans trading in the Indian Ocean. However, in consequence of the massacre of Amboyna where servants of the Dutch East India Company massacred servants of the EIC, fortresses became more important for the overseas trade in the eyes of the company (Watson 1980a: 78).

The company was not only coping with the political changes in northwestern India; it also experienced escalating problems with interlopers who wanted to trade into India in a regulated company. The latter included members of the Levant Company whose trade had come under increasing strain during the 1670s, when the EIC began to import cheaper silk to England. The different views on trade were expressed in a series of pamphlets during the 1670s. Thomas Papillon published a pamphlet named *The East-India-Trade a Most Profitable Trade to the Kingdom and Best Secured and Improved in a Company and a Joint-Stock*. Here he, as the title suggests, went to great length to describe the EIC's joint stock as the most important trade for the nation. The pamphlet was a direct response to the 1676 pamphlet *Tvvo Letters Concerning the East-India Company*, in which two fictional characters – a barrister and a country gentleman – discuss the soundness of investing in the EIC. The barrister advises the country gentleman not to invest as the people controlling the EIC were not liable for the investors and the 'Company may be bold at Sea and Land to make Warr against whom they please in the Indies, to build Forts and Castles, and to take Mens Persons and Goods there by force of Arms'. The end of the quote is not foreshadowing the war between the company and the Mughal Empire but refers instead to the EIC's practice of confiscating the ships and goods belonging to interlopers (Anon 1676b). Yet, before

Thomas Papillon answered the thinly veiled accusations of monopoly put forward in the pamphlet, an anonymous defender of the EIC also answered the *Tvvo Letters* directly. In the pamphlet *An Answer to Two Letters Concerning the East-India Company*, the author suggested that the Dutch had been the authors of the former pamphlet, to secure the calico trade for themselves. He continued by underlining the need for fortresses to secure the trade. This could only be done by trading in a joint stock:

> Further, Suppose there be a known Trade, that may be very advantageous to the Kingdom, and that for the obtaining and settling and carrying on of which there is a necessity to be at a vast Expence, to settle and keep Factories and Agents in several places, and with several Princes and on Occasion by Warre to force those Princes to perform their Capitulations, and to erect Forts and maintain Garrisons for security of the Trade, as also to cope with and prevent the designs of Enemies that would debarre the English of such a Trade.
>
> (Anon 1676a: 10)

The call for war and force against princes who did not live up to the promises of the farmans or capitulations was in thread with the call for use of force by the company servants overseas. The governor of Bombay, Gerald Aungier, had been advocating peaceful means through most of his tenure in Bombay, but 1676 proved to be a year of change for him as well, and he made it clear to the company's committees in London that 'the times now require you to manage your general commerce with your sword in hand' (Watson 1980a: 78). A new discourse was slowly evolving inspired by the experiences of the servants on the ground in India and Asia. Thomas Papillon was less bombastic regarding the use of force in his answer to the 1676 pamphlet the following year. He, like the anonymous pamphleteer, argued that the joint stock model was necessary for trading into India due to the strength of the multitudes of kingdoms and princes in the Far East. He found that 'there is no coming for any European people to any place in those Countreys for Trade, without making Presents to the Kings, Princes, Governors, and great Men at their first coming, and obtaining their license and permission'. This indicates Papillon was not unfamiliar with the concept of having to gift lavishly to obtain a better position abroad. In other words, the notion of having to gift sums of money to Charles II would not have been foreign to Papillon. With the words 'those Countreys' he does indicate a difference in the understanding of us and them – between England, maybe even Europe and 'those Countreys'. However, it is not indicated in the text that this practice of gifting is immoral, wrong or limited to the overseas. This issue of gifting or bribing is not likely to have caused any larger disagreement between the two former business partners, which has otherwise been claimed (Papillon 1887: 81–84).

Moreover, he wrote that 'there is a necessity of purchasing or hiring some great House to abide in for the security of their persons and goods, during their abode, at every respective place' (Papillon 1677: 14). The need for purchasing a great house for the security of the personnel overseas underlines the relative weakness of the English nation in the setting abroad. The European and English presence in India and the East Indies meant little to the people of Asia: the Europeans were only a drop in the ocean of merchants active in the Bengali waters. A few Asian people were worse off by the European presence, and a few were better off, but the vast majority of people were utterly unaffected in their everyday life (Ogborn 2008: 79). Papillon continues his argument of the necessity of a joint stock and that the company's monopoly should be upheld as the company already 'have been at vast Charges and Hazards, not only to procure a freedom and liberty of Trade, with many great Privileges and Immunities'. Moreover, in an effort to secure its trade by maintaining so-called great houses and warehouses in some places 'as at Fort St. George, Bombay, and St. Helena', it was necessary 'to make considerable Fortifications, and to keep large Garrisons' (Papillon 1677: 14). The purpose of the considerable fortifications is somewhat unclear: it could serve as protection both from the other Europeans in Asia and from arbitrary rule by Asian rulers. At the bottom line, in Papillon's opinion, trade to India could flourish only after agreements with the emperor, kings and princes in the Far East and through a joint stock with the capability to build and maintain essential structures. However, in Papillion's vision, trade should be conducted through negotiations with the locals and not by force. The discussions about the trade to India, and thereby also the monopoly of the EIC, only escalated into the 1680s.

In 1681 the Levant Company published its allegations against the EIC after presenting the said allegations to the Parliament. The primary criticism was concerning the form of trade – the joint stock model – which was seen as omitting too many people from the trade and concentrating the important trade to India in the hands of a few (Anon 1681). Josiah Child answered the Levant Company's allegations promptly in the 1681 pamphlet *A Treatise Wherein Is Demonstrated, I. That the East-India Trade Is the Most National of All Foreign Trades.* Child stated, like Papillon and all other EIC pamphleteers before him, 'That there is a necessity of a Joynt Stock in all Foreign Trade', but only 'where the Trade must be maintained by Force and Forts on the Land; and where his Majesty cannot conveniently maintain an Amity and Correspondence by Embassadors; and not elsewhere' (Child 1681: 5). Child openly pointed out that forts and force were needed to trade to India in a different way than Papillon does it.

There was a clear difference between the discourse of Thomas Papillon, who acknowledged the need to gift the Moghul and the many princes and kings of the Far East to obtain trading privileges, and that of Josiah Child. In the case of Papillon, it seems the fortifications were to be used in a defensive strategy to maintain a foothold for trading. Child viewed force a necessity and the only viable solution to secure the foreign trade for England. The aforementioned 'Force and Forts' were meant to serve dual purposes. The primary objective of the forts and force was to protect against the local powers – petty princes and governors – against the other Europeans, in particular, the Dutch, and against English interlopers trading to India. However, the second objective was to be able to raise revenue from the locals who were living under the jurisdiction of the forts (IOR E/3/90: 171–5). The changing reality of Indian politics, continued reliance on powerful Indian portfolio capitalists and an increased threat from English interlopers facilitated a change of personnel within the EIC. One of the most important fault lines appears to have been the discourse of force. However, the discourse of force and military power was not the EIC and Josiah Child's sole approach to trade in the East Indies in the tumultuous 1670s and 1680s. Simultaneous with the worsening situation in India, and increasing troubles with interlopers, the company took a diplomatic approach to trade. In May 1682, eight ambassadors arrived from the Sultanate of Banten, in present-day Indonesia, and Sir Josiah Child was very keen to instil onto the Privy Council that only the company should deal with the ambassadors while they were in England (London Gazette). The EIC hoped to secure the foreign diplomats' support and protection of English trade against the Dutch, but the ambassadors had come without executive powers and therefore the company's ambitions to obtain trading privileges were thwarted. Soon after, events in Asia further worsened the EIC's situation overseas. The Dutch helped the Sultan of Banten to maintain power against his son, the 'young king', and while doing this they removed all other Europeans trading in Banten (Stern 2011: 69–70). The company was urging its servants in India to leave their inclination to 'womanish pity' and assume the political government, which had been bestowed upon them by Charles II (IOR E/3/91: 5). To avoid similar fates like that of Banten, the company's new policy of force was underlined and the company in London urged its factors in Madras 'strengthened & fortifie the Fort and Town by degrees that it may be Acruable against the Assault of any Indian Prince & the Dutch power of India' (IOR E/3/90: 160–2). The company servants were convinced that to secure the Asian trade for the future it was necessary to change their strategy. In the coming decades the company's committees in Leadenhall Street came to the same conclusion.

In conclusion, the close connections between English merchants in India and Indian portfolio capitalists made a significant impact on the Court of Committee in London and influenced a change in the company's politics and commercial strategy. The dependence on cooperation in India not only led a renewed discussion of the importance of a forceful presence in Asia but also meant attempting to ally the company closer to the Armenian community. In 1688, simultaneously with the company's unsuccessful campaign against the Mogul Empire, the company signed an agreement with prominent Armenian traders on them carrying trade from India and Persia (IOR B/39, 133–5). The deal offered to the Armenians cheap shipping and wide-reaching rights in India, which indicate how important it was for the EIC to develop a network beyond the control of the Indian portfolio capitalists.

The Marathas, the increasing influence of powerful portfolio capitalists particularly in South India and the competition with the Dutch and English interlopers for the favour of the Asian rulers meant that a revision of the company's commercial strategy was necessary. The relations between Europeans and Indians were reported back to England and the Court of Committee, but the interpretation of these relations and the most favourable way to proceed differed greatly. Within the company, different visions of trade were promoted and exemplified by Josiah Child and Thomas Papillon, and though both visions perceived the joint stock model and promoted fortifications as necessities to secure the trade, they had different opinions on the use of force. In Papillon's vision, the forts were merely a defensive measure, whereas Josiah Child was more inclined to promote the use of force and saw the forts as more offensive structures. Child's vision was closer to the advice conveyed by the company's servants abroad, as exemplified by Aungier's words from 1676. The change in discourse regarding force inspired by the events overseas meant that the company needed more than mere merchants: what was needed was, as expressed by the governor of Bombay, Gerald Aungier, men with the abilities of a 'souldier, Lawer, Philosopher, Statesman and much lesse a Governour' (Stern 2011: 83–84). This was not only true among the company servants in the East but, as also pointed out by Child in his 1681 pamphlet, just as true regarding the people directing the company's business in London. During a period when the EIC was in a weak position overseas and trading on the mercy of numerous powerful actors in India, the servants overseas fanned the flames of divergence within the boardroom in London. The result was a change of commercial policy, which during the 1680s would lead to wars against Siam and the Mogul Empire endangering English overseas trade even more than before.

References

Manuscript

EIC Court Minutes: 1687–90. IOR B/39.

EIC Factory Records, Bombay: various years beginning 1670. IOR G/3.

EIC Letter Books: various years beginning 1682. IOR E/3.

Miscellaneous papers relating to the East India Company's affairs with which Thomas Papillon was connected: 1677–84. Kent Archives, Maidstone. CKS U1015/015.

Oxenden Papers: 1684. BL Add MS 40698.

Papers Relating to the EIC: 1682–1701. BL Add MS 22185.

Rawlinson Letters. Bodleian Library, Oxford Mss Rawl. Lett.

Streynsham Master Papers: 1640–1724. IOR Mss EUR E210.

Will of Jeremy Sandbrooke: 1705. TNA: PROB 11/481/374.

Print

Anon. 1676a. *An answer to two letters concerning the East-India Company London.*

———. 1676b. *Tvvo letters concerning the East-India Company London.*

———. 1681. *The allegations of the Turkey Company and others against the East-India-Company, relating to the management of that trade presented to the Right Honourable the Lords of His Majesties most Honourable Privy Council, the 17th of August London.*

Anon. 1691. *Companies in Joynt-Stock unnecessary and inconvenient: free trade to India in a regulated company, the interest of England. Discours'd in a letter to a friend*: [1691].

Batchelor, Robert K. 2014. *London: the Selden Map and the making of a global city, 1549–1689.* Chicago: University of Chicago Press.

Bond, Maurice. 1976. *The diaries and papers of Sir Edward Dering, Second Baronet, 1644 to 1684.* London: H.M.S.O.

Chaudhuri, K. N. 1978. *The trading world of Asia and the English East India Company, 1660–1760.* Cambridge: Cambridge University Press.

Child, Josiah Sir. 1681. *A treatise wherein is demonstrated, I. That the East-India trade is the most national of all foreign trades. II. That the clamors, aspersions, and objections made against the present East-India Company, are sinister, selfish, or groundless. III. That since the discovery of the East-Indies, the dominion of the sea depends much upon the wane or increase of that trade . . . IV. That the trade of the East-Indies cannot be carried on to the national advantage, in any other way than by a general joynt-stock. V. That the East-India trade is more profitable and necessary to the Kingdom of England, than to any other kingdom or nation in Europe.* London: Printed by J.R. for the Honourable the East-India Company.

Coleman, D. C. 1963. *Sir John Banks, baronet and businessman. A study of business, politics, and society in later Stuart England.* Oxford: Clarendon.

Cook, Harold John. 2007. *Matters of exchange: commerce, medicine, and science in the Dutch Golden Age*. New Haven, CT: Yale University Press.

Das Gupta, Ashin. 1979. *Indian merchants and the decline of Surat, c.1700–1750*. Wiesbaden: Steiner.

De Krey, Gary Stuart. 1985. *A fractured society: the politics of London in the first age of party 1688–1715*. Oxford: Clarendon.

de Sola Pool, Ithel, and Manfred Kochen. 1978. 'Contacts and Influence', *Social Networks* 1: 5–51.

Fryer, John. 1698. *A new account of East-India and Persia, in eight letters: being nine years Travels begun 1672, and finished 1681 . . . With maps, etc*. London: R. R. for R. Chiswell.

Gordon, Stewart. 1993. *The Marathas 1600–1818*. Cambridge: Cambridge University Press.

Hasan, Farhat. 1991. 'Conflict and Cooperation in Anglo-Mughal Trade Relations during the Reign of Aurangzeb', *Journal of the Economic and Social History of the Orient* 34(4): 351–360.

———. 1992. 'Indigenous Cooperation and the Birth of a Colonial City: Calcutta, c. 1698–1750', *Modern Asian Studies* 26(1): 65–82.

Lawson, Philip. 1993. *The East India Company: a history*. London: Longman.

Letwin, William Louis. 1959. *Sir Josiah Child, merchant economist: with a reprint of brief observations concerning trade, and interest of money, etc. [With a portrait.]*. Boston: Baker Library, Harvard Graduate School of Business Administration.

Marshall, P. J. 1976. *East Indian fortunes: the British in Bengal in the eighteenth century*. Oxford: Clarendon.

Master, Streynsham Sir, and R. C. Sir Temple. 1911. *Diaries, 1675–1680, and other contemporary papers relating thereto*. London: Murray.

Ogborn, Miles. 2008. *Global lives: Britain and the world, 1550–1800*. Cambridge: Cambridge University Press.

Ogilby, John. 1673. *Asia*. London: Printed by the author.

Papillon, A. F. W. 1887. *Memoirs of Thomas Papillon, of London, merchant (1623–1702)*. [S.l.]: Beecroft.

Papillon, Thomas. 1677. *The East-India-trade a most profitable trade to the kingdom and best secured and improved in a company and a joint-stock: represented in a letter written upon the occasion to two letters lately published insinuating the contrary*. London.

Pearson, M. N. 1976. 'Shivaji and the Decline of the Mughal Empire', *The Journal of Asian Studies* 35(2): 221–235.

Pincus, Steven. 2009. *1688: The first modern revolution*. New Haven, CT: Yale University Press.

Richards, John F. 1990. 'The Seventeenth-Century Crisis in South Asia', *Modern Asian Studies* 24(4): 625–638.

———. 1993. *The Mughal Empire*. Cambridge: Cambridge University Press.

Scott, William Robert. 1910. *The Constitution and Finance of English, Scottish and Irish Joint-Stock Companies to 1720*. 2 vols. Cambridge: Cambridge University Press.

Sharm, Yogesh. 1998. 'A Life of Many Parts: Kasi Viranna: A Seventeenth Century South Indian Merchant Magnate', *The Medieval History Journal* 1: 261–290.

Stern, Philip J. 2011. *The company-state: corporate sovereignty and the early modern foundation of the British Empire in India.* Oxford: Oxford University Press.

Subrahmanyam, Sanjay, and C. A. Bayly. 1990. 'Portfolio capitalists and the political economy in early modern India', in Sanjay Subrahmanyam (ed.) *Merchants, markets and the state in early modern India*, pp. 242–265. Oxford: Oxford University Press.

Veevers, David. 2013. '"The Company as Their Lords and the Deputy as a Great Rajah": Imperial Expansion and the English East India Company on the West Coast of Sumatra, 1685–1730', *The Journal of Imperial and Commonwealth History* 41(5): 687–709.

Watson, Ian Bruce. 1980a. 'Fortifications and the "Idea" of Force in Early English East India Company Relations with India', *Past & Present* (88): 70–87.

———. 1980b. *Foundation for empire: English private trade in India 1659–1760.* New Delhi: Vikas.

3 The East India Company and the shift in Anglo-Indian commercial relations in the 1680s

Michael Wagner

In this chapter, I will examine a period that I believe was pivotal in the evolution of Anglo-Indian commercial relationships: the 1680s. In this decade, mutual commercial interests in England and in India led to significant developments, which promoted a greater integration of the English and Indian economies.

Although the major debates about the nature of Anglo-Indian relationships have tended to focus on the eighteenth century, historians have recognized that the period immediately preceding and following the English Glorious Revolution of 1688 saw important changes in the East India Company (EIC) and the policy of the English government regarding India. Om Prakash (1998: 211) observed that the 1680s marked the start of a qualitative improvement in the trade of the EIC as well as the Dutch East India Company. However, the gains in trade during the first half of the 1680s came to an abrupt halt for the EIC towards the end of the decade as the company became engaged in a losing war (sometimes known as Child's War) with the Mughal Empire. The commercial motives of this war remain difficult to comprehend, and the aggression of the EIC is perhaps best explained by political changes in England. Philip Lawson (1987: 50) saw the combination of EIC governor Josiah Child's belligerent leadership and the aggressive imperial policy of the late Stuart regime leading to a distinct shift in approach in the 1680s. This view was echoed by Steve Pincus (2009: 373), who noted the strong relationship between Child and James II. Despite the disruptive impact of the war on trade in the late 1680s, there were some important developments in the decade, which provided the foundation for closer financial linkages between England and India.

To illuminate these changes, I will start with an overall review of the developments affecting the EIC and its trade with India. An understanding of the nature of the EIC's business, particularly the concentration of economic interests in the company, is necessary to understand the political debates concerning the EIC in the late seventeenth century as well as the reliance of the English government on the EIC as a source of valuable 'loans' to support the cost of wars with France. Developments within the Mughal Empire also acted to increase the importance of Anglo-Indian trade. Escalating taxes and growing demand for silver within the empire increased the importance of Western trade, especially trade with the EIC. I will then focus on developments in Madras. Madras is interesting as a case study in this period because as K. N. Chaudhuri noted, 'Between 1660 and 1680 the centre of gravity in the company's commercial policy moved to the south, from Surat to Madras' (1978: 53). A number of financial institutions and commercial practices were introduced in Madras, which were not dissimilar to contemporary developments in England. In this regard, the expansion of the activity of the EIC's mint was particularly important for the extension of the company's operations generally in India, but especially in Bengal.

Politically, the early 1680s was not an easy time for the EIC in England. Josiah Child's appointment as governor of the EIC in 1681 occurred during a period of mounting criticism of the company. Most contemporary criticism of the EIC revolved around two issues. The first was the quantity of bullion and coin that it exported. The political concern about the export of treasure affected the EIC for almost its entire life as a company and also affected the Russia Company in the eighteenth century (Wagner 2014). In the case of the EIC, its exports of silver were seen as a substitute for the export of English manufactured goods, especially woollen cloth. The situation was exacerbated by the fact that the main import of the EIC, calicoes, acted as a substitute for English manufactured garments made from woollen cloth and silk. The second criticism of the EIC concerned the exclusivity of the company, especially the limited number of shares that were available for purchase by the investing public. These criticisms were at the heart of the Levant Company's attack on the EIC in the early 1680s. The Levant Company accused the EIC of finding it 'more to their advantage to trade with money at interest than to enlarge their own stock' and also accused the EIC of trading with the 'treasure of the nation, dividing to themselves what sums they please' (1681: 3). Because the EIC constrained the number of its shares and paid high dividends, the price of the company's shares more than quadrupled between 1672 and 1681 (Chaudhuri 1978: 512). This clearly benefitted the company's existing shareholders but frustrated potential investors seeking to share the spoils. For the overall EIC trade with India, gold became considerably less important than silver in the 1680s and relatively unimportant from the 1690s onwards. However, as discussed later in this chapter, gold remained important in certain regions of India, such as Madras, which traditionally employed gold-based currency (Chaudhuri 1968: Table 1). The general increase in the importance of silver in the 1680s was driven by both the growth of trade and the fiscal demands of the Mughal Empire. Over the course of the seventeenth century, the Mughal state's revenue demand more than doubled (Richards 1993: 186). Land taxes, which represented about 90 per cent of Mughal taxes, were typically paid in silver rupees. The main routes by which American silver reached the Mughal Empire were Persia and the Red Sea, but direct trade with Europeans, such as the EIC and the VOC (the Dutch East India Company), was growing in importance as a source of silver supply. By the 1680s, almost 20 per cent of the silver bullion imports into the Mughal Empire came via the EIC (Haider 1993: 323).

By far the major supplier of silver to the company in the 1680s was Thomas Cooke. Cooke formed a powerful combination with Josiah Child. They were the two largest shareholders in the company, and they dominated the EIC in the 1680s and early 1690s. In 1691, Child and Cooke owned over 12 per cent of EIC shares between them (IOR H/2, list of stockholders for 1691), and Child's son married Cooke's daughter the same year. Cooke began the first of several terms as EIC governor in 1692. Like Child, Cooke was a controversial figure and he was accused of bribery in connection with the renewal of the company's charter in 1693. The power of the London goldsmiths who supplied silver to the company, such as Cooke, only waned after 1696 when the EIC changed its policy and bought silver from suppliers in Amsterdam and Cadiz (Chaudhuri 1968: 491).

Larger investors were becoming more prominent in the company in the late seventeenth century. Between 1675 and 1691, the percentage of EIC stock held by individuals with more than £2,000 of par value shares almost doubled (Davies 1952: 296). This situation only started to change somewhat after 1693 when the government required that new stock be issued. By 1699, the year after the founding of the rival New East India Company, Child and Cooke had very dramatically reduced their shareholdings and the largest shareholders were Alvaro and John Mendes DaCosta and Peter Henriques junior (IOR H/2, list of stockholders for 1699). Although a number of Sephardic Jews had large holdings in EIC stock in the 1690s and Jews would also invest in the New East India Company when it was founded in 1698, it should be noted that, by the time the United Company was formed in 1709, Jews held only a little over 12 per cent of EIC stock, similar to the holdings of Child and Cooke in 1691 (Dickson 1967: 268). Typically, these Jewish shareholders had interests in the EIC's trade and were not purely financial investors. Henriques was an important customer of the EIC who bought a range of goods, including calicoes and pepper (IOR, L/AG/1/5/6 Cash Book 1678–1682). The Mendes DaCostas were involved in several businesses that affected the EIC, especially the importation of gold from Portugal that was subsequently re-exported to

India (Yogev 1978: 39, 109). An act of Parliament in 1698 that prohibited EIC stockholders from engaging in private trade in diamonds limited the expansion of Jewish influence within the EIC because the one area of Anglo-Indian commerce where Jews were dominant in the late seventeenth century was the importation of diamonds (Yogev 1978: 98).

The EIC was viewed by the English government as an important source of financing. Custom duties on the company's growing imports were a significant source of royal finance. In addition, the company loaned £170,000 to the government in the 1660s as government spending rose during the first two Anglo-Dutch Wars. In 1698, the New East India Company loaned £2 million to the government at 8 per cent interest. This was the entire amount of the share subscription to the new company. With the creation of the United East India Company in 1709, additional stock of £1.2 million was issued, and the entire amount of new capital was loaned to the government at no interest, reducing the interest rate on the consolidated government debt of £3.2 million to 5 per cent (Scott 1910: 152–92).

While the government demanded loans equivalent to the par value of EIC stock, the EIC relied upon its bonds and other borrowing for its working capital. EIC bonds were highly attractive investments. They were secure, and there was a ready market for the securities. While the bonds were nominally issued for terms of six months, they were both renewable (by investors) and redeemable (by the company). These features contributed to their price stability in the market (Marco and Malle-Sabouret 2007). East India and South Sea bonds, as well as the notes of the Bank of England, were all, in effect, secured by the debt owed them by the government (Dickson 1967: 409). In 1721, the government went further and placed statutory restrictions on the quantity of bonds that the EIC was allowed to issue, limiting them to the value of the company's loans to the government. Therefore, in practice, EIC bonds were government bonds by another name.

The reliance upon bonds and other short-term borrowing for its working capital meant that a very large proportion of the company's cash flow consisted of either borrowing or repaying debt. For example, for the year 1682, the company's total cash outflow was some £2.2 million (IOR L/AG/1/5/6). Of this total cash outflow, half (£1.1 million) went towards the repayment of principal on borrowings. Interest payments amounted to £33,700. The exact amount of outstanding debt in 1681 is not known, but in that year, the EIC claimed that its debt at interest was £550,000, and the EIC's records for 1685 indicate debts of £569,244 (EIC 1681: 10; IOR H/4: 23–25). Interest payments of £33,700 would represent interest of about 6 per cent on £550,000 (Dickson 1967: 411). The Levant Company also claimed that, at times, the EIC was able to borrow at an interest of 3–4 per cent (Levant Company 1681: 4). This was true, but, in practice, the company frequently adjusted the interest rates on its bonds (IOR B/37: 28). The fact that the repayment of principal totalled £1.1 million suggests that, notwithstanding the renewability feature of the bonds, they were normally held for about six months. To meet its ongoing working capital needs, the company borrowed £1.4 million in total in 1682. Therefore, it is not altogether surprising that a central plank of Josiah Child's view of political economy was that the government should act to keep interest rates low. Child argued that low interest rates were a key to the development of the Dutch economy, but they were also particularly beneficial to the EIC and its major shareholders. Given the EIC's capital structure, the ability to borrow at low interest rates was essential in keeping interest payments on the company's considerable debt at a reasonable level and low interest rates contributed to a very high valuation of the company's shares (along with the policy of intentionally constraining the number of shares issued and paying out very high dividends).

In addition to the large sums required to repay its debts, another salient feature of the company's cash outflow in 1682 was the payment of £661,000 (about 30 per cent of total cash outflow), which went to Thomas Cooke and Co. for gold and silver. Suppliers of silver were also the biggest lenders to the company. In 1685 'Mr. Cook' (presumably Thomas Cooke) and William Atwill (a goldsmith and silver supplier to the company) were owed some 13 per cent of the EIC's total debt (IOR H/4: 23–25). In total, therefore, about 80 per cent of the company's cash outflow went either to repay debt or to buy treasure.

The remaining cash outflow of about £440,000 went towards operational expenses, of which trade goods (excluding silver) accounted for £137,000 (Chaudhuri 1978: Appendix 5, Table C3). About half of the expenditure on trade goods was for broadcloth (Chaudhuri 1978: 512; IOR L/AG/1/1/9, 128). This was by no means an insignificant sum in the context of the late seventeenth-century trade, but it was dwarfed by the purely financial operations of the company. There was, however, another very important component of the company's cash outflow, and that was expenditure on shipping services. The company was paying well over £100,000 per year to ship owners (IOR L/AG/1/1/9: 55–71). These payments for the freight of commodities represent only a fraction of the potential return from ship ownership. Ship owners appointed ship masters. Ship masters, in turn, were permitted a certain level of private trade on their own account (which was difficult to strictly enforce) and could also influence which other private trade cargoes were carried in their ships.

Private trade, particularly private trade in diamonds, was, of course, where the real money was for senior employees of the company. The 'nabobs' who returned to England did not acquire their fortunes from their company salaries. While a portion of private trade was financed with Indian capital, Soren Mentz's (2005) work has illustrated the importance of English capital and linkages to the city of London in the financing of private trade. Madras was the centre of the Indian diamond trade, and a community of Jewish merchants, who normally acted as commission agents for their partners in London, established themselves in Madras in the 1680s (Love 1913: 486). Furthermore, private trade networks were very much linked to Amsterdam as uncut diamonds were typically imported to London and then sent to Amsterdam for cutting and polishing.

The concentration of economic interests in the EIC's business was not restricted to its investors and suppliers of silver and ships. The composition of the company's commodity imports to England has been well documented, but less well understood is the role of large wholesale buyers of the EIC's commodities in England. The fact that sales were conducted via auction suggests a fair and open buying process, but it is important to recognize that the auctions took place over an extended period. For example, the auctions in October 1682 took over a week to conclude. This lengthy process increased the likelihood that large buyers would know each other's interests and be able to set market prices. The company's biggest customer in the early 1680s was Robert Woolley. Woolley bought about £80,000 of goods from the EIC annually in the early 1680s (IOR L/AG/1/1/1/9: 289–304). Woolley was a wealthy broker who, in 1682, was a member of the London Common Council and was estimated to be worth £30,000 (Woodhead 1965: 180). Woolley's brokerage activity led him to produce London's first regularly published price list for commodities, known as a price current, starting in the 1670s (Price 1954). Given the range of commodities in which Woolley dealt, the price current acted as a form of advertising for his business. Thus, English imports from India contributed in a direct way to the establishment of a business press in London.

Working relationships with business people and politicians were as vital for the EIC in India as they were in England. The following discussion concerning Madras illustrates that, as was the case in England, it was political relationships that were most problematic in India. Although business relationships appeared to be much more under the control of the company than political relationships, business relationships were not entirely immune to political influence. Increasingly in the 1680s, as the political landscape changed in southern India, the business infrastructure that evolved began to resemble that of England.

In the 1670s, the EIC's relationship with Indian merchants in Madras was dominated by a single figure, the chief merchant known variously as Kasi Viranna, Hasan Khan or, as the English called him, Cassa Verona. Viranna controlled the hinterland around Madras that supplied textiles to the EIC. He was able to establish a quasi-monopoly on the supply of textiles to the EIC at Madras by advancing money to artisans in the surrounding countryside and securing access to their production. Viranna was also the undisputed leader of the large Indian settlement at Madras known as 'black town' by the English (the English settlement at Madras was known as 'white town'). Black town was essentially a commercial settlement that was largely free of the political influence of the sultanate of Golconda, which controlled the territory around Madras. In addition to his roles as a businessman and civic leader, Viranna was an astute politician. He facilitated the private trade of senior EIC officials in Madras, which allowed them to return to England with riches far beyond what they might have expected to save from their modest salaries (Mentz 2005: 115, 120). Despite the very useful services that Viranna provided to the EIC in Madras, company officials in London disapproved of his dominant position. Both Streynsham Master and William Gyfford were made aware of the unease of the court of directors with Viranna's power when they were appointed to the governorship of Madras in 1675 and 1682, respectively. Gyfford received a letter from the then EIC governor, William Thompson, which stated 'You must give your new men you propose to deal with full assurance to protect them against the threats of Verona, who is grown so potent by our indulging him, that he menaces and frighteth persons from offering to deal with you' (Fort St. George 1914: EIC to Gyfford, 5 January 1681).

Viranna's death in 1680 marked a turning point in the relations between the EIC and Indian merchants at Madras. After Viranna's death, the EIC entered into contracts with groups of Indian merchants, sometimes referred to as 'joint stock companies'. These associations were not like Western joint stock companies, but they did involve pooling of capital among Indian merchants. Not only did this new relationship give the EIC greater leverage in its relations with Indian merchants, but the customary practice whereby the EIC had advanced money to Viranna to enable him to contract with his suppliers was now ended. As Miles Ogborn noted, with Viranna's death it became possible for the English at Madras to 'impose conditions on the merchants at Madras which were much more in the company's favour' (2008: 93). In particular, the EIC was now able to withhold payment until it had received a substantial portion of the supplies for which it had contracted (Arasaratnam 1966: 87). This development is consistent with Tirthankar Roy's argument that the idea and practice of contract was the real business innovation that the EIC introduced in India (2012: 208–9). Roy has observed that contracts were not unknown in India but the scale and complexity introduced by Europeans was without Indian precedence.

In 1682, Streynsham Master was accused of illegal private trading and removed as governor of Madras. Under Master's governorship, relations between the EIC and the local administration around Madras had been poor. While Golconda was not ruled by the Mughals, it had been required to pay an annual tribute to the Mughals since 1635 (Richards 1993: 138). The sultan of Golconda, Abul Hasan Qutb Shah, was Muslim, but several of his key ministers, particularly those concerned with tax collection and finance, were Brahmins. The person in charge of the area that included Madras was a Brahmin called Podela Lingappa. Lingappa was a thorn in the side of Streynsham Master. Lingappa was not appeased by the token gifts offered by the EIC (cloth, horses, etc.) but instead wanted both one-time and annual payments in the local gold coinage, known as pagodas. When Master refused, Lingappa blockaded Madras's food supplies in 1679 and cloth supplies in 1680. The appointment of William Gyfford to replace Master as governor of Madras improved relations with Lingappa, and peace was achieved when Gyfford agreed to pay him a one-time fee of 7,000 pagodas (about £3,000) and a further 1,200 pagodas annually. For his efforts, Lingappa was given greater responsibility in the Carnatic region under Golconda's rule.

While Gyfford was repairing relations with Lingappa, one of his early initiatives was the establishment of a bank in 1682 at Fort St. George (Fort St. George 1914: 28 August 1682). This was the first Western-style bank established in India. The bank was authorized to accept deposits up to £100,000 (this would have made it one of the larger banks in London during this period). The remit of the bank was not only to serve company employees. The bank was open to business from people living in and around Madras, including Portuguese depositors. The bank paid 6 per cent interest on deposits of not less than six months. Unfortunately, this was an unattractive rate in India and the bank was not a success. The maximum legally allowable rate of interest on loans in England had been capped at 6 per cent since 1651. English interest rates were still much higher than Dutch interest rates, but they were only about half the prevailing rates in India. For example, in 1681, the Madras factory failed to secure local loans at 10 per cent (Fawcett 1955: 68). Fortunately company employees were not compelled to use the bank. In 1680, employees were given the option of transferring money to London via bills of exchange drawn on the company (Watson 1980: 77). This option was particularly attractive to employees engaged in private trade. In 1682, the ease of private trade was further enhanced when all persons were given the right to export silver and gold to India upon payment of a 2 per cent commission. In addition to the bank, the EIC set up an office in Madras in 1687 to insure ships going from India to England (Love 1913: 543). The bank and the insurance office were not the first and were by no means the most important financial institutions established by the EIC in Madras.

The evidence suggests that a mint was established at Fort St. George shortly after its founding in 1640 (Love 1913: 543). The currency in this part of India was gold-based, unlike Mughal territory where the main currencies were the silver rupee and smaller copper coins. Initially, the mint at Madras produced the gold coins used locally such as the pagoda. Consequently, whereas silver was the EIC's main export to the rest of India, the main export to Madras during this period was gold. For example, in 1677, three ships were sent to Madras, each with a cargo worth about £60,000, and roughly 80 per cent of that cargo consisted of gold for the mint (Fort St. George 1911: 12 December 1677). The more coin produced by the mint, the greater would be the local money supply and the lower the market rate of interest. This hurt the business of local moneylenders/bankers, known by the English as *shroffs*, but they found ways to adapt. H. D. Love described how shroffs hoarded the lower-value coins known as *fanams* prior to a new issue of pagodas by the mint. This raised the market price of fanams relative to pagodas. The shroffs then sold fanams at a profit once the mint released pagodas into the market. Shroffs were also able to exploit the fact that the minting of gold pagodas was a competitive business in Golconda. The Dutch had a mint at Pulicat, some thirty-five miles up the coast from Madras, which also produced gold pagodas. When pagodas produced by the English and Dutch mints had different gold content, this created arbitrage opportunities for local moneylenders. The EIC committee members in London regularly requested that samples of Madras and Pulicat minted coins be sent to them for analysis. When the gold content of the Madras pagodas was found to be greater than that of the Pulicat pagodas, the EIC court of directors admonished the Fort St. George administration for squandering gold resources (Fort St. George 1916: 6 April 1683).

The factory at Fort St. George was encouraged by the EIC committee in London in 1675 to expand its activities by seeking permission from the sultan of Golconda to mint silver and copper coins, but permission was denied (Fort St. George 1911: 24 December 1675). By the mid-1680s, Golconda's power was waning. Mughal–Golconda relations had been strained since 1683 when Golconda refused to remit tax revenues to the Mughals. In 1686, the Dutch declared war on Golconda, and, more important, the Mughals invaded Golconda. That year, the EIC took advantage of Golconda's weakness, and, under the authority of James II, the Madras mint began production of silver rupees, which were identical to Mughal coins. In 1687, the Mughals conquered Golconda. Further development of the Madras mint was temporarily arrested by Josiah Child's war with the Mughals. Although the EIC was easily defeated by the Mughal army and merchants from the EIC had to prostrate themselves before Aurangzeb and beg for the reinstatement of trading rights, the actual financial punishment of the company seems lenient – 150,000 rupees (less than £20,000) plus damages (Robins 2006: 50). Clearly, the Mughals still saw value in an ongoing relationship with the EIC. In fact, the Madras mint was given the authority in 1692 by Aurangzeb's son, Prince Karn Baksh, to mint silver as well as gold coins (Love 1913: 508). This opened up a vast new market for the coins of the Madras mint in the larger part of India that used silver- rather than gold-based currency.

It is worth reflecting on why the EIC would want to operate a mint at Madras and then would want to produce silver rupees. One of the initial functions of the mint was to pay company employees. Local employees had salaries quoted in pounds, but they were paid in gold pagodas made at the company mint. The company was able to set the nominal exchange rate between pounds and pagodas at a level that typically overvalued the pagoda and consequently underpaid employees (Love 1913: 504–5). However, there were other more important benefits to the company than short-changing its employees. The alternatives to minting its own coins were to either deal with local shroffs or have coins minted at the Mughal mints. Borrowing locally could be done only at interest rates that were far higher than in England, and, even if the company had treasure on hand, the local supply of coins was unpredictable. Going to the Mughal mints could be a lengthy and relatively expensive process. Minting its own coins gave the company a steady and relatively inexpensive supply of currency. Furthermore, the ability to mint silver rupees in Madras and export them to Bengal was an important step in the development of the EIC's trade in Bengal. The mint at Bombay, which was established in 1672, also eventually exported silver coins to Bengal. The export of silver rupees to Bengal by the EIC's mints helped break the minting monopoly of the Jagat Seth merchant house in Bengal, and the EIC mints eventually displaced the Mughal mints in the Indian financial system. As K. N. Chaudhuri described, 'The disposal of the treasure was effected with remarkable smoothness and regularity' (1978: 189). Business boomed at the Madras mint in the eighteenth century.

In conclusion, the late seventeenth century saw a transformation in Anglo-Indian commercial relations. Some of this transformation was driven by changes within the EIC. The 1670s and early 1680s were a prosperous period for the company, and although this run of prosperity was disrupted by the EIC–Mughal war of the late 1680s, the company's economic potential was evident. Most of the economic interests in the company were concentrated in relatively few hands. The company's share and bond ownership, the supply of precious metals and shipping services to the company, and even the purchase of the goods brought back from India, were all dominated by a few. The opportunities in private trade also saw senior company servants returning from India with increasingly large fortunes. This combination of prosperity and exclusivity exposed the company to growing criticism within England and meant that the New East India Company was prepared to loan the government £2 million for a licence in 1698. Furthermore, the United Company was in no position to deny the government's requests for a further loan of £1.2 million in 1709. As the EIC was an important source of English (and British) government's finance, one can argue that Anglo-Indian commerce in the late seventeenth and early eighteenth centuries was an integral component of the 'English' financial revolution. The changes within the Mughal Empire had at least as significant an impact on commercial relations. The Mughal expansion in southern India and the increasing tax demands of the Mughal authorities meant that Western trade became more important to India as a source of precious metals. As the case of Madras demonstrates, this led to the introduction and expansion of financial linkages between England and India starting in the 1680s. In Madras, the EIC expanded the activities of its mint, set up a bank, introduced insurance services, began to remit proceeds of private trade to England via bills of exchange and introduced more formal contracts in its dealings with Indian merchants. In London, Indian imports also provided the basis for the establishment of a business press. Furthermore, stronger Anglo-Indian financial linkages had repercussions in Amsterdam, which became an important market for the purchase of treasure by the EIC, as well as an integral link in the networks of private trade in diamonds that involved EIC employees.

Were these developments evidence of an Anglo-Indian partnership? In a sense they were. This was not a period during which the English could simply impose their will on India. There may not have been mutual admiration between Indian and English merchants, but there were compatible interests on both sides of Anglo-Indian commercial relationships. The example of Madras suggests that the nature of the Anglo-Indian partnership was changing in the 1680s from a very large dependency of the EIC on powerful local merchants such as Kasi Viranna to one where the company had more latitude to expand its operations as long as these did not run counter to Mughal interests. By and large, the growth of Anglo-Indian trade in the late seventeenth century benefitted both the English and Mughal administrations while offering opportunities for leading participants on both sides of the trade to amass great personal wealth. While Anglo-Indian trade did become, as George Osborne put it, a 'one way street', under the British Raj, that was not always the case. The establishment of closer financial linkages between England and India in the 1680s was not a prerequisite for, but certainly aided, the process of the expansion of British economic influence in India.

The accounting year ran from 1 July to 30 June. The figures for 1682, therefore, represent results for July 1681–June 1682.

References

Manuscript

EIC Accountant General Records: various years beginning 1682. IOR L/AG.
EIC Accounts: 1671–1685. IOR H/4.
EIC Court Minutes: 1682–1684. IOR B/37.
EIC Lists of Adventurers: 1694–1699. IOR H/2.

Print

Arasaratnam, S. 1966. 'Indian Traders and Their Trading Methods (c.1700)', *Indian Economic and Social History Review*, 2(4): 85–95.

Chaudhuri, K. N. 1968. 'Treasure and Trade Balances: The East India Company's Export Trade, 1660–1720', *The Economic History Review*, 21(3): 480–502.

———. 1978. *The Trading World of Asia and the East India Company 1660–1760*. Cambridge: Cambridge University Press.

Davies, K. G. 1952. 'Joint Stock Investment in the Later Seventeenth Century', *The Economic History Review*, 4(3): 283–301.

Dickson, P. G. M. 1967. *The Financial Revolution in England*. London: Macmillan.

EIC. 1681. *The East India Company's Answer to the Allegations of the Turkey Company and Others against the East India Company*. London.

Fawcett, C. 1955. *The English Factories in India*. 4 vols. Oxford: Oxford University Press.

Fort St. George. 1911–29. *Despatches from England*. 11 vols. Madras: Government Press.

Haider, Najaf. 1993. 'Precious Metal Flows and Currency Circulation in the Mughal Empire', *Journal of the Economic and Social History of the Orient*, 39(6): 298–367.

Lawson, P. 1987. *The East India Company: A History*. London: Longman.

Levant Company. 1681. *The Allegations of the Turkey Company and Others against the East-India Company*. London.

Love, Henry Davison. 1913. *Vestiges of Old Madras 1640–1800*. 2 vols. London: Murray.

Marco, P. Nogues and C. Vam Malle-Sabouret. 2007. 'East India Bonds, 1718–1763: Early Exotic Derivatives and London Market Efficiency', *European Review of Economic History*, II: 367–94.

Mentz, Soren. 2005. *The English Gentleman Merchant at Work: Madras and the City of London, 1660–1740*. Copenhagen: Museum Tusculanum Press.

Ogborn, Miles. 2008. *Global Lives: Britain and the World, 1550–1800*. Cambridge: Cambridge University Press.

Osborne, George. 2014. 'Good Days Are Coming.' Speech in Delhi, https://www.gov.uk/government/speeches/chancellors-speech-in-india-good-days-are-coming (accessed on 27 July 2015).

Pincus, Steven. 2009. *1688: The First Modern Revolution*. New Haven, CT: Yale University Press.

Prakash, Om. 1998. *European Commercial Enterprise in Pre-Colonial India*. Cambridge: Cambridge University Press.

Price, J. M. 1954. 'Notes on Some London Price Currents, 1667–1715', *Economic History Review*, 7(2): 240–50.

Richards, J. F. 1993. *The Mughal Empire*. Cambridge: Cambridge University Press.

Robins, Nick. 2006. *The Corporation That Changed the World*. London: Pluto.

Roy, Tirthankar. 2012. *The East India Company: The World's Most Powerful Corporation*. New York: Penguin USA.

Scott, W. R. 1910. *The Constitution and Finance of English, Scottish and Irish Joint-Stock Companies to 1720*. 2 vols. Cambridge: Cambridge University Press.

Wagner, Michael. 2014. 'Misunderstood and Unappreciated: The Russia Company in the Eighteenth Century', *Russian History*, 41(3): 393–422.

Watson, Ian Bruce. 1980. *Foundations for Empire: English Private Trade in India, 1659–1760*. New Delhi: Vikas.

Woodhead, J. R. 1965. *The Rulers of London, 1660–1689*. London: London & Middlesex Archaeological Society.

Yogev, Gedalia. 1978. *Diamonds and Coral: Anglo-Dutch Jews and Eighteenth-Century Trade*. Leicester: Leicester University Press.

4 Indian merchants, company protection and the development of the Bombay shipping pass regime, c. 1680–1740

Tristan Stein

In early 1725, cruisers belonging to the East India Company's Bombay presidency seized four South Asian merchant vessels sailing between Gujarati ports and Calicut that had neglected to take out company shipping passes (IOR P/341/6: 40, 60). For several years the government of Bombay had attempted to establish its authority over navigation on the west coast of India and to prosecute its maritime rivalry with regional rulers and power-holders by seeking to require ships in the region to take out company passes and pay a duty for those instruments. The council and president of Bombay had recently concluded that the time had arrived to enforce the use of the company's shipping pass more aggressively and now decided to make an example of the four vessels, as 'if we defer longer to use some Acts of Severity they will pay little regard to the Orders we may publish in future' (IOR P/341/6: 40). The council accordingly resolved to require the shipowners to pay a total of 800 rupees for the release of the vessels. This action, together with the subsequent arrest and fining of other Asian vessels, had the desired effect. The Bombay council reported to the East India Company's directors in August 1725 that the preceding months had witnessed a notable increase in requests for company passes (IOR E/4/459: 442–3; IOR Orme MSS 121: 111v–112r).

During the opening decades of the eighteenth century, the shipping pass emerged as a critical tool for expanding Bombay's maritime power and encouraging the city's commercial development (Elliott 2013). From the arrival of the Portuguese in Asia to the ascendance of the British in India at the end of the eighteenth century, first the Portuguese *cartaz* and then the Dutch *pascedul* and English pass were among the most notable expressions of European maritime power around the Indian Ocean world (Prakash 1998: 140–3; Thomaz 2001). These instruments, 'part passport, part protection racket', were licences issued to ships sailing around the Indian Ocean that manifested an aggressive claim to maritime jurisdiction over trade and navigation and that sought, in the British case, 'to fold those ships into a sort of Company security regime and establish deference to Company sea power' (Stern 2011: 43–44). Yet, in seeking to establish the dominance of its pass over regional navigation, the government of Bombay added to the wider jurisdictional and commercial complexity of the western Indian Ocean. European and Asian maritime powers on the west coast of India competed to establish the primacy of their shipping passes and pass regimes, and merchants navigated among these rival powers in a search for security and protection. Under these conditions, and despite instances like the condemnation of the Gujarati vessels mentioned earlier, the history of the Bombay shipping pass in the first half of the eighteenth century reveals both the enduring ability of South Asian authorities to shape the organization of Indian Ocean navigation and the success of South Asian merchants in manipulating the pass system to their own ends.

The Bombay pass regime was a system of protection and maritime control that rested on negotiation with South Asian merchants and shipowners, as well as on the exercise of naval force, and that demonstrated the extensive intermingling of British and Asian commercial interests underlying the expansion of British commerce and corporate power. In this respect, it was indicative of the character of the Indian Ocean pass system more broadly, which, as Lauren Benton has emphasized, rested on the delicate balance of European power at sea and vulnerability on land; the shipping pass formed the basis for a maritime order that lay at the intersection of European and Asian authorities (Benton 2010: 141). On the one hand, the pass system was an expression of European naval power and an instrument of maritime authority, wherein European powers required Asian merchants and shipowners to take out passes to avoid attack. On the other, Asian rulers and officials successfully required Europeans to grant passes to their subjects and to protect their navigation and trade. Merchants in Surat negotiated the terms under which they took out British passes, and Maratha commanders at the end of the 1730s forced the Bombay government to accept treaty terms that substantially reshaped the nature and workings of the British pass regime. Most crucially, the development of that regime in the first decades of the eighteenth century suggests that long-term significance of the pass lay in the protection it promised to South Asian merchants and shipowners as well as in the claims to maritime control that it manifested.

This chapter traces the history of the East India Company's shipping pass regime on the west coast of India during the first half of the eighteenth century and the role of Anglo-Indian interactions in the progress of that system. It begins by recounting the early evolution of the English East India Company's pass in the seventeenth century and then demonstrates how maritime competition in the early eighteenth century between the British and regional power-holders, especially the Maratha admiral, Kanhoji

Angria, led the Bombay presidency to transform the company's shipping pass into a tool of maritime power by seeking to require Asian vessels on the west coast of India to take out their passes. It also shows that merchants at Surat and other Indian Ocean ports negotiated the terms under which they took out company passes and illustrates how the protective value of the pass encouraged the intermixing of British and Asian commercial interests. The chapter concludes by briefly examining the relationship between the development of the Bombay pass regime in the opening decades of the eighteenth century and its emergence as a system of imperial power in the latter half of the century.

I

Shipping passes and maritime passports were a ubiquitous feature of early modern Indian Ocean and global navigation and commerce. In Europe, the Mediterranean and Asia, mediaeval rulers granted safe conducts to merchants and travellers and to the captains of ships to certify to whose subjects a vessel and its cargo belonged and to request other sovereigns to allow a vessel and its contents to pass freely and without harm. With an eye to the control of trade and navigational routes, the Mamluks issued passes to vessels sailing in the Red Sea and rulers on the west coast of India granted licences and safe-conduct passes to ships from at least the fourteenth century (Thomaz 2001; Prange 2011: 1276). Subsequently, seventeenth-century marine treaties among European states established passports as a primary tool for identifying ships at sea while agreements between European states and the corsairing powers of North Africa established the Mediterranean or 'Turk' pass as an essential feature of Mediterranean and Atlantic navigation through the early modern period (Stein 2015: 608–9, 612–4). The emergence of the Indian Ocean shipping pass system thus both rested on Asian and European mediaeval precedents and paralleled the development of other regional passport regimes as states and empires sought to regulate growing levels of maritime trade and violence.

Despite such precedents and parallels, the early modern Indian Ocean shipping pass system constituted a unique set of regional regulatory regimes. Whereas passes previously and elsewhere served primarily to identify vessels and, hopefully, to ensure their safe passage, the arrival of the Portuguese transformed the Indian Ocean pass into an aggressive means through which both European and Asian powers sought to exert a jurisdictional claim over sea lanes and the movement of ships and goods. During the sixteenth century, the Portuguese used the pass to establish their control over key Indian Ocean trade routes. In the seventeenth and eighteenth centuries, European and Asian powers followed the Portuguese in using the pass as a tool to exert jurisdiction and control over trade and commerce (Prakash 1998: 140–1). The English and, more especially, the Dutch adopted the pass soon after their arrival in Asia. Through the early modern period, though, the use of passes rested on the balance of European power at sea and weakness on land. The Mughal governors of Surat, for example as well as local officials and rulers elsewhere, regularly insisted on the provision of passes as part of diplomatic negotiations and forced the English and other Europeans to grant passes to vessels belonging to powers with which they were in a state of hostility (Foster 1642–1655: 3; Foster 1651–1654: 179).

During the seventeenth century, the English pass served primarily as an instrument of identification and a request for safe conduct. Although the form of English passes, especially in the seventeenth century, frequently differed based upon where they were being issued, they shared common features. Passes identified the vessel carrying them, its owner and master and sometimes described the voyage the ship was making. In the case of passes granted at Madras in the late seventeenth century, the Council of Fort St. George (1910–1946) did 'desire and intreat all Persons in other parts of India that are subjects to his Majesty our Soveraigne Lord the King, and all our friends and Allys to suffer' the vessel bearing the pass to proceed without 'any let, hinderance, Seizure, or molestation' (Madras Diary: 75, 77). The pass thus served as an instrument that identified the vessel carrying it as one belonging to English or company subjects or to the subjects of a power with which the company was in alliance or a state of peace. In their form, these documents were more safe-conduct passes than instruments for the control of trade or navigation. Unlike Portuguese or Dutch passes, English passes rarely proscribed vessels from carrying particular cargoes or mandated that vessels call at specific ports. The value of the pass lay in the power of the company to withhold it and in the extension of an element of company protection to the vessel carrying it. Such protection depended, in turn, on how effectively the company could oblige other powers to respect its passes.

The emergence of the English pass as a key instrument of Indian Ocean navigation proceeded in line with the development of the company as an Indian Ocean power. Local conflicts with Asian rulers led to acts of reprisal and violence and to requests to company officials from Asian merchants and shipowners for passes to guarantee 'their quiet returne' (Foster 1630–1633: 284; Foster 1634–1636: 50). In the context of company diplomacy and war making, company agents used passes to restrict vessels from trading with the company's enemies. During a period of conflict with Malabar rulers in the early 1660s, for instance, the company's agents at Surat issued passes that called for English vessels to allow the ship carrying them to pass freely '[p]rovided you finde them nor aney of them tradeing in the Portes of Cannanor nor Callicute' (IOR E/3/27: 32r). Nevertheless, through much of the seventeenth century, the English company struggled to establish the effectiveness of its passes. Though Asian vessels obtained English passes in an effort to secure their vessels from the Portuguese and Dutch, English agents frequently complained of how the Dutch or Portuguese seized vessels despite the English passes they carried (IOR G/3/6: 70–71). During the 1660s, the East India Company engaged in lengthy and ultimately fruitless negotiations with the Dutch to establish the mutual observance of their respective passes (TNA: CO 77/11: 76r-v; BL Add MS 28093: 168v–169r).

It was only during the 1680s and 1690s that the growth of the commercial and naval power of the English East India Company transformed the English pass into an instrument of maritime power comparable to the Dutch and Portuguese passes. For the company's directors and its agents overseas, the pass was a means to combat the growing problem of interloping and to assert more effectively company jurisdiction over both British and company subjects in Asia (IOR G/19/21: 7v). In 1688, President John Child and the council at Bombay directed that all ships sailing under English colours were to take out passes yearly and to pay a duty of a rupee per ton for liberty to trade and the company's protection (Fort St. George 1688: 16). This measure was clearly directed primarily at private English vessels, 'in Consideration of the Privileges to trade in India' and 'as an acknowledgement for the treatey, favour and kindnesse and to Contribute towards their great Charges' (IOR E/3/47: 145r–46r). Yet the increasingly bellicose stance of the company towards the Mughal Empire and other Asian polities also increased the importance of the English pass for Asian merchants and shipowners anxious to avoid the seizure of their property and vessels. During the company's wars against Siam and the Mughal Empire in the late 1680s, the company's pass offered some protection from its own cruisers and prize courts. The company's Bengal prize court, for example, released the *Diamond* on the basis, in part, that the vessel carried a pass from the council at Fort St. George certifying that it belonged to subjects of Golconda (IOR E/3/47: 11v–12r).

With the growth of English maritime power, the shipping pass increasingly served to mediate between the company's threats of violence to its foes and promises of protection to its friends and allies. The growing problem of 'piracy' in the 1690s, in the form of both depredations by European vessels and attacks launched by Arabian and South Asian rulers on Mughal shipping, further encouraged the company's agents to expand the use of its passes (Stern 2011: 134–8). In 1694, the Bombay president John Gayer advised Samuel Annesley, his counterpart at Surat, regarding the company's pass, 'From English we may demand it, and I think it no way unreasonable for Countrey Ships that sail not under our Colours we must take what we can get.' Gayer further encouraged Annesley to warn Mughal officials and country merchants that the company would be 'severe' with vessels that failed to take out its passes, 'For that we doe not know who they are, if we meet them with out att sea, especially att this time when there are so many pirates' (IOR E/3/50: 355r). Although the company's agents used such threats to induce Asian vessels to take their passes, they also used passes to extend the company's protection to merchants taking up residence in its settlements and to merchants with whom they did business. In 1700, Thomas Pitt lamented to Edward Littleton that one of their South Asian counterparts had lost his goods when the vessel carrying them was seized by the Portuguese for want of a pass, 'which they might have had if they had asked for it' (BL Add MS 22842: 134). With the growing strength of the company, its pass offered the vessel bearing it the promise of the backing of a major maritime power in what were becoming increasingly dangerous and complicated seas.

II

Through the seventeenth century, the English shipping pass served primarily to identify vessels as belonging to the company's friends and allies and as an instrument for the suppression of interlopers. In the second decade of the eighteenth century, the East India Company pass became a tool of maritime control. This transformation was the product of both the expansion of company power and Anglo-Indian maritime and political competition on the west coast of India. Beginning at the end of the seventeenth century and continuing through the early decades of the eighteenth, the Maratha military commander, Kanhoji Angria, carved out a space for himself as a political force on India's west coast by threatening Mughal and European shipping from fortified strongholds and seeking to impose his pass on coastal navigation. Although the British disparaged Kanhoji as a 'pirate', he was, in fact, an emerging political ruler who sought to establish a maritime regime not unlike that to which the company itself aspired (Stern 2011: 186–8; Elliott 2013). It was to challenge Kanhoji's growing power, establish its own maritime predominance and fund convoys and naval campaigns that the Bombay presidency sought for the first time to force its pass on all Asian navigation on the west coast of India and to expand Child's pass duty to foreign vessels. The result was the development of a more aggressive pass regime of maritime control and protection. The response of South Asian merchants and authorities to this new regime underscored, however, the extent to which the use of passes in practice depended on the balance of European and Asian powers.

The rise of Kanhoji Angria transformed the political environment around Bombay. Although the Bombay presidency entered into peace agreements with him early in the eighteenth century wherein each agreed to refrain from attacking the other's vessels, the presidency's practice of granting passes to Mughal vessels and Kanhoji's efforts to force his own pass on coastal navigation led to regular conflict (Elliott 2013: 195). Kanhoji protested that Bombay's insistence that any vessel freighted by the company or its agents ought to be considered as 'English' deprived him of valuable prizes. At the core of the contest between Bombay and Kanhoji were questions both of maritime dominance and of the extent to which the company could extend its protection to Asian vessels. Kanhoji predicted in a letter to Bombay's governor, Charles Boone, that if he once allowed an Asian vessel to sail freely because it carried the company's pass and British goods, 'tomorrow your Excellency will say that you have a mind to Freight Fifty or a hundred Ships of the Surat Merchants, if so what occasion have they to take the Pass they always took of me?' (IOR P/341/4: 77). Bombay depended, however, on such country vessels for provisions and for the private trade of the British merchants and agents resident there. The result of disagreements as to what constituted a legitimate prize was disputes and reprisals that produced a series of wars between the company and Kanhoji and his successors that lasted until the middle of the century.

Although it had little success in combating Kanhoji's forces directly, Bombay presidency's long-running conflict with him encouraged both the rise of British naval and military power on the west coast of India and the development of the shipping pass into an instrument through which the company asserted its authority over navigation along the west coast of India (Elliott 2013: 193). The organization of convoys and outfitting of cruisers at once displayed company naval power and brought Mughal and South Asian navigation under company protection. In February 1717, the East India Company's directors approved a plan proposed by the Bombay president and council to extend Child's pass duty to passes given to Asian vessels at Surat and elsewhere and advised 'You may well defend the taking that Duty because of the new Expenses you are at to protect their trade' (IOR E/3/99: 207r; Chaudhuri 1978: 123). Although the agents at Bombay did little to act on this resolution for several years, this plan directly linked, for the first time, the provision of passes to the company's emerging maritime security regime on the west coast of India.

The continuation of Bombay's contest with Kanhoji Angria and the growing expense of that conflict subsequently led the presidency to extend its pass regime over regional navigation. In so doing, it tied the shipping pass to the commercial development of Bombay itself and sought to use its pass system to attract vessels and trade to the city. In early 1723, the council notified the company's directors that it intended to replace the existing tonnage duties levied on vessels trading to Bombay from Surat and other ports to the north with pass duties. According to the council, the custom duties levied at Bombay were deterring vessels from coming to the city. Conversely, the council believed it had 'as good right' to oblige country vessels to take its pass as the Portuguese; moreover, the duty it intended to levy in exchange for the use of the pass 'may near if not quite Compensate for relinquishing the Tonnage' (IOR E/4/459: 175; IOR P/341/5: 15 March 1723). This approach shifted the burden of the presidency's duties and the source of its revenues away from the commerce of Bombay and onto the country trade more broadly. It also suggested an ambitious attempt to use the shipping pass to establish Bombay's commercial and political predominance on the west coast of India. In May 1723, the council notified the company's directors that it intended to extend the new tonnage duty to the vessels of Surat (IOR E/4/459: 202).

The Bombay presidency's plan to expand the pass regime and to enforce the use of its passes at Surat threatened, however, the balance between European and Mughal powers that underlay the operation of the shipping pass system. Levying a duty for passes issued and collected at Bombay was straightforward. It was a different matter at Surat. Although Mughal authority over the city was waning and its commerce increasingly suffered as a result of political instability, Surat in the early 1720s was still the commercial centre of western India (Das Gupta 1979: 7–8, 139–48). Surat's merchants had, moreover, a long history of negotiating the terms of their relationships with both the Mughal governors and European companies that depended on their financial services and commercial cooperation (Nadri 2009: 12–13, 22). Merchants and shipowners at Surat took out European passes, but they were accustomed to doing so largely on their own terms. 'It is pretended', the British factory at Surat reported regarding the operation of the pass system in 1723,

> that the European nations being powerful at Sea the Merchants do ask passes from those settled in this City to show to the Commanders of such ships as they may happen to meet at Sea that they might have no disturbance from them. (Orme MSS 127: 184–5)

Yet the only charges the Dutch, French and British had previously required for passes were small fees paid to the factory secretaries. Only the Portuguese levied a formal duty in exchange for Portuguese passes and that was widely evaded. In September 1723, the company's chief broker at Surat, Laldas Parak, warned that the plan to collect additional fees for the issuance of passes served only as a 'means to stop our busines and disgust the Governor & Merchants of Serving us' (IOR Orme MSS 127: 191).

The effort of the Bombay presidency to extend its new pass regime to Surat failed in the face of resistance from Surat merchants and Mughal officials. The governor of the city, Momin Kahn Dehlami, objected to what appeared to be an explicit assertion of the company's maritime jurisdiction, 'supposing there is no right to levy dutys on the King's [Mughal Emperor's] Subjects' (IOR Orme MSS 127: 184). In response to such opposition, the Bombay council threatened to withhold passes and planned to blockade Surat. Yet the stopping of trade at Surat cut both ways since the trade of the city dwarfed that of Bombay and it was impossible for the British either to dispose of the company's woollen goods or to provide cargoes for the company's homeward-bound ships without access to Surat and the cooperation of the city's merchants (IOR P/341/5: 237–8). It was thus the British who gave in after the Surat merchants threatened to withhold their trade altogether if not granted passes at the customary rates. In the face of opposition from the Mughal authorities at Surat and fearful that the company might be blamed at the Mughal court for any decline in the trade of Surat, the council at Bombay relented and agreed to distribute its passes as normal (IOR E/4/459: 275; IOR P/341/5: 237–8).

As a system of maritime control, the British pass regime thus remained dependent both on Mughal cooperation and on negotiation with Surat merchants over the terms of company protection. The result was an uneven pass regime that impacted South Asian merchants differently based on the relative power of their rulers. During the 1720s, the regular appearance of cruisers sailing out of Bombay and the periodic seizure of vessels without passes induced a growing array of merchants and local rulers to seek out the company's passes and to pay the duties required for them (IOR E/4/460: 98; IOR E/3/104: 227v). The presidency's aggressive approach to its passes also meant that company's agents were able to deploy the threat of refusing passes to South Asian merchants or rulers as a means to put pressure on weaker regional polities (IOR P/341/8: 487–8; IOR P/341/9: 307–8). Yet, although the company's directors and agents continued to aspire to bring the Surat merchants under the new conditions of the pass regime, they were unable to effect this. In 1726, the council at Bombay instead recommended that the company continue its 'indulgence' of granting passes free of the tonnage duty to merchants at Surat rather than risk any interruption to its trade at that port (IOR E/4/460: 38; IOR E/3/106: 115v).

The example of Bombay's contests with Surat merchants over passes underscores the pass regime's character as a system of maritime organization that depended on the balance and intersection of British and Asian authorities as well as on the exercise of British power. Surat merchants, moreover, were not alone in their ability to negotiate the terms of company protection. In early 1728, the council at Bombay advised the company's directors that they had taken the company's agent in the Persian port of Gombroon to task for exceeding his orders in requiring payment of the tonnage duty in exchange for the company's passes, since they had not intended that duty to extend to any but those merchants trading along the west coast of India, 'who do more particularly Benefit in a Secure Navigation by Means of our Cruizing Vessels'. In light of the unsettled conditions of the Persian Gulf and the corresponding need to maintain a naval force in the Persian Gulf, the government of Bombay confirmed the duty at Gombroon but desired that it be 'Levy'd by Consent of the Subjects & Government rather than by Compulsion' (IOR E/4/460: 139). A year later, when the head of the company's factory at Basra reported that he could not induce the merchants there to take our English passes at the price sought, the council of Bombay directed the agent to issue out 'our Permits on the merchants terms, rather than disgust them'. The council also sent orders to Gombroon instructing the company's agent there to lower the pass duties 'if the Merchants require it' (IOR E/4/460: 267).

III

During the 1720s and 1730s, the Bombay presidency established a notable, if uneven, pass regime on coastal navigation in western India. The annual revenue the Bombay government raised from pass duties increased from 720 rupees in 1724 to 6,184 rupees in 1736, indicating a substantial increase in the distribution of passes. Even this latter sum compensated, however, only for a fraction of military and naval costs that ran into the hundreds of thousands of rupees (IOR P/341/9: 247–8). The Bombay council's dream of the pass regime serving as a major revenue source remained unfulfilled. Meanwhile, even though the shipping pass system was a critical manifestation of corporate political power, it provided 'only a loose set of rules for much more complex and layered arrangements' (Benton 2010: 142). In the Indian Ocean, as around the early modern world, merchants and shipowners showed remarkable creativity in navigating politically contentious waters and captains regularly sailed with several different passes and flags. British traders and company agents hired and freighted South Asian vessels, and South Asian merchants and shipowners, in turn, sought out the protection and advantages conferred by flying the company's flag and carrying the company's pass (Furber 1965: 8–9, 32–34; Prakash 2007: 225). The varied use of the company's pass by British merchants and agents and their South Asian counterparts underscored the commercial interconnections upon which British trade at Bombay and around Asia depended.

In theory, the shipping pass stood as the centre of a system of European maritime control. In practice, both South Asian merchants and corporate agents used passes freely to their own commercial ends. South Asian merchants and shipowners – together with their European counterparts who sailed and traded in the same waters – navigated a complex and dangerous maritime world. The Dutch and Portuguese sought to enforce the use of their passes in the seas surrounding their possessions, as did Kanhoji Angria and the other Maratha commanders who were carving out their own power bases. South Asian merchants and shipowners took out British passes and those of other European powers, in search of some measure of protection and security in uncertain waters. Even Kanhoji Angria's own subjects found ways to benefit from the protection of British passes. In 1729, for example the council at Bombay condemned two Bombay vessels that had been freighted by Kanhoji's agents to make an example of them, 'having reason to believe this has been but too frequent a practice' (IOR Orme MSS 121: 11r; Elliot 2013). Two years later the council at Bombay refused to restore a vessel to a merchant despite the British pass it carried, since the merchant, who was described as an inhabitant of Surat in the pass, was well known to be a subject of Kanhoji. As before, the council complained 'that Passes are frequently obtain'd in this fraudulent manner for the Benefit & Protection of our Enemy's Vessels' (IOR P/341/7: 64–65). Such cases were, moreover, typical of a nebulous and fluid maritime environment in which extensive 'cross-national' connections and partnerships were common. Bombay's cruisers sometimes seized ships for failing to take out company passes or for carrying Kanhoji's that were owned by multiple merchants who were subject to different rulers. Under these conditions determining the provenance or subject affiliation of vessels was often difficult (IOR P/341/8: 348–52; Elliott 2013: 196–7).

Despite the council of Bombay's periodic condemnation of technically abusive and fraudulent practices, British agents and merchants themselves adopted flexible approaches to the company's pass. As the Bombay government sought to impose its pass on regional navigation, the company's servants provided passes for the Asian vessels they freighted, a practice that was essential to the success of their private trade but a source of concern for the company's directors, who worried that such collaboration allowed Asian merchants to enjoy farman privileges reserved for the company and its agents and might produce disputes with Mughal authorities at Surat (Prakash 2007: 225). In early 1727, the company's directors forbid the granting of passes to foreign vessels after they received news that a 'large Moors ship' had traded in Bengal without paying Mughal customs duties on the basis of a pass given to it by two British private merchants (IOR E/3/104: 87r–v). The directors probably did not, in fact, intend for this order to apply to the pass regime as a whole. Instead, they sought to put an end to the practice of using passes to make foreign vessels appear to be the property of the company or its agents. The Bombay council, in turn, responded by observing that the country trade on the west coast of India offered limited opportunities for the company servants at Bombay and that they, unlike their counterparts at Madras or Calcutta, were obliged to hire South Asian vessels to carry on their private trade. Indeed, the expansion of private British trade from Bombay during this period depended both on the use of Asian ships and on collaborations with South Asian merchants (Furber 1965; Prakash 2007: 222–3; Davies 2014: 63). The council further explained that Asian vessels freighted by the company's agents were considered British by Asian authorities, assuring the directors '[t]hat Ships so hired & employed by your Servants, Navigated with an English Commander & Officers under your Pass & Colours have at all time been deem'd English ships by the sundry Country Governments' (IOR E/4/460: 259). The council of Bombay's explanation of what constituted a 'British' ship echoed its earlier dispute with Kanhoji over the provision of company protection to Asian vessels and further demonstrated the close relationship between British trade and Asian navigation.

The extent of company protection for Asian vessels within its security regime varied considerably. While the government of Bombay considered vessels freighted by company agents to be 'English', it took pains to explain to merchants at Surat that the pass did not represent an acceptance of responsibility for the vessel bearing it, but instead 'only recommend the safety of them as our Friendship or Resentment on such as shall molest them having our pass shall be regarded' (IOR E/4/459: 234). The efficacy of company protection during the first half of the eighteenth century was also often limited. Although Bombay's campaigns against Kanhoji led the presidency to institute convoys for the protection of coastal shipping and stimulated the development of its naval forces, its government complained regularly of difficulties in securing navigation. In early 1727 the council of Bombay warned the company's directors that their inability to maintain the presidency's fleet had allowed Kanhoji to seize several vessels that had not taken his pass (IOR E/4/460: 78). On the other hand, diplomatic support from the government of Bombay sometimes allowed the company's subjects and pass-holders to recover ships and cargoes seized by other powers. In the mid-1720s, the company's courts at Bombay helped an Asian inhabitant of the island to reclaim a vessel that had been seized years earlier by the Portuguese, much to the consternation of the Portuguese viceroy at Goa (IOR P/341/6: 10 February 1727). A decade later, the president of

Bombay similarly entered into a lengthy dispute with the Portuguese after a vessel belonging to an inhabitant of Bombay was seized for failing to take out a Portuguese pass (IOR P/341/8: 414, 416–23, 428–30).

Cases like these reveal the potential appeal, despite its limits, of company protection for South Asian merchants. Moreover, even though the shipping pass was indeed part of a 'protection racket', it was subject both to manipulation on the part of South Asian merchants and their British counterparts and to negotiation with merchant communities and political authorities. As a result, the operation of the pass system depended as much on the commercial strategies of merchants and shipowners as on the will and orders of the company. Diplomatic efforts of Bombay's governors on the part of South Asian merchants and shipowners and disputes over the extension of the company's privileges and protection to Asian merchants revealed, meanwhile, the increasingly complex relationship between company authority and a growing range of subjects and protégés.

IV

During the second half of the eighteenth century, the growth of company power gradually transformed the shipping pass regime and established the dominance of the British pass regime on the west coast of India. Through the first half of the eighteenth century, the Bombay pass regime rested on a balancing of European and Asian commercial interests and political powers. Bombay's military weakness and the continued rise of the Maratha empire brought an end to Bombay's pass duty in the late 1730s, when orders from the company's directors and a treaty with the Marathas forced the government of Bombay to limit its passes to the company's own agents and subjects. In the following decades, though, South Asian merchants sought out the company's pass and protection by relocating to Bombay as conditions on the west coast of India and at the port of Surat deteriorated in the face of Mughal–Maratha conflict and the continued decline of Mughal power (Das Gupta 1979; Subramanian 1996: 49–54, 130). As Bombay's military and naval strength grew, the pass regime emerged as a unilateral extension of protection over company subjects and dependants.

The demise of Bombay's pass duty demonstrated again the ability of Asian merchants and authorities to define the operation of the British shipping pass regime. By the late 1730s, it was clear that the government of Bombay lacked the power to impose its pass on Asian navigation. In 1737, the council of Bombay advised the company's directors that the limited resources of the Bombay presidency had led South Asian merchants to question the utility of passes and the duties they paid for them: 'Many of those people think it very hard to be obliged to take Our Pass on such terms, pleading that without them their Vessels & Boats wou'd be as safe from any of the Pirates who infest the Coast' (IOR P/341/9: 247–8). Meanwhile, despite their earlier support of Bombay's aggressive pass regime, the directors worried that defending the reputation of the pass would lead to unacceptable diplomatic and military costs and entanglements. In 1738, they ordered the presidency to revise its pass regime and to restrict the distribution of passes by limiting them to vessels belonging to the company's agents and British merchants: 'As the Passes which you Grant may truly be called Passes of Protection, We order that in future they be only given to the Ships belonging to and which are the Property of our own European Servants and Licenced Free Merchants' (IOR E/3/107: 226v). Meanwhile, in 1739, the government of Bombay entered into negotiations with the Maratha general Chimnaji Appa following dramatic Maratha successes against Portuguese possessions near Bombay. Although it considered the resulting articles as 'farr from being upon equal & moderate terms', the Bombay council had no choice but to accept them as it did not have 'Force sufficient' to 'enter on any means of Opposition to them' (IOR P/341/10: 239). The treaty forbade the British from granting their passes to the vessels of foreign subjects and thus reinforced the director's orders, limiting the protection of British passes to vessels belonging to the company's own servants and subjects.

These restrictions on the distribution of passes substantially altered both the nature of the British pass regime and the relationship between subject status and company protection. Both the Marathas and the company's directors sought to disassociate the pass from claims to maritime control or jurisdiction and to render it instead a document for identifying the vessel carrying it as the property of British subjects. Notably, the directors specifically cited the Mediterranean pass, an instrument that functioned as an identifying passport and that European rulers – in theory – granted only to those who were their legitimate subjects, as the model for their conception of the revised pass regime (Stein 2015). In place of the company's official pass, its agents were to grant vessels belonging to the subjects of foreign sovereigns identifying certificates, which did not bear the company's seal, in order to enable the company's own cruisers and vessels to differentiate friend from foe at sea (IOR E/3/107, 226v). Since these certificates did not carry any claim to company protection, the directors also ordered that the council of Bombay abandon its pass duty altogether (IOR E/3/108: 158r). In the following decades, the government of Bombay altered its approach to the shipping pass accordingly and regularly asserted its intention to limit passes to individuals 'under our immediate protection' (IOR P/341/27: 516). In the late 1760s, the government of Bombay, together with the directors in London, specifically rejected proposals on the part of agents at Basra to grant passes to foreign vessels in exchange for payment of a fee (IOR R/15/1/1: 4r; IOR E/4/998: 6–7; IOR E/4/464: 80).

Yet even as the government of Bombay sought to restrict the distribution of passes, the movement of South Asian merchants to Bombay brought a growing number of subjects and protégés under the company's 'immediate protection'. The growth of company power and the movement of South Asian merchants to Bombay during the second half of the eighteenth century transformed the presidency's pass regime, turning a system that had rested on negotiated and multilateral foundations into one of imperial protection that gradually eliminated rival claims to maritime authority on the west coast of India (Layton 2013: 88–93). Although the ability of Maratha commanders to dictate treaty terms to the government of Bombay in 1739 underscored the limits of Bombay's military and naval strength, the balance of power on the west coast of India very gradually shifted in Bombay's favour over the following decades. In 1756, the government of Bombay, with the assistance of Maratha forces aligned against Kanhoji, drove one of his heirs from his coastal stronghold, and, three years later, the British gained partial control of Surat itself (Stern 2011: 191–2). Meanwhile, in the face of political instability, South Asian merchants relocated to Bombay or placed themselves under the company's protection at Surat and other ports (Subramanian 1996: 52–54, 130; Nadri 2009: 78–80). Both the East India Company's directors and the government of Bombay had long realized that the presidency's success depended on attracting merchants and inhabitants. The directors accordingly balanced their restrictions on the distribution of passes to foreign vessels with encouragement that the council at Bombay make efforts towards '[a]lluring all sorts of people to live under your Protection' (IOR E/3/108: 158r). Bombay's commercial and economic development across the eighteenth century was largely a function of the decision of South Asian merchants to seek out opportunity within that port city and to place themselves under British protection (Subramanian 1996; Davies 2014: 62–63). By the end of the century, the efforts of Bombay's government to maintain the efficacy of a pass system that now incorporated an array of subjects and protégés became a motive for military action and the suppression of coastal powers that threatened vessels carrying company passes (Layton 2013: 92).

The ambitions of the government of Bombay in the early eighteenth century to establish a protection regime on the west coast of India anticipated this subsequent rise of the British pass to regional dominance. The development of the shipping pass regime depended as much on the ability of Bombay to attract South Asian merchants to its protection as it did on the imposition of that protection on them. In this respect, although the eventual primacy of the British pass stemmed from the late eighteenth-century expansion of British military and naval power, it also had roots in the more complex character of the earlier pass system, in which merchants shopped for protection and negotiated the terms under which they took out passes. Much as Asian merchants and political authorities had forced the government of Bombay to give up its efforts to force its pass upon navigation along the west coast of India, so they were responsible for the emergence of a new protection regime in the second half of the eighteenth century as they sought out company protection in an unstable and uncertain commercial and political environment. The development of the pass regime in the latter part of the century also represented, however, a significant departure from its earlier history. Asian merchants, especially at Surat, showed an impressive ability to navigate and resist the rise of British power through the end of the century (Nadri 2009: 78–83). The global expansion of the British Empire nevertheless transformed the multilateral and negotiated regimes that had previously shaped British interactions with extra-European peoples into systems of imperial control. With the growth of company power, the protection of the company's pass increasingly ceased to be a matter of negotiation and instead became contingent on subjection to the company state.

References

Manuscript

Additional Manuscripts (Add Mss): 22842 and 28093. BL.
Bombay Public Proceedings: various years. IOR P/341.
East Indies Original Correspondence: Volume 11, 1668–1670. Colonial Office, TNA: CO/77.
EIC Correspondence with the East: various years. IOR E/3.
EIC Factory Records, Bombay: 1669–1710. IOR G/3.
EIC Factory Records, Fort. St. George (Madras), 1655–1758. IOR G/19.
EIC Letters Correspondence with India: various years beginning 1709. IOR E/4.
Orme Manuscripts: 121 and 127. IOR.

Print

Benton, Lauren. 2010. *A Search for Sovereignty: Law and Geography in European Empires, 1400–1900.* New York: Oxford University Press.
Chaudhuri, K. N. 1978. *The Trading World of Asia and the English East India Company: 1660–1760.* Cambridge: Cambridge University Press.
Das Gupta, Ashin. 1979. *Indian Merchants and the Decline of Surat, c. 1700–1750.* Wiesbaden: Franz Steiner Verlag.

Davies, Timothy. 2014. 'English Private Trade on the West Coast of India, c. 1680–c. 1740', *Itinerario*, 28(2): 51–73.

Elliott, Derek L. 2013. 'The Politics of Capture in the Eastern Arabian Sea, c. 1700–1750', *International Journal of Maritime History*, 25(2): 187–98.

Fort St. George [Madras Diary]. 1910–46. *Diary and Consultation Book*. 86 vols. Madras: Government Press.

———. 1915. *Letters from Fort St. George. Vol. 2: 1688*. Madras: Government Press.

Furber, Holden. 1965. *Bombay Presidency in the Mid-Eighteenth Century*. London; Bombay Printed: Asia Publishing House.

Layton, Simon. 2013. 'The "Moghul's Admiral": Angrian "Piracy" and the Rise of British Bombay', *Journal of Early Modern History*, 17(1): 75–93.

Nadri, Ghulam A. 2009. *Eighteenth-Century Gujarat: The Dynamics of Its Political Economy, 1750–1800*. Leiden: Koninklijke Brill.

Prakash, Om. 1998. *European Commercial Enterprise in Pre-Colonial India*. Cambridge: Cambridge University Press.

———. 2007. 'English Private Trade in the Western Indian Ocean, 1720–1740', *Journal of the Economic and Social History of the Orient*, 50(2/3): 215–34.

Prange, Sebastian R. 2011. 'A Trade of No Dishonor: Piracy, Commerce, and Community in the Western Indian Ocean, Twelfth to Sixteenth Century', *American Historical Review*, 116(5): 1269–93.

Stein, Tristan. 2015. 'Passes and Protection in the Making of a British Mediterranean', *Journal of British Studies*, 54(3): 602–31.

Stern, Philip J. 2011. *The Company-State: Corporate Sovereignty and the Early Modern Foundations of the British Empire in India*. New York: Oxford University Press.

Subramanian, Lakshmi. 1996. *Indigenous Capital and Imperial Expansion: Bombay, Surat and the West Coast*. Delhi: Oxford University Press.

Thomaz, Luis Filipe F. R. 2001. 'Precedents and Parallels of the Portuguese *Cartaz* System,' in Pius Malekandathil and Jamal Mohammed (eds.), *The Portuguese, Indian Ocean, and European Bridgeheads, 1500–1800: Festschrift in Honour of Professor K. S. Mathew*, pp. 67–85. Tellicherry: Institute for Research in Social Sciences and Humanities of MESHAR.

Part II

Religion, society, ethnographic reconnaissance and inter-cultural encounters

5 'God shall enlarge Japheth, and he shall dwell in the tents of shem'

The changing face of religious governance and religious sufferance in the East India Company, 1610–1670

Haig Smith

In the early spring of 1618, while waiting aboard the *Royal James* in the Swally Basin, the East India Company (EIC) chaplain and scot, Patrick Copland, complained about the conduct of a fellow chaplain, Mr Goulding. Writing back to the company, Copland lamented Goulding's unchristian conduct, alluding to the preacher's midnight jaunts among the local female population, leading him to conclude that 'such preachers can never persuade Japheth to come and dwell in the tents of Shem; well may they harden them in their idolatry' (Foster 1906–1927: 1.26). Copland refers here to the evangelical prophecy of Genesis 9:27 in which Japheth (gentiles) would be allowed to enter the tents of Shem, a euphemism for conversion into God's chosen church. However, by placing this comment in the context of the religiously pluralistic environment Copland and the EIC were operating in, it does more than merely allude to the evangelical aspirations of one man, but highlights the nuances in the difficulties and solutions that the EIC and its officials faced when dealing with religion in the Indian subcontinent over the seventeenth century. When Copland discussed preachers hardening Indians in their own faiths, he was not reducing subcontinental religious agency to the whims of the EIC chaplains, but rather he exposed the power and religious strength of the Indian people. EIC officials were very cautious not to overstep their own position upsetting 'Japheth's faith', damaging their own commercial, religious and political positions in India.

As one of the most enduring images of English commercial and corporate expansion during the seventeenth century, the EIC not only laid the foundations that established one of the largest corporations in history, but also the beginnings of what David Armitage has labelled Britain's

'Protestant, commercial, maritime and free' Empire (2000: 8). It was under the company's management that ideas about English governance were exported abroad, and in the face of the foreign and unfamiliar strains of new exotic geographies, experimented and adapted upon to ensure the commercial success. One such social construct that was exported en masse was the Protestant faith. The church and its officials not only adopted the role of enforcers of the religious Protestant authority in a religiously pluralistic land, but also the moral authority of the Protestant English Company. Like all other servants of the company, its chaplains in the first decades of the company's existence encountered and tackled issues that were unfamiliar and alien from their traditional role back in England. The holder of the office of chaplain was expected to find pragmatic solutions to combat the religious, secular and environmental hazards that the Asian subcontinent presented through cross-cultural and religious interactions. Whether this came from the religiously distinct and varied communities of India, the threat of apostasy or the diverse Protestant community created within the company itself, the corporate chaplain in the pre-Braganza years was seen as a constant given in the company to ensure good moral and secular guidance.

The functional pragmatism of the corporate response was then gradually mirrored in that of the company's religious governance. As the century wore on, the company came to face new pressures, primarily surrounding the changing from a body that governed English company servants abroad to one that held jurisdictional power over English, European and Indian peoples of varying faiths, and so sought to develop new solutions to confront these challenges. From the chaplain's clerical administration of English officials in pre-Braganza years to the cosmopolitan religious governance of the company in the years that followed the acquisition of Bombay, company officials both religious and secular transplanted practicable solutions to organisational problems onto complex moral and theological motivations. During the first half of the century company leadership, whether in London or in India, with stoic directness ordered chaplains to merely 'deal with' the problems created by the denominational variation of the EIC community, as well as environmental issues of daily life in India. Similarly the absence of any recognisable English enforcement or ecclesiastical structure in India encouraged the company leadership to reduce the complex moral and theological problems that company officials faced. Almost after the first voyages, the EIC was acutely aware of the implications of apostasy and the moral behaviour of its personnel as well as the prospect of evangelism; its leadership sought to deal with these issues by developing the role of the EIC chaplain over the seventeenth century into a corporate 'moral' police force. The presence and immediacy of these alien pressures meant that the focus of the company was to maintain the presence of any form of Protestant liturgy rather than that of one Protestant sect. The effect of this was that for much of the seventeenth century the chaplaincy was busy ensuring the spiritual wellbeing of the Anglo-centric population of the company to be concerned with any outward 'aggressive' policy of evangelism. Instead for commercial and practical reasons the company and its chaplaincy adopted a form of passive evangelism based upon the moral example rather than coercion, believing that by the effective moral policing of its own it could convert others. In the years that followed the company's acquisition of Bombay and Madras, religious governance moved beyond the remit of just the chaplain, becoming more than a tool to ensure the good behaviour of the company's English personnel, developing into a device that the company could utilise to govern over an increasingly cosmopolitan population that encompassed a variety of faiths. Although still maintaining its core identity as an English Protestant company, the EIC's religious governance came to a face value representing multiple faiths, in which the company sought to encourage migration and commerce into its jurisdiction through a religious policy of sufferance.

Company officials both religious and secular who ventured abroad to India entered an environment that in many ways had been for hundreds of years defined by its religious diversity. Many scholars such as Susan and Christopher Bayly have gone to great lengths to illustrate the impact traditional religious variation in India had on shaping eighteenth-century English imperialism (Bayly 1988, 1989, 1999). Building upon a discussion started by the Baylys, this outlook uses their analytical framework to bring the discussion away from the eighteenth century into a pre-imperial environment, the seventeenth-century corporate world. It also focuses upon how responses to religious variety in Indian society, by both the Mughal emperors and their Maratha counterparts, shaped and to some extent was emulated by EIC officials, in the formulation of the company's own religious policy during the seventeenth century. It also highlights the role of a varied Protestantism within the EIC, and how the company, as well as India, provided the cultural, religious and political space outside of the narrow confines of the religious establishment in England to embrace a Protestant plurality.

1610–1660

Mughal and Maratha context

Many of the EIC's chaplains and personnel were to comment on religious sufferance in the Mughal Empire. In an account of his time at the Mughal court, Thomas Roe wrote that Jahangir, the Mughal emperor, in a drunken declaration announced that 'Christians, Moores, Jewes, he medled not with their faith; they came all in louve, and he would protect them from wrong' (Foster 1899: 2.382). Gradually, many in the EIC began to suggest such a policy of religious sufferance offered by the Mughal emperors was what allowed for their 'tyrannical government there to be more easily endured' (Terry 1655: 418). Many of those who ventured to India in this early period often wrote back, perplexed by the exotic combination of religious toleration and freedoms with Mughal despotism. Edward Terry, chaplain to Thomas Roe, commented upon this while recalling a debate between Thomas Coryate and a Muezzin, in which he suggested that Christians were theologically better than Muslims as they believed in the one true God. The chaplain goes on to write that Coryate was lucky to be in India for 'every one there hath liberty to profess his owne Religion freely and if he please may argue against theirs, without feare of an inquisition' (Terry 1655: 271). Such an approach towards religious governance was later considered as an important element in ensuring the company's commercial mission, and so EIC officials adopted similar ideas of sufferance in the company's policies towards religious governance. Although the religiously cosmopolitan atmosphere, that Jahangir and his father Akbar had created in the growing Mughal Empire, proved difficult at times for English visitors to grapple with, it was to provide the ecumenically extensive foundations for the EIC's early policies towards religious governance. Similarly, to Susan Bayly, conclusions on the origins of caste, the adoption of religious sufferance as a tool of governance by the EIC, not only came from external English factors of a Protestant plurality, but primarily from an interaction with, and the adoption of, policies and ideas that had their foundations firmly in the attitudes of the leadership of the Indian subcontinent (1999: 25–63).

As Christopher Bayly has pointed out, Akbar and his advisors at the Mughal court agreed that not only Islam but also the many different faiths represented in India society, particularly Hinduism, 'should be in a constant' and 'fruitful dialogue' (1999: 17). The aim was to politically solidify bonds between Muslim Mughal leadership and the Hindu population, reinforcing the Mughal emperor's power. This was a policy that Akbar's son Jahangir followed; his grandson Shah Jahan made a token move away from the liberalism of his father and grandfather; he, however, continued to maintain some religious suffrage towards non-Muslims, patronising Hindu festivals, in particular the Ratha-Yatra at the Jagannath Temple, Puri (Eaton 2001: 71). For the early Mughal emperors, particularly the court of Akbar, both Hindu and Muslim political and social ideas merged. The author of the political work the Akhalq-I Jalali highlighted the wisdom of Hindus, while Akbar's *Ibādat Khāna* (or Hall of Prayer) harked back to a long Mughal tradition of interfaith dialogue and discussion in the emperor's court (Bayly 1988: 14; Alam and Subrahmanyam 2009: 463). By the seventeenth century the 'universalising vision' of the Mughal court, which had its foundations in Akbar's political and religious ideas, went beyond the beliefs of the indigenous Hindu society or the Islamic culture of the Mughals, to 'help balance the body politic' (Bayly 1988: 12). Religious sufferance then had a tradition in the ideological governance of the early-seventeenth-century Mughal emperors and their governments; however, other Indian leaders, particularly the Marathas, also adopted this policy of religious sufferance.

The role of the Bhakti movement and its bent towards religious sufferance in the evolution of Maratha society has been thoroughly discussed by historians, highlighting the role of interaction and dialogue between the invading Islam of the Mughals and Hinduism, particularly the Bhaktiism of the Marathas (Bayly 1988: 23–26; Gordon 1993: 19–21). The importance of the Bhakti saints in achieving social integration was vital in the emergence of Maratha self-rule, which, Bayly has argued, 'would not have been possible' without them (1999: 23). They espoused doctrinal ideas that not only broke down the traditional differences between Hindu sects, while also encouraging an outlook, which emphasised comparability with other faiths, particularly Islam. Stewart Gordon has pointed out that this dialogue between faiths was established along the lines of doctrinal similarities, calling attention to the fact that although the adoption of Islamic culture and Hindu sects varied geographically and individually, as a whole they 'found the ideas of faith common to both Bhakti and Islam' (Gordon 1993: 19). This form of syncretisation of faith can be seen in the popularity of ideas of Brotherhood that were central to Islam, which also were appealing to Hindus especially those who followed the Bhakti movement, who were encouraged by the Islamic theological critique of caste. While Muslims were openly included in Maharashtra social and religious order, as geographically Islamic and Hindu holy sites overlapped, on top of this, historians have pointed out that Marathi Islamic poets and thinkers such as Shah Muntoji Bahami and Husain Ambar Khan proved influential, along with Hindus in the establishment of a Maratha culture in the face of Mughal aggression (Kulkarni 1970: 338–9; Gordon 1993: 19). Even the famed Hindu leader of the Maratha cause Shivaji ordered that no mosque be destroyed or sacked.

For the Maratha and Mughals alike, religious sufferance was a tool of interaction that encouraged, or at least tried, to foster a certain level of goodwill between the contrasting faiths of leadership and people. Whether sufferance took the form of religious syncretisation, freedom to practice individual faith, or the offering of political and cultural influence to the wider religious community, it was a pre-existing tool of governance in the Indian subcontinent prior to the arrival of the EIC. Early Mughal and Maratha leaderships were acutely aware that to secure power in a religiously diverse environment, some form of religious accommodation would be required. This Indian subcontinent policy of religious sufferance did not solely evolve out of EIC's own religious experience but had its foundations within the interactions of Indian leadership with religion in the late sixteenth and seventeenth centuries.

Theological and Protestant plurality

Although at its core the EIC remained a commercial enterprise with profit maximisation as its main mission, the religious interests and concerns of its early leadership ensured that religious governance and a theologically diverse chaplaincy would play a part in the company's evolution. The corporate structure of England's seventeenth-century overseas expansion provided the means, in the words of one member of an American company, to render 'spirituall things for their Temporall' offering 'advantages and benifitts', that ensured that their spiritual and financial exchanges would succeed (Winthrop 1931: 2.146). Illustrating that the fluid interchange of temporal commerce was not parallel, but interwoven, with spiritual matters as the nonconformist divine Henry Wilkinson wrote in his treatises on debt:

> How should true Religion, and the Gospell sincerely preached, (for which the world hates us, and yet without which our life would be tedious, and a very shadow of death) bee defended by his power against the malice of the Divell and his instruments, if all the springs and fountaines of the Kingdom did not constantly runne into the Ocean of his Treasury?
>
> (Wilkinson 1625)

For many like Wilkinson the only way that the nation, and importantly the Protestant faith, could succeed was to ensure that the treasury was kept full. Wilkinson's image of the 'Ocean of his Treasury' reveals a shift from the previous century that increasingly placed goals that would lead to national prosperity in the hands of an ever-expanding international and global commercial network. This network was initially religiously Protestant, however, paradoxically as their corporate jurisdictions increased so did the diversity of religion.

From the outset the company embodied the denominational variation of England attracting a broad spectrum of the Protestant population, which was reflected in its leadership. Its first governor, a moderate puritan and ally of the earl of Warwick, Sir Thomas Smythe was heavily involved in the company for over eighteen years and continued in high office from 1614 to 1621 at the king's request. Over the same period Smythe's political rival Sir Edwin Sandys took up an active and often influential role in the company. A high Anglican, son of the bishop of Worchester and accused Catholic convert, Sandys had long been a controversial figure especially after his book, which called for the toleration of Catholics as well as the need to unite all the Christian churches, was published, supposedly without his permission (Sandys 1629: 194–222; Rabb 1998). Similarly, the company attracted the attention of the influential ecclesiastical Abbott family. The youngest of five brothers, Maurice, was involved in the running of the company for forty years and was at varying points a merchant, director, deputy-governor and finally governor from 1623 to 1636. It was through Maurice that his eldest brother, the archbishop of Canterbury, George (another elder brother Robert was also the bishop of Salisbury) was able to have a voice in the company. A Calvinist, the archbishop took a deep interest in individual and group commerce; however, it was primarily his fascination with the interaction of the English between non-Europeans and other Europeans in the Far East that interested him. Daniel O'Connor has argued that above all else the archbishop and his successor Laud both valued their correspondence with Anglican chaplains, Abbott in particular, with the Roe embassy by which he received the observations of the religions of the Indian court (2012: 4–6). Although its primary aims were to maximise profit, the religious sentiments of the company's leadership provide an insight into the broad Protestant spectrum that was incorporated into throughout the company. The variation of Protestantism, whether acute or moderate, represented by those who held top-ranking positions in the company, not only illustrates the Protestant diversity of the EIC but reflects why the company chaplaincy was ecumenically diverse, as company leadership was involved in the selections of ministers.

This variation in Protestant beliefs, at every level of the company, meant the EIC was far more pluralistic in its Protestantism. Differences in Protestant ecclesiastics rather than being seen as a threat were but in fact the opposite, using a collective Protestantism as a force to unify and govern. As Peter Lake has pointed out in his works on dispute in the early Stuart church, particularly the puritan community in London, that the variation of theological ideology discussion created an 'arena of lay activism and, at least potentially heterodox, doctrinal debate' (2001: 5). When transported aboard, the English Protestantism was allowed further religious expression, even more so the overseas provided a space in which religious governance could be conducted through 'heterogeneity, dispute, experimentation and, often toleration' (Games 2008: 253). Despite the fact that it would take some time for this tolerationist form of religious governance to become universal, from the outset the EIC adopted incredible leniency towards English Protestant ministers. Although little is known about the first chaplains of the EIC due to the scarcity of the records, over the century approximately ninety-nine ministers were appointed to go out to India or remain on the fleet (McNally 1976). Although it is unclear as to which Protestant church these men chose to practise their Christian faith, it is clear that the majority were made up of Anglicans such as Sir Thomas Roe's chaplain Edward Terry. However, from those that can be traced there was a broad array of Protestants present in the company, such as the two Presbyterian chaplains Samuel Tutchin and Patrick Copland, as well as a number of Anabaptists. This array of different ministers, with varying theological and liturgical backgrounds, caused several problems that often affected the social cohesion of the company's servants upon ships or in the factory.

One of the most prolifically mentioned chaplains of the company, Patrick Copland, highlights the assortment of theological backgrounds that made up the early EIC chaplaincy. Originally a graduate from St. Andrews University, Copland is one of the earliest and well-known EIC chaplains. Despite being a Scottish Presbyterian he was asked by the company to serve on four voyages between 1612 and 1621, before leaving for Bermuda and becoming a Congregationalist during the 1630s. Copland is mostly remembered or canonised in the history of the EIC for instigating the first company conversion in 1618 of an Indian boy who was later named Peter Pope by James I who thought it a witty response to the Catholic presence in India. However, Copland's fame outside the company did not mean that he avoided controversy or criticism from within. Following a battle of Jakarta on Christmas day in 1618, Copland's sermon was accused of being so influential that he 'dissanimated' the sailors who refused to fight against, the Dutch, their fellow Protestants. While on another occasion he was asked by the company's directors, who respected his opinion, to report upon the conduct of the captain of the fleet (O'Connor 2012: 38). Copland not only offers an example of both the influence and the power of the company chaplain but also highlights the awareness of the chaplain to their secular and evangelical roles as well as bringing to light the broad church that made up not only the clergy of the EIC but also its Protestant community.

Apostasy

As part of the acclimatisation process, the company gradually became more aware of, and worried about, the prospect of its English personnel converting.

The letter books of the EIC report cases that demonstrate how the company was primarily concerned with either the conversion of English subjects or specifically its own personnel, reinforcing the idea that evangelism for much of the seventeenth century was an internal mission. Evangelism was encouraged by example rather than coercion, so as to not endanger the company's relationship with educated middlemen such as European converts, Jews and Armenians as well as Hindus and Muslims on whom it relied. One particular case involved a recently employed Portuguese convert to Islám who had become an 'enemy of the Jesuits' and had recently come into the employ of the factor at Agra, Thomas Kerridge. Worried by his status as a converted European, Kerridge wrote the letter to ensure his employment, as he wished to keep him in service writing that as a European convert he did 'more business in an hour than his banyan in a day' (Foster 1896–1902: 1.283–4). As a Portuguese convert to Islam, his coming into the employment of the company was not an issue, as his apostasy had only brought disgrace to his nation, not the English one. However, the prospect of an Englishman in the company committing apostasy was one that both the company's secular and religious leadership feared deeply.

Edward Terry warned of the appeal of Islam to many Europeans, as well as those who practised the religion, claiming that it was the liberty and toleration it afforded towards the marriage rights of men that encourage conversion and 'hinder the settlement and growth of Christianity in those parts' (1655: 428). Indeed marriage posed several problems for the company, which ranged from the legality and religious sanctity of the marriage to the issue of the subject identity of not only the couple but any children born from the union. The Levant Company certainly had to deal with two cases in the 1630s when the company received a letter from a vizier concerning rumours that company officials were trying to send back the wife and children of an Englishman who married a native. Such an act was considered 'contrary to the Noble Law' of the Ottoman Empire, as through the act of marriage the English merchant had forfeited his right as subject of the English Crown to be one of the Ottoman Empire (TNA: SP105, 109 f., 265).

Although it would most probably be impossible to quantify how many English persons converted over this period, it can be presumed that the number was small, since relatively few occurrences are recorded. Despite this, it was a constant worry of officials in any company working abroad, who believed that it could be prevented only by the presence of religious leadership (O'Connor 2012: 221–40). Not only was the company worried about the spiritual ramifications to conversion but also the implications of an individual's conversion on foreign opinions toward the nation and national identity of the individual. In the spring of 1649 President Breton wrote of his grief to 'imparte unto you a sad story' of how one man's apostasy had brought both 'dishonour to our nation, and (which is incomparably worse), of our Christian profession' (Foster 1906–1927: 8.260). The man in question was Joshua Blackwell, a factor at Agra, whose conversion to Islam at the time left him according to Breton 'irrecoverably lost' (Foster 1906–1927: 8.260). Breton's surety that Blackwell was beyond reformation was not only based on religious fatalism but on an acknowledgement of Mughal farmans, which prevented any interaction that would lead to the reconversion of Englishmen who had become Muslim. Over the next year Blackwell became a frequent character in company dispatches between Surat and London, with factors being updated to his 'poore and wretched temporall condicion' (Foster 1906–1927: 8.294). Yet despite Breton's assertion he was beyond 'redemption', in the months that followed Blackwell initiated a series of correspondences that would lead to him being readmitted into the company and the Protestant community it represented (Foster 1906–1927: 8.299). Even 'upon the acknowledgement of his sin and promise of perseverance in his Christian profession' Blackwell faced problems that led to him being sent back to England despite his protests. In a letter to Blackwell, the chaplain of Surat, William Issacson, who had been placed in charge of Blackwell's readmittance into their society, explained how it would be difficult for the company to continue employing him as he would be 'subject to the abuse of every Mahometan that knowes your condition' (Foster 1906–1927: 8.302–4).

It was not just conversion to Islam or Hinduism that the EIC was guarded against; it was also ever-conscious of the presence of Catholicism. In 1648 one of the factors at Fort St. George reported back with great urgency to the company that the grandson of the founder of the Fort had 'turnd Papist rouge' and fled to Sao Tome (Foster 1906–1927: 8.298). The company replied by sending letters to the viceroy to return him to India, and in event that failed Thomas Breton was sent to 'require him' (Foster 1906–1927: 8.298). Even after the Treaty of Braganza in the 1660s, which effectively allowed Catholics to openly practise their religion in India (specifically Bombay), the EIC treated conversion as a serious threat. Indeed it was so wary of the possibility of Catholic conversion that any catholic priest accused of trying to convert or converting an English subject was immediately classed as an enemy of the company and as so was placed under investigation (Stern 2011: 104–6). For the EIC it was the chaplain who was the first line of defence against conversion, and thereby securing the subjecthood of its personnel, and whose particular 'stamp clerical approval could mitigate' the 'collective peril' of religiously patchwork society the English found themselves in (Games 2008: 223). Blackwell and Cogan's tale is not one that stands in isolation with conversion or at least the threat of it as

G. V. Scammel has pointed out, remaining an ever-present peril in the minds of EIC leadership (1992; Stern 2011: 105). The links between religious faith and identity meant that conversion posed a serious threat to EIC leadership, as it perceived itself to be the governing body that represented the English national identity abroad. Conversion then was not only a disgrace to one's country and faith but was a threat to company governance, as it removed Englishmen out of the company's sovereignty, weakening its position and commercial aims. It was then not only the chaplains' godly duty but also their corporate mission to prevent apostasy.

1661–1701

The marriage of Charles II to Catherine of Braganza brought with it the first major jurisdictive acquisition of the English in the Indian subcontinent, acquiring Bombay in 1661. By the beginning of the eighteenth century England had obtained control of Bombay, Madras and Calcutta; with these territorial acquisitions the English obtained jurisdiction over a growing population that was religiously cosmopolitan. The company's religious concern no longer only stretched to its Protestant plurality, but its government came to rule over Muslims, Hindus, Parsis, Armenians, Jews and Catholics. In light of this, its officials would have to develop and adapt a policy of religious governance that would include these new populations into the wider English world. It was in the cultural exposure of EIC officials to the religious world of the Indian subcontinent, as well as the pluralistically Protestant community that they had created over the previous sixty years, that it began to form a policy of religious governance that embodied sufferance. This policy, as previously mentioned, had its foundations in early-Mughal and Maratha religious governance as well as growing out of the company's Protestant plurality, but also came out of the demands of local religious groups to have a vocal say in English territories. Company officials were quick to present this policy of sufferance as their own invention of benevolence, which offered religious protection in the face of Mughal and Iberian religious injustice.

In opposition to Indian and European prejudice

Written two years into the War of Twenty-Seven Years, the acting governor of Bombay, Richard Keigwin, wrote in *The Articles of Agreement between the Governor and Inhabitants of Bombay* guaranteeing 'the inhabitants the liberty of Exceriseing their Respective Religion' (IOR E/3/43). This statement had been part of a series of moves that had been initiated by both George Oxenden and Gerald Aungier from the late 1660s, offering widespread religious suffrage; however, the timing of Keigwin's articles helps to illustrate the much wider reasoning for the EIC's religious policy. As early as 1665 Henry Gary in a letter to Henry Bennet, Lord Arlington, wrote of the economic benefits of granting religious liberty to the people of Bombay, proclaiming 'bulyd them pagados and mesquitas to excersise theyr religion publiquely in, noe doubt then but this will bee made a very famous and opulent port' (Foster 1906–1927: 12.51–2). By the time Keigwin was publishing the articles, the policy of religious sufferance was well established in Bombay; however, drawn up during a time of religious dislocation encouraged by conflict, these articles are illustrative of much wider post-Braganza EIC policy on religious governance. Their publication was an advertisement for the religious governance of the EIC to Hindus and Muslims fleeing from persecution and conflict between the Mughal and Maratha states. Similar to the Mughals in the late sixteenth and early seventeenth centuries, the English officials adopted religious sufferance to secure the aims of the company. By continuing the policy of religious sufferance established by the Mughals and Marathas, but advertising it as an English institution, EIC officials hoped to ensure the success of the company's commercial and financial mission, inviting local migration through the prospect of religious sufferance and protection.

In 1665 Sir Josiah Child did not draw upon Indian government for a link between religious sufferance and trade; rather he did allude to the closest European counterpart, the Dutch, pointing out that in India liberty in religion grew out of the necessity for liberty in trade and property, writing that English success was down to their willingness to 'allow an Amsterdam of Liberty in our Plantations' (Child 1693: 150–1). Although the influence of the Dutch on EIC official's ideas towards religion and religious governance was influential, the policy of sufferance, as previously suggested, came from sixteenth- and early-seventeenth-century Indian leadership. By the middle of the seventeenth century, Indian, or more so Mughal, leadership, under Aurangzeb, provided the means for the EIC to advertise its governance as being a religiously benevolent alternative to the local Indian as well as Iberian governments. It has previously been easy to fall into a trap in South Asian history of overemphasising historical moments in India religio-political past and thereby misrepresenting the reasoning behind what to modern readers would be seen a nocuous decisions. Aurangzeb's reintroduction of the *Jizya*, a poll tax upon non-Muslims (which had been abolished by Akbar for being prejudicial), in 1679 is one such example of where overemphasis has led to misrepresentation in the historical discussion. Whether seen as financially forcing Hindus to convert to Islam, or a policy to encourage support from loyal Muslims in his empire, Aurangzeb's motivations to reintroduce the Jizya has long been debated by historians on its role in the conflicts of Indian subcontinent in the late seventeenth century (Sarkar 1928: III: 249–50; Chandra 1969: 322–40). However, despite its contested position in Indian politics during this period, the Jizya does conversely offer the intellectual space to see the adoption of religious sufferance by EIC officials as a tool of governance. The company as an olive branch offered religious freedom to Hindus who migrated to Bombay and Madras; religious sufferance became an integral part of the EIC response to Aurungzeb's reintroduction of the tax. Religious sufferance actively encouraged Hindus to migrate to safety in land under EIC jurisdiction, fleeing the financial burden of the Jizya, but also bringing with them, to the great benefit of the English and the company, their own financial and commercial links.

Similarly, religious sufferance also provided EIC leadership with the governmental apparatus to present itself as being the compassionate alternative to other traditional European parties in the area, particularly the Catholic Portuguese. Although in recent years the severity of Catholic inquisition in Goa has come under question, its imposition was real in the mindset of the local population and EIC officials, who sought to use it to encourage resettlement to English-owned territory (Neill 1984: 231). The religious administrative centre for the Portuguese, Goa, had been a bishopric since 1534; the inquisition formally began in 1560 with the arrival of the first archbishop Gaspar de Leao Pimental, although an outward policy of aggressive evangelism began in 1542 with the arrival of the Jesuit Francisco Xavier (Ames 2000: 195). The most influential and long-reaching policy began seventeen years after Xavier's arrival and involved the forcible conversion of Hindu orphans. The law of 1559 gradually became more flexible encompassing not just orphans but children whose fathers had died were taken, and in the process the church could confiscate the parents' property (Priolkar 1961: 127–40). By encroaching upon both the religious and property rights of Indians, the Portuguese provided the company with the perfect opportunity to pit themselves as the benevolent other, allowing Hindus to escape the Catholic inquisition in neighbouring Goa. In two letters to Surat, the deputy-governor of Bombay, Henry Young, expressed his deep concern over the practices of Roman Catholics in forcibly converting Indians not just in Goa but also in Bombay, which he suggested was 'sending of scareing off the island to their Inquisition' (Foster 1906–1927: 13.218). The EIC policy of sufferance then was to provide not only an alternative space for Indians to flee both Indian and European governance but also the opportunity for the company to present English Protestantism evangelism, as a benevolent passive counter to aggressive and prejudicial ministry of the Portuguese Catholics.

For the religious and secular leadership of the EIC, Protestant evangelism was to play an important role in securing the company's relationship with the Indian community, as being a positive alternative to other European commercial companies. In 1665 Young wrote that the aim of Catholic ministers was not only to prevent people from migrating to the island but also in response to the forced conversions of Indians by the Portuguese that 'noe Christian made, though forcibly (mocke) baptized' (Foster 1906–1927: 13.219). For the company in India, the Portuguese provided them with a European contemporary who accentuated the difference between the Catholic evangelism taking place in Goa and their own passive evangelism. Unlike the zeal and heavy-handed evangelism of Catholic religious government, the EIC's primary objective was to demonstrate their difference through passive religious governance, at the head of which the chaplain would establish an 'effective church', and thereby 'a well ordered and morally unassailable Protestant society' (Stern 2011: 117–8). However, as the early EIC was quick to realise, this required a lot more policing than was first expected, leading factors to plead with the company to send chaplains to counter the fact that its personnel were 'dangerously disordering themselves with drink and whores' (Stern 2011: 117–8; Keay 1993: 48). Accounts of drunkenness and debauchery among the company's personnel were frequent and of serious concern to the company and its image. Personnel across the company, from chaplains to captains and merchants to governors, expressed concerns about the difficulty of governing such an 'irregular and almost incorrigible scum of rascals'. Their main concern about the 'ungodly behaviour' of personnel was the prejudicial effect that it had upon their commercial aims, as it damaged the company's image and reputation among local populations (*CSPC* 1617–1621: 264).

One chaplain recalled, during his time in India, that local people had complained about the conduct of the English sailors and merchants who came ashore. He went on to write, mimicking the broken English they spoke, 'Christian religion, Devil religion, Christians much drunk, Christians much do wrong, much beat, much abuse others.' For Terry the behaviour of the EIC personnel was the 'most sad and horrible thing' especially when he considered 'what scandal there is brought upon the Christian religion' of the company and country (1655: 239). To ensure that the trading mission of the company was successful, it needed to ensure the good behaviour of its personnel; this therefore fell to the company chaplains. In one letter, the company official told the chaplain that the 'civil behaviour is very requisite for begetting love and estimation amongst those heathenish people', and to do this his primary aim was to 'settle such modest and sober government' to ensure godly behaviour and thereby a godly example of passive evangelism and fulfilling secular and ecclesiastical roles (Terry 1655: 239; O'Connor 2012: 48).

Civic governance

The company's policy towards religious governance was also not only fuelled by the external forces of Indian and European politics, or Protestant evangelical requirements, but by the internal pressures of Indian people who now fell under EIC jurisdiction. This approach builds upon the work done by Arthur Fraas but places it firmly in the context of the seventeenth century, when Indian legal, social and political agency in English's jurisdictions was secured by the power of religious and cross-religious groups, as well as the EIC's policy to define people (for better or worse) within these religious groupings (2011). In the lead-up to the handover of Bombay, EIC intelligence reported that groups of the local inhabitants had offered to 'deliver up the island in spight of the Portingalls' (Foster 1906–1927: 11.143–4). These local inhabitants on several occasions continued to vocally exercise themselves politically under English rule, both within and across their religious communities, reinforcing as well as pushing the boundaries of the EIC policy of religious sufferance. One year before King Charles II signed the charter handing over the control of Bombay to the company in 1667, 123 Christians, 84 Hindus and 18 Muslims presented the king with a petition outlining the abuses of the Portuguese, in particular the fact that there was no religious tolerance and only Roman Catholicism was acceptable. The petition then goes on to ask the king to prevent the government of Bombay from allowing any discussion to 'alienate us from your government' (Khan 1922: 451–4). While in Madras, from Streynsham Master's term as governor onwards, the company adopted a policy of significant inclusion. In 1678 Master reorganised the choultry courts from two justices to three, while by the 1690s the English mayor of the town was supported by numerous aldermen and burgesses, a number of whom were made up of different Indian religious and ethnic groups: one Armenian, one or two Jews and Portuguese, Hindus and one Muslim (IOR E/3/92: s172–3). Ames argues that the governors Cooke, Lucas and Gary, as well as Presidents Oxenden and Aungier, adopted de facto religious tolerance, fuelled by the need for the company to appease religious groups within the port. Under the governorship of Gerald Aungier in 1673 the council of Bombay proposed that for the better regulation of government, encouraging migration and appeasing religious groups, it should offer them their own councils, writing that Muslims, Hindus and Portuguese should have their own chief and council and 'may be impowered to have a perculiar regard and care of their owne cast to accomdate and quiet all small differiences and quarrels which mat happen amongst them' (IOR G/3/2/159). By politically solidifying religious sufferance in the governance of Bombay and other towns that came under the EIC's jurisdiction, company officials not only secured their own aims but also met those of local Indian peoples.

Practical issues

On top of dealing with the religiously cosmopolitan environment of India, EIC officials had to find practical solutions to environmental issues that affected the religious practice and governance of its ecumenically diverse English and European employees. As an essential element of the majority of Protestant sects was the active observation of group or collective worship however, like all aspects of life in India, this encountered practical problems due to denomination divisions that often flared into debates between factors. After being accused by Joseph Hall for disobeying the company's orders, by only observing divine worship on the Sabbath and not every day, Shem Bridges, the local company chief, eloquently observed that in India it was difficult to find a religious direction that pleased all, writing, 'It will bee difficult to calculate an Ephemerides that will serve all Meridians.' Bridges was not only highlighting the problems theological unity faced, but the practical issues of environmental factors that company servants faced in their new surroundings. Factories were areas in which space was shared between English company servants and indigenous workers, meaning that private worship was either difficult or impossible to conduct, as there was no area where 'at prayer wee may not bee disturbes or gazed on by the Workmen and Collyes that are continually about the factory'. Similarly spaces were often allocated for dual use; as Shem points out there was no place to entertain local dignitaries and EIC leadership or hold events other 'than the hall which must bee our Church'(IOR E/3/45). Indeed this became a problem that was openly recognised by company leadership both within India and back in England, with a chapel being requested for and built in Madras and Surat between 1661 and 1664 (Foster 1906–1927: 11.199). The temperature was also an issue, as Bridges pointed out that only one service on a Sunday could be expected as 'in these hot countries, for neither a mans spirits nor voice can hold touch here with long dutyes'. These environmental impracticalities encouraged ministers and company servants to adapt their methods, encouraging shorter sermons, which even then according to some were still 'thought too much by some' (IOR E/3/45). The effect of this was that Bridges points out despite company orders for all 'men or company to heare divyne service', many refused to even turn up to church, with on character and nonconformist friend of Hall even breaking the Sabbath and working (Foster 1934: 95).

Similarly the factory records are littered with incidents in which factors complained that company officials in London were sending out ministers who did not conform to their beliefs. Following the appointment of four ministers to Surat and Coromandel Coast in 1668, the factors at Bombay wrote back to general court, vexed that prior to ministers being sent out, the council had recognised 'that the principles of religion owned and practised by your servants in Surat and at Bombay differ much from the opinions professed by the gentlemen you have sent us' (Foster 1906–1927: 13.248). Although at the time they agreed 'it our dutys . . . to treat the said gentlemen with all civility and due respect' to 'embrace them with the arms of brotherly love', sometimes the denominational differences flared into arguments. Following his appointment to Masulipatam, which lasted a year, Rev. Walter Hook (one of the four ministers mentioned earlier) was sent to Fort St. George where his refusal to read from the Book of Common Prayer or follow the traditional Anglican liturgy caused dissension in the factory. The argument that took place over two days concluded with the chief factor, Mr Jersey, walking out of church and establishing his own prayer meetings in his house. But despite that argument and any ecclesiastical differences initially reported in any letters, Smithson writes that the minister Hook 'had gained very much the affections of most English here' (Foster 1906–1927: 13.284–7). While externally the altercation was practically dealt with by the president at Madras George Foxcroft who pointed out that Hook could not be dismissed and that all sides were to blame, ordering that peace and unity through a group meeting was now to be established. Foxcroft had essentially instructed all parties to 'deal with it'.

Despite the difficulties of environmental factors and theological divisions, one of the primary roles of the chaplain for the leadership of the company was to ensure that the observation of sermons was maintained, as these not only were the primary form of outward religious worship but also served the purpose of bringing together the EIC personnel into one collective. Not only from these meetings were men and women told how to behave but they also served to ensure that the factors, chief merchants and captains could govern a group of people by arranging that they collectively met twice a day. These meetings then were at their core method or form of what could later be described as Hobbesian social control, with the chaplaincy and religious governance applying an external restraint upon humanity's inherent social evils and indulgences. Although the influence of these meetings is hard to quantify, they were considered by the company's leadership an effective method of control. In 1614 David Midelton received a commission that ordered prayers to be read morning and evening both on land and at sea, ruling that only through sickness could these group meetings be missed (Foster 1896–1902: 3.57). Company leadership even dictated that group religious observation be held on a household level, declaring in 1615 that good government in household could be established 'observing due times of common prayer' and that this was the only way to ensure that 'servants be kept from disorderly gadding to rack houses, etc' (Foster 1896–1902: 3.108). For the company's leadership the spiritual influence of these meetings was of utmost importance; however, equally important was their use as a method of social control where local EIC leadership could gather collectively personnel and police their collective behaviour. The chaplains were to remind people of the company's moral code and law, reminding every man 'to abandon as much as possible those vices which custom has glued just to his inclination' (*CSPC* 1630–1634: 399). By providing the company's personnel with a sermon that reinforced the religious governance of the company, the chaplain not only was of benefit to the company but provided 'strong meat, for all growing Christians', fulfilling his two roles, spiritual and temporal (Terry 1655: 463).

Conclusion

By the end of the century religious sufferance had a strong tradition in Indian and EIC political and religious governance. It had been used both as a tool for political leadership, such as the Mughals, Marathas and EIC leadership, to establish and obtain commercial or political power and by local populations and religious groups to promote their own independence within political systems. For the chaplains of the EIC, keen to fulfil both their ecumenical and secular responsibilities, religious sufferance helped not only to establish a broad Protestant community in India but also encouraged them to adopt a passive form of evangelism, one that embraced conversion by example. This is not to say that Protestant evangelism did not take a proactive form; however, it was not until the end of the century that an impassioned policy of propagation began to emerge. The policy of sufferance did have its detractors: as Aparna Balachandran has pointed out, opinion of the corporation was 'mired in oriental corruption and laziness', an assertion that was aimed at the whole company, including its chaplaincy (2008). It wasn't until 1689 and the chartering of the Society for the Promoting Christian Knowledge (SPCK) and the Society for the Propagation of the Gospel (SPG) in 1701 that a concerted effort was made by the English to establish a state-driven evangelical agenda. Although these organisations, as well as others of a similar vein, had not been developed into the missionary societies that we have come to associate with India until the middle of the eighteenth century, their establishment marked the shift in reception towards the policy of sufferance and towards one where conversion became both a religious and political motivation.

Throughout the seventeenth century Shem's tent remained open, and Japheth was not only encouraged to enter an environment in which religious governance was familiar but also did so on his own terms. The policy of EIC officials to adopt religious sufferance was openly used to encourage Japheth's migration into their jurisdiction enlarging their population, while those religious groups also sought to push the company into further expanding religious and political sufferance. The Indian social and religious environment not only encouraged Shem's tent to embrace subcontinental political and religious differences but also forced English Protestants to embrace their own plurality, something that had not happened until the end of the century within England itself, while ensuring that they remained within the Protestant church. Although the level of religious inclusivity, and freedom of practice, was not to last more than half a century after the 1700s, this pre-colonial period tells us a great deal about the religious and political flexibility corporations in the seventeenth century could exercise abroad, while also highlighting the importance external societies had on the making and adoption of policies.

References

Manuscript

EIC Correspondence with the East: various years. IOR E/3/43–92.

EIC Factory Records, Bombay: 1674–1681. IOR G/3/2.

Levant Company Minute Books: 1616–1638. TNA: SP105, 109 f., 265.

Print

Alam, Muzaffar and Subrahmanyam, Sanjay. 2009. 'Frank Disputations: Catholics and Muslims in the Court of Jahangier (1608–11)', *The Indian Economic and Social History Review*, 46(4): 457–511.

Ames, Glenn J. 2000. 'Serving God, Mammon, or Both? Religious vis-à-vis Economic Priorities in the Portuguese *Estado da India*, c.1600–1700', *Catholic Historical Review*, 86(2): 193–216.

Armitage, David. 2000. *The Ideological Origins of the British Empire*. Cambridge: Cambridge University Press.

Balachandran, Aparna. 2008. 'Of Corporations and Caste Heads: Urban Rule in Company. Madras, 1640–1720', *Journal of Colonialism and Colonial History*, 9(2).

Bayly, C. A. 1988. *Indian Society and the making of the British Empire*. Cambridge: Cambridge University Press.

———. 1989. *The Origins of Nationality in South Asia: Patriotism and Ethical Government in the Making of Modern India*. Oxford: Oxford University Press.

Bayly, Susan. 1989. *Saints Goddesses and Kings: Muslim and Christians in South Indian Society 1750–1900*. Cambridge: Cambridge University Press.

———. 1999. *Caste, Society and Politics in India from the Eighteenth Century to the Modern Age*. Cambridge: Cambridge University Press.

Calendar of State Papers Colonial, East Indies, China and Japan, Vols. III–VIII 1617–1634. TNA.

Chandra, Satish. 1969. 'Jizyah and the State in India during the 17th Century', *The Journal of Economic and Social History of the Orient*, 12(3): 322–40.
Child, Sir Josiah. 1693. *A New Discourse on Trade*. London.
Eaton, Richard M. 2001. 'Temple Desecration and Indo-Muslim States', *Frontline*, 5: 70–77.
Foster, William (ed.) 1899. *The Embassy of Sir Thomas Roe to the Court of the Great Mogul, 1615–1619*. London: Hakluyt.
———. (ed.) 1906–1927. *The English Factories in India, 1618–1669*. Oxford: Oxford University Press.
———. (ed.) 1934. *The Voyage of Thomas Best to the East Indies, 1612–1614*. London: Hakluyt.
———. (ed.) 1986–1902. *Letters Received by the East India Company From Its Servants in the East, 1602*–1617. Oxford: Oxford University Press.
Fraas, Arthur M. 2011. 'They Have Travailed into a Wrong Latitude: The Laws of England Indian Settlements, and the British Imperial Constitution. 1726–1773'. Unpublished Ph.D. dissertation, Duke University.
Games, Alison. 2008. *The Web of Empire: English Cosmopolitans in an Age of Exploration, 1560–1660*. Oxford: Oxford University Press.
Gordon, Stewart. 1993. *The Marathas 1600–1818*. Cambridge: Cambridge University Press.
Keay, John. 1993. *The Honourable Company: A History of the English East India Company*. New York: Harper Collins.
Khan, S. A. 1922. *Anglo-Portuguese Negotiations Relating to Bombay, 1660–1677*. London: Oxford University Press.
Kulkarni, A. R. 1970. 'Social Relations in the Maratha Country in the Medieval Period', *Indian History Congress Proceedings*, 32(1): 231–269.
Lake, Peter. 2001. *The Boxmaker's Revenge: 'Orthodoxy', 'Heterodoxy' and the Politics of the Parish in Early Stuart London*. Stanford, CA: Stanford University Press.
McNally, S. J. 1976. *The Chaplains of the East India Company*. London: India Office Records.
Neill, Stephen. 1984. *A History of Christianity in India: The Beginnings to AD 1707*, Vol. 1. Cambridge: Cambridge University Press.
O'Connor, Daniel. 2012. *The Chaplains of the East India Company 1601–1858*. London: Bloomsbury Academic.
Priolkar, A. K. 1961. *The Goa Inquisition*. Bombay: Bombay University Press.
Rabb, Theodore K. 1998. *Jacobean Gentleman: Sir Edwin Sandys, 1561–1629*. Princeton: Princeton University Press.
Sandys, Sir Edwin. 1629. *Europae Speculum: Or, a View or Survey of the State of Religion in the Westerne Parts of the World*. London.
Sarkar, Jadunath. 1928. *History of Aurangzeb*. 3 vols. Calcutta.
Scammell, G. V. 1992. 'European Exiles, Renegades and Outlaws and the Maritime Economy of Asia c. 1500–1750', *Modern Asian Studies*, 26(4): 641–661.
Stern, Philip J. 2011. *The Company State: Corporate Sovereignty & the Early Modern Foundations of the British Empire in India*. Oxford: Oxford University Press.

Terry, Edward. 1655. *A Voyage to East-India*. London.
Wilkinson, Henry. 1625. *The Debt Book: Or, a Treatise Upon Romans 13 ver. 8. Wherein Is Handled: The Civil Debt of Money or Goods, and Under It the Mixt Debt, as Occasion Is Offered: Also, the Sacred Debt of Love*. London.
Winthrop, J. 1931. *Papers*, ed. Stewart Mitchell. Vol. II. Boston: Massachusetts Historical Society.

6 Maritime society in an early modern port city

Negotiating family, religion and the English Company in Madras

Mahesh Gopalan

In the first half of the seventeenth century, agents of the English East India Company were exploring various locations along the southern Coromandel for the establishment of a factory. The commercial success of the Dutch East India Company at Pulicat and the Portuguese at Santhome, respectively, influenced the choice of the English East India Company, who selected the region around Pulicate Lake and the Palar River. After surveying the region north of Pulicat and further south, these officials eventually settled on a location between the Triplicane (Cooum) and the Elambore Rivers, and in 1638 they received a grant from Venkata Nayaka to establish a factory there. Thus began the English establishment at Madras, which began as a small trading outpost and grew into a fortified company factory called Fort St. George and was supported by a rapidly growing urban settlement extending beyond the fort walls. Over the next three decades, the English settlement at Madras attracted many of the Portuguese, Indo-Portuguese and other residents from places like Santhome and surrounding areas and therefore became a notable site of cross-cultural dialogue. The growth of English commerce and the declining fortunes of Santhome shaped the English Company's interaction with local producers, merchants and European free traders who now sought to relocate their business from the English port. It resulted in the growth of the urban settlement and a growing distinction between the white and black town. By the eighteenth century the spaces that offered Madras a distinct physical identity grew to include surrounding villages like Triplicane, Chetput, Nungumbakum, Egmore and the Portuguese commercial centre of Santhome (Love 1913; Neild 1979; Watson 1980; Marshall 1998).

In the seventeenth century the English East India Company also underwent a significant transformation. Through periodic renewals of its charter, the company secured a number of privileges from the English Crown, which empowered it to project itself not just as a trading entity with a monopoly over East India trade, but also as a bona fide representative of the English Crown, acting on its behalf in the region. This, in turn, influenced the company's engagement with local political groups and led to the consolidation of its administrative, economic and political powers, and eventually to the emergence of the 'company state' (Stern 2011). During the seventeenth and eighteenth centuries, the company actively competed with local political elites for political and judicial rights, land revenue, control over production and other economic flows (Mines 2001).

This chapter examines European society at Madras during this period of transition, when the nature of English presence shifted from being commercial to distinctly political. It analyses the social conditions of those living in Madras and its impact on the altering political, physical and notional spaces that defined the settlement. It argues that the company state at Madras emerged from a multi-layered engagement between the company officials in the port city, their superiors in London, the local political elites operating within the region and the diverse residents of Madras.

Reordering traditional family structures: maritime English society in early modern Madras

In the second half of the seventeenth century, the port of Madras was associated with a frequent movement of people, and admixtures were reordering traditional family structures and social practices (Love 1913; Marshall 1997; Jayawardena 2009). This created a society that sought new markers of social order and social identity through discarding old hostilities, embracing new notions of togetherness and establishing new familial and social hierarchies. As argued by Patrick Manning, the interplay of family structures and migrations in the Indian Ocean during this period constituted a 'frontier' for families. There existed a variegated series of zones where patterns of family life changed in response to the arrival and departure of migrants and where people lived in close proximity/intimacy with and shared family ties with 'others' – people they self-classified as different from themselves, according to several criteria. This maritime society at Madras was not one defined by lineage, but by new markers of hierarchy and mobilization: ethnicity, birthplace, legal status, religion and racial categorization (Manning 2013: 300–10). These new criteria came to define the status and rank of individuals and contributed to the creation of social and political spaces within which further transformations could occur.

The nature of work for many employees in the English East India Company required them to serve across various stations dotting the Bay of Bengal, forcing them to leave their families behind at Madras. In addition, there were company employees in the region who were separated from their families in Britain. The company records contain many references to requests by various individuals to be reunited with their families, whether within the Bay of Bengal region in South Asia or in Britain. In one such instance, Mr Thomas Winter, a resident of Madras, requested that his son and daughter be brought there from England so that they could spend some time with him. In another example, the wife and three daughters of Mr Cole sailed from England to join him at Madras (Fort St. George 1910–1946: 25). Mr Ralph Ord, the company school master and later a free merchant at Madras, requested for leave to go to Madapollam to see his sister who had settled there after having recently been married to Mr James Wheeler (Madras Diary 1681: 44). On two occasions in the 1680s, John Bugden applied to the council for permission to bring his wife from Bengal to Madras. In another such case John Hart, who had been serving the company at Madras, applied to bring his wife from Surat. The last two examples mentioned earlier pertain to individuals not in the service of the company but those who had been granted permission to conduct trade on their private accounts (Madras Diary 1681: 18). In some cases matrimonial ties were finalized in England. For example in 1675, Mary Barber who set sail from England for Madras with her maid was sent to be the wife of Jonathan Pace (Fort St. George 1670–1677: 25).

There were soldiers separated from their families whose wives claimed part of their salary in England (Madras Diary 1683: 35). In 1673, the daughter of Nicolo Gomes appealed to the company for help after her father, a company soldier, was killed accidently. She petitioned that she was of a marriageable age but in a poor financial condition. Many individuals in Madras supported her cause, and she was made a recipient of company charity (Madras Diary 1672–1678: 18). In another instance, the widow of Mr Sam Tutching petitioned the company for the balance of her husband's salary and gratuity (Madras Diary 1672–1678: 34). In 1690, Mary Sterling applied to the company for some maintenance, since her husband was dying, and she was too poor to sustain herself. She cited her father Captain Francis's service to the company as a reason that she ought to be given some assistance (Madras Diary 1690: 6).

Throughout this period, there were many complaints regarding the shortage of eligible European women as marriage partners for European men working in the East. The Portuguese, and later the English and the Dutch, all sent young women from Europe to their settlements in the hope that they would marry their employees and help establish their families in the East (Penny 1900; Love 1913). The settlements in the East were predominantly male and not seen as safe places for women. It was difficult for many married employees of the company to bring their families from England. In addition there were regulations about bringing their wives when they travelled from one settlement to another. At the same time many of the company's unmarried employees used the opportunity of being away from established social networks in Europe to court women of European and native origin in the East and to establish households in the region, as many could not afford to maintain European wives. In places like Madras marrying Indo-Portuguese women were a feasible option for many, but such decisions were taken only after factoring in various business and financial considerations, like inheritance and transfer of assets.

The social flux of this period also impacted the working conditions of company employees. It affected the company garrison, where officers were constantly faced with instances of indiscipline. In 1678 the accidental death of an English soldier, Thomas Savage, within the company garrison arose from the punishment ordered by the sergeant John Waterhouse on account of indiscipline. Corporal Edward Short was a co-accused. Thomas Savage was found drunk at three o'clock in the afternoon, and he abused the sergeant in charge of the *choultry* guard, who decided to initiate disciplinary action. Corporal Edward Short, acting on orders given by Sergeant Waterhouse, tied Thomas Savage to his cot. However, Savage continued to be abusive, and Waterhouse ordered that his neck and knees be bound till three or four inches of a match was burnt out. Unfortunately, when the knot was released the soldier was found to be dead. An enquiry was instituted because witnesses testified that the corporal tying the knot did not actually know how to go about it, and the sergeant was too headstrong to consider requests that the drunken soldier be given an opportunity to apologize. Other witnesses claimed that the sergeant dismissed their pleas to the effect that the drunken soldier would die if subjected to such harsh punishment. Different accounts of the episode began to circulate widely, adding to the tensions within the garrison. The issue of drunken behaviour was a concern all across the company establishment. Drunkenness among company employees can be seen as a possible strategy of coping with the working conditions in the East and with the pressures of the newly emerging social system. The agent and council eventually decided to avoid further tensions within the garrison and sent the accused to England aboard the *New London*, in custody of its Captain George Erwin (Madras Diary 1678–1679: 1–5). Apart from offering an insight into the tensions in the work space, this story illustrates the growing pressures on the English East India Company to establish a judicial system at Madras.

Like most early modern port cities the social conditions at Madras were such that individuals were living away from familiar, traditional family settings, thrown into a protracted engagement with a local society shaped by the sea and the way of life that it supported. Many found themselves thrown into the 'rough life' of maritime trading communities, as opposed to the supposedly gentle, cultured life of an imagined and constantly re-configured 'home', which acted as a counterpoise to their existential reality. The social world of the 'rough life' of the early modern maritime port city was composed through reports of bad behaviour of 'horrid' swearing and profanation of the name of God, drunkenness, uncleanliness and sexual immorality. While England served as a marker defining a secure social and political world, the regions of Asia, the Indian Ocean and ports like Madras were represented through images of uncertainty, difficulty, fear, death, confusion and indiscipline.

The changing social world at Madras and its attendant socio-economic tensions brought the institution of the family and marriage into sharper focus. It redefined interpersonal relations and institutional engagements with the larger society. New social support systems emerged, endorsed by the company, which could help the European society at Madras to cope with the difficulties of living away from home. Administrative and religious institutions like the Protestant Church, the civic administration bodies and the judicial apparatus came to play an important role in offering such social support, engaging with the growing inequalities and thus re-defining families and individuals associated with the early modern maritime world. Throughout the course of the seventeenth and eighteenth centuries, the English East India Company had to develop responses to such stimuli. It established judicial and political institutions in the late seventeenth century, which increasingly came to govern social interactions (Marshall 1997, 1998; Mines 2001). The company formulated rules for the children of soldiers and for the children born of mixed marriages between Protestant and Catholics and between Englishmen and native women (Fort St. George 1670–1677: 47). Thus, the company made social, political and legal interventions and shaped the Protestant moral economy that governed European society in Madras.

Formalizing the company's social gaze: regulating the social world at Madras

In the last three decades of the seventeenth century, the English East India Company presided over the formalization of the administrative, political and social spaces, which is seen by many scholars as marking the beginnings of the company state (Lewansowski 1977; Neild 1979; Marshall 1998; Brimnes 1999; Stern 2011). The court of directors formally declared Madras a 'city' and instructed the governor of Madras to institute a civic administration and a civil legal system (Fort St. George 1686–1692: 11). These formal administrative, judicial and civic institutions established by the company in late-seventeenth-century Madras were restricted to the English residents. However, to exercise its sovereign claims over Madras, the company needed to create institutions whose economic and political control extended over all residents, not just the English. During this period the company administrators claimed sovereign rights from diverse sources like royal grants by the king of England, royal farmans issued by the local Nayaka ruler, the Marathas, the rulers of Golconda and the Mughals, and from various commercial or political agreements the company made with governors and officials representing the dominant political elite in the region. The company officials were aware that these rights, sourced from a multiplicity of authorities, were not absolute and could be withdrawn at will. Therefore, they were always cautious about overreaching the limits of their power (Mukund 2005).

To organize the social and moral world of its employees, the English East India Company sought to enforce discipline and to introduce rules that governed their daily life. For the purposes of such an engagement, the company differentiated between the public and private spheres of its employees. Regulations centred on issues such as the residence of company employees in private accommodation outside the fort played an important role in organizing living space, individual behaviour and the social order. The company feared that residing outside the fort would make its employees prone to corruption, drunken behaviour, gambling and so forth. Officials faced many difficulties in checking what was described as the 'unruly behaviour' of its employees. But due to a shortage of suitable accommodation within the fort, a few exceptions were made till the company's houses within Madras and other factories were enlarged. Furthermore, company employees and other British persons residing outside the fort often purchased property privately and thus developed their own personal economic interests, which could run counter to those of the company's enterprise. Such activities may have been a natural outcome of their long-term decision to settle in the East in general and in places like Madras in particular. However, it became a serious concern for the company, because many such employees declined postings in places not of their choice. Resultant anxieties prompted the directors to decree that those violating their transfer orders ought to be made to return to England (Malleson 1911: 262). Although the order was in keeping with previous action taken against employees who violated company rules, such punitive action was not very easily undertaken, and on most occasions the company was forced to negotiate a settlement.

The company simultaneously sought to establish a moral order in which the Protestant chaplain played a central role, in close association with the church. This, in turn, led to the criss-crossing of private and public roles of various individuals within this socio-religious space in Madras (Penny 1904). The company did not merely appoint chaplains; it also despatched numerous copies of Bibles and catechisms for distribution in the hope of facilitating larger changes in society and promoting the Protestant church (Fort St. George 1670–1677: 120). On behalf of the company, the English agent, Streynsham Master, laid the foundations for the St. Mary's Church within the fort. Since the establishment of the fort, the company dining hall had served as a makeshift church, and this was the first attempt by the English East India Company to establish a formal religious space within the fort. Residents of Madras made financial contributions on private account towards the construction of St. Mary's, consolidating the role of the church as a symbol of the Protestant socio-cultural assertion in Madras (Madras Diary 1678–1679: 65). In 1677 Streynsham Master ordered that the general code of conduct for the company's servants be displayed in the hall and be universally binding for all company employees in Madras and across the Bay irrespective of their religious and racial identities (Malleson 1911: 9–10). These rules were meant to discourage company employees from 'unchristian like behaviour and disorderly practices' and to re-enforce 'Protestant' ways. The English Company was not averse to the use of religion as part of its attempt to develop a comprehensive system of social discipline and was gradually ordering the social and moral economy through the articulation of a universal code of conduct with moorings in a distinctly Protestant worldview.

The company's larger social intervention in the direction of curbing 'unruly' and 'un-Christian' behaviour of its employees and other residents of Madras extended to the functioning of 'entertainment houses'. The company felt compelled to address complaints about the activities of company employees after working hours and to simultaneously explore ways of generating administrative revenue through the imposition of taxes on economic activities. It banned gaming houses, forbade residents of the town and the fort from frequenting these places late at night and introduced fines to penalize those who continued to defy this law (Fort St. George 1678–1679: 68). It also introduced a licencing fee for entertainment houses, the making and sale of arrack and the sale of betel leaf. By bringing certain forms of economic activity within the scope of regulation, and giving them de facto legitimation, the company produced an official discourse about what was to be considered permissible and within the purview of its moral gaze.

Formalizing socio-political spaces in early modern Madras: establishing a civil legal system and the Madras city cooperation

These processes were deepened through the establishment in the late-seventeenth-century Madras of a civic administration, a civil legal system and judicial courts empowered to pronounce judgment on matters after trial (Penny 1904: 62). The company thus sought to organize the urban world of Madras, with its diverse range of inhabitants. In the 1670s (when these legal systems were put in place), the company identified groups that were gradually incorporated under the jurisdiction of these new civic and legal institutions, thus ensuring that they remained socially, culturally, economically and politically subordinate to the English. Instead of excluding these groups, the company chose to appropriate the non-English European and Indo-European populations residing in Madras and the surrounding regions. Through the instrumentality of the newly established courts, the company could oversee certain economic aspects of daily life in the city. The choultry court included three company officials, the customer, the mint master and the paymaster who sat in court on Tuesdays and Fridays (Penny 1904: 62; Love 1913: 404). It was expected to register all sentences in Portuguese and maintain a register of all alienations and sale of slaves, houses, gardens, boats and ships (Madras Diary 1678–1679: 7). A higher court of appeal known as the court of judicature was also established. It consisted of the governor and the council and heard cases of great importance or of a value of more than fifty pagodas. The court of judicature met in the company chapel on Wednesdays and Saturdays, as did the other courts on designated days. The customary use of the chapel as a space for the convening of courts during this period can be read as an attempt by the company to appropriate ecclesiastical authority for political purposes and confer its credence upon newly instituted institutions of legal and judicial power.

The courts established in Madras during the late seventeenth century allowed the company mechanisms for control over all forms of economic activity and offered legitimation to the emerging moral economy. This produced a new vocabulary for the assertion of English sovereign rights over the emerging cityscape, albeit with limited reference to the daily life of European inhabitants and the subjects of the English Crown. The company also acknowledged the preferability of imposing local laws over non-Europeans and those not in the employ of the company. There was thus a distinct differentiation between matters that fell under the jurisdiction of the company and those that did not. A similar distinction was made with respect to various forms of economic activity, separating those activities that had a direct or indirect impact upon the company's economic interests from those that did not. The company carefully enumerated the individuals, activities and political rights that it sought to assert and undertook to protect. The courts of law and the city cooperation settled competing claims on the legitimacy of English law. This resulted in a general differentiation between European and non-European and subjects of the English Crown and other denizens, along with variations in the application of English laws and local laws. The articulation of such social, economic and legal differentiations through court judgements played a crucial role in the production of a new urban social space. The company state's claim to sovereign powers in seventeenth-century Madras was not seamless and overarching: it was textured and qualified by such a layered understanding of the company's interests and jurisdiction, as interpreted in light of the newly emerging moral economy. Thus, attempts by the company to define and to institutionalize its authority over various forms of economic space within Madras need to be situated in this context.

The company's engagement with the residents in the port city went beyond the tasks of establishing discipline, enumerating economic activities and establishing civil and economic courts of law. The establishment of the Madras city corporation institutionalized the company's attempts to regulate urban spaces and helped to separate its commercial arm from the administrative one. The requirement for a city corporation did not emerge out of a general need to exercise sovereign authority over the port city. Rather it arose from specific discussions on the issues of registration of property and the maintenance of the city and its defences and the need to enumerate and regulate the economic, religious and cultural world of urban Madras. The authority to establish the corporation was derived through the charters of 1661, 1683 and 1686 (Love 1913; Srinivasachariar 1939). The office of the mayor was established in 1687 (Love 1913: 497). The order creating the city corporation issued by the governor and the company stated that it was merely following 'the practice of other European nations in India'.

At first glance the establishment of the Madras city corporation can be seen as an administrative imposition of an English institution over the city and its populace. However, its establishment was also attended by issues like the appointment of coolies to clear dirt from the town and the imposition of a tax for the same. Certain residents living outside the fort, mostly non-European, objected to this and demanded that the company first list the number of houses at Madras. However, there arose fears that an official count of houses would prompt the local political elite to demand a greater rent from the English and lead to protest against the formal collection of taxes. Instead it was suggested that it be done informally, as done during festivals and other celebrative occasions, varying according to the castes and the streets that they lived in (Madras Diary 1678–1679: 86). Although the English agreed to this arrangement, they insisted on counting the European households and officially collecting a tax from the Christian house owners who lived in the town (Madras Diary 1678–1679: 93). The court of directors continued to insist on a formal and proper system of taxation. They had received reports about taxes being charged in other European settlements under the Dutch, Portuguese and native governments and were eager to implement a similar system. The directors reminded the officials that it was their duty to charge the residents for the 'protection and preservation from wrong and violence', but left the decision to the agent and council (Fort St. George 1681–1686: 10). Nonetheless, they also pointed out that 'to make the English nation as formidable as the Dutch or any other European nation in India, there was a need to exhibit some political skill to ensure that all fortified possessions of the company repaid their full charges and expenses' (Fort St. George 1681–1686: 166). It was suggested that a wall be constructed around the black town, a section of the settlement inhabited by weavers, painters, local traders (Chettis), Armenians and some Portuguese (Fort St. George 1681–1686: 13). It was hoped that such a wall would secure the economic holdings of the company and various individuals associated with it (Madras Diary 1681–1686: 154). The company also ordered that all the houses, godowns and buildings within the garrison town should be registered and that due taxes be paid. It imposed regulations on the sale and purchase of new houses (Madras Diary 1690: 56–57). The jurisdiction of the corporation was restricted to the town of Fort St. George, commonly known as the Christian town, and the city of Madrassapatam and territories within a radius of ten miles from Fort St. George. The mayor's court was empowered to try all cases, civil or criminal, and to impose fines, imprisonment or corporal punishment as penalties (Love 1913: 98–99). The establishment of civil and mayoral courts and of the city corporation shows that the English East India Company was gradually developing a formal presence at Madras. These institutions did not necessarily fashion a new political order, but they played an important role in laying the foundations for further change. They represent a phase in which the company could begin to imagine and articulate its concerns in a manner very different from earlier occasions. The establishment of these institutions and the manner in which they could intervene in the social and economic life of the port city offered scope for a further expansion of English political imagination in the region.

Negotiating family, religion and administration in an early modern port city

It is evident that for the English Company the fortified factory at Madras primarily represented a commercial space where it engaged with merchants operating in the region. For much of the seventeenth century its concerns were restricted to securing this commercial space and ensuring a regular, un-interrupted supply of commodities into the fort and its subsequent periodic loading on company ships. But, for the company employees and the residents of Madras, the fort was more than a space of work: it was part of what they would have seen as a home city where they and their families resided, a space where the economic life emanating from the port shaped their political, professional and social worlds. This urban space became home to a large number of local European and non-European residents who were connected in diverse ways to the English Company's commercial enterprise. These groups grafted their own religious and social traditions on the urban space at Madras. The contestations within this urban space helped these groups develop their own unique and shared cultural and political symbols through which they expressed themselves (Caplan 1995; Brimnes 1999, 2003; Mukund 2005; Gross, Vincent and Liebau 2006).

Thus, like many early modern port cities, Madras represented a cosmopolitan space that offered various groups an opportunity to engage with the European commercial enterprise (in this case, the English commercial enterprise). The English Company officials at Madras in their recognition of these spaces and their cosmopolitan character gradually altered the company's presence in the region. They ensured that this process helped not only forge a better strategy towards engaging with emerging social tensions in the early modern port city but redefine the nature of company presence in the port city.

References

Armitage, David. 2004. *The Ideological Origins of the British Empire.* Cambridge: Cambridge University Press.

Bowen, H. V., Elizabeth Mancke and John G. Reid (eds.). 2012. *Britain's Oceanic Empire: Atlantic and Indian Ocean Worlds, c. 1500–1850.* Cambridge: Cambridge University Press.

Brimnes, Niels. 1999. *Constructing the Colonial Encounter: Right and Left Hand Castes in South India.* Richmond: Curzon Press.

———. 2003. 'Beyond Colonial Law: Indigenous Litigation and the Contestation of Property in the Mayors court in Late Eighteenth Century Madras', *Modern Asian Studies* 37(3): 513–50.

Caplan, Lionel. 1995. 'Creole World, Purist Rhetoric: Anglo-Indian Cultural Debates in Colonial and Contemporary Madras', *The Journal of the Royal Anthropological Institute* 1(4): 743–62.

Fort St. George [Madras Diary]. 1910–46. *Diary and Consultation Book.* 86 vols. Madras: Government Press.

Fort St. George. 1911–29. *Despatches from England.* 11 vols. Madras: Government Press.

Gross, Andreas, Vincent Y. Kumaradoss and Heike Liebau. 2006. *Halle and the Beginning of Protestant Christianity in India, Volumes I–III.* Halle: Verlag der Franckeschen Stiftungen.

Jayawardena, K. 2009. *Erasure of the Euro-Asian: Recovering Early Radicalism and Feminism in South Asia*. New Delhi: Social Scientists' Association, Women Unlimited.

Lewansowski, Susan J. 1977. 'Changing Form and Function in the Ceremonial and the Colonial Port City in India: An Historical Analysis of Madurai and Madras', *Modern Asian Studies* 11(2): 183–212.

Love, H. D. 1913, repr. 1996. *Vestiges of Old Madras*. New Delhi: Asian Education Service.

Malleson, G. B. 1911. *Diaries of Stryensham Master*. London: John Murray.

Manning, Patrick. 2013. 'Frontiers of Family Life: Early Modern Atlantic and Indian Ocean Worlds', in Richard M. Eaton, Munis D. Faruqui, David Gilmartin and Sunil Kumar (eds.), *Expanding Frontiers in South Asian and World History: Essays in Honour of John F. Richards*, New Delhi: Cambridge University Press.

Marshall, P. J. 1997. 'British Society in Indian under the East India Company', *Modern Asian Studies* 31(1): 89–108.

———. 1998. *The Eighteenth Century, Oxford History of the British Empire*. Oxford: Oxford University Press.

Mines, Mattison. 2001. 'Courts of Law and Styles of Self in Eighteenth Century Madras: From Hybrid to Colonial Self', *Modern Asian Studies* 35(1): 33–74.

Mukund, Kanakalatha. 2005. *The View from Below: Indigenous Society, Temples and the Early Colonial State in Tamil Nadu 1700–1835*. New Delhi: Orient Longman.

Neild, Susan M. 1979. 'Colonial Urbanism: The Development of Madras City in the Eighteenth and Nineteenth Centuries', *Modern Asian Studies* 13(2): 217–46.

Penny, Mrs. Frank. 1900. *Fort St. George Madras: A Short History of Our First Possession in India*. London: Swan Sonnenschein & co.

Penny, Rev. Frank. 1904. *The Church in Madras Being the History of the Ecclesiastical and Missionary Action of the East India Company in the Presidency of Madras in the Seventeenth and Eighteenth Centuries*. London: John Murray.

Srinivasachariar, C. S. 1939, repr. 2000. *Madras 1639–1939*. New Delhi: Asian Education Service.

Stern, Philip J. 2011. *The Company-State: Corporate Sovereignty and the Early Modern Foundations of the British Empire in India*. New York: Oxford University Press.

Watson, Ian Bruce. 1980. *Foundation for Empire: English Private Trade in India 1659–1760*. New Delhi: Vikas Publishing.

7 'Domesticity' in early colonial Bengal

Ruchika Sharma

> [A] sum of forty sicca rupees per month during the life of my female friend Peggy who has lived with me many years. She is a native of India and the mother of my only son John.
>
> (IOR L/AG/34/29/8)

This is the will of John Henderson, senior surgeon of the Second Regiment of European Infantry, written in 1792. He also left his remaining fortune – bonds, cash, Peggy's jewels and clothes – to her only. This will, like many others, gave out various bequests and details of personal finances, as well as the instructions to the executioners of his will. However, it also points to certain interesting aspects of the interpersonal relationship established between John Henderson and a native woman, known as Peggy.

By the mid-eighteenth century, despite the presence of the English East India Company (EIC) and a considerable amount of trade, Bengal continued to be a Mughal Subah. Before 1756, as Ghulam Husain Khan noted, the English were known in Bengal 'as only Merchants' (1969: 2). In addition to the political vacuum, the rivalries among the European companies were largely responsible for the changing character of the English EIC from a commercial to a political one. After the Portuguese and Dutch, in the eighteenth century it was the French who emerged as a major challenger to the English EIC. The Anglo-French rivalry became apparent in southern and eastern India, where the English and French took the sides of rival claimants for the thrones of the Nawab of Arcot and the Nizam of Hyderabad. War ebbed and flowed across southern India with little intermission from 1746 until the complete English victory brought the fighting to an end in 1761 (Prakash 2002: 8). Even before complete victory over the French in south India, the British had gained supremacy in Bengal after the battle of Plassey in 1757.

By 1760, Bengal had an Indian ruler backed by the EIC. In 1764 the British defeated the Mughal emperor and his ally, the Nawab of Oudh, at Buxar (Dyson 2002: 8). This was used by the British to gain considerable political leverage over Bengal. The EIC thereby obtained *diwani*, or the revenue administration, of Bengal, Bihar and Orissa. It never denied the authority of the Mughal emperor but just like any other independent 'successor state' began to manage the administration of these three regions. Thus by 1765 the company was de facto sovereign in Bengal: it had become the ascendant military power in the region, and it had acquired the *diwani*, the right to collect territorial revenues estimated to be worth between £2 million and £4 million per annum in the provinces of Bengal, Bihar and Orissa (Bowen 1989: 187). C.A. Bayly holds that the English EIC benefitted from this time of flux and opportunity, where it could play off one state against the other while it offered its own services in the Indian 'military bazaar' (Bayly 1988: 48). According to Bayly, the increase in the volume of the textiles in the triangular trade between Britain, China and India made Bengal, and specifically Calcutta, extremely important to British interests.

The second half of the eighteenth century in India was marked by the emergence of the English EIC as an empire. The beginnings of the EIC may have very well been purely commercial and financial, but the company gained political undercurrents as and when the time was correct, both in terms of the available opportunity and a shift in the policy of the EIC. As we have seen, the reasons that it valued its colonies initially were for commercial purposes. As Ronald Hyam puts it,

> [I]t was a politically 'mercantilist' trade in colonial raw materials, especially those strategic naval supplies which would make possible self – sufficiency in time of war. In order to extract such materials from the periphery (or overseas world) it might be necessary to plant settlers or impose order on indigenous chaos by establishing formal rule. But then two imperatives followed ineluctably. What you held you had to defend against rivals. And what you defended you began to value for its own sake; irrespective of the original intention.
>
> (Hyam 1999: 30–31)

The stiff competition facilitated the need for political leverage. The increasing use of military force may have been made necessary by rivalries with other European trading companies, but it was extended to the Indian ruling potentates, first for their internal struggles and then to subjugate them at a political level. Forming a vicious circle, the same political control was used to press for even more commercial subsidiaries and monopolies subsequently. In many ways, the regime of Warren Hasting as the leader of the British in India continued the kind of complex negotiated political relationships the pre-colonial regimes had relied on (Wilson 2008: 53). This quest to understand and thus administer newly acquired areas was not only what it appeared. It seemed that the idea was to go ahead with continuities in the existing customary practices. It began with a promise to protect the caste and property of its Hindu and Mohammedan subjects under Warren Hastings (Cassels 1988: 63). This protection involved ruling 'the conquered in their own way . . . to reconcile British rule with Indian institutions' (Mukherjee 1968: 79). It seemed like a policy of non-intervention, but it also meant studying the Indian past the way they wanted to see it, which was based on the religion of its rulers. There was an attempt to interpret Indian society in an idealised indigenous form, as seen by British orientalists. Nigel Leask terms this process as a combination of a bit of both 'reverse acculturation' and codification or 'recuperation' of Indian manners and institutions (1992: 9).

The company's courts were offering a law that was wholly alien to those to whom it was applied, not because the substance of the law had been consciously changed but because of what the company had selected as the 'established laws and usages of the country' and the manner in which they were interpreted (Marshall 1987: 129). This was the time of enlightened 'orientalists' as well as the nabobs – the former discovering India and the latter living in India. Theon Wilkinson in his book *Two Monsoons* justifies this proximity with India by citing enforced separation, which, he says, resulted in the 'stranded' officers becoming Indianised. Smoking a hookah became commonplace; adopting native customs and modes of dress, normal; keeping *bibis* (mistresses), socially acceptable, especially as officers below the rank of major were strongly discouraged from marrying (Wilkinson 1976: 46). Wilkinson also mentions an extremely high mortality rate of the British in India. Among the various reasons, one very important reason was that their lifestyle, dressing and diet were not in keeping with the Indian weather. Thus the 'Indianisation' of the British male was the gradual result of two factors – the need to know India (to govern it) and physically encountering the Indian ways of life.

E.M. Collingham's work, based on the physical experiences of the Raj, does not consider the Indianised nabob a fictional character, but a reality of the 'Anglo-Indian' life. According to her, the two important questions the British faced in their early days of the empire were first, how to govern India, and second, how to survive the hostile environment. The codes of behaviour, whereby there was certain proximity between the British and the India in the second half of the eighteenth century, were made possible as a result of these two needs. Therefore the Indianisation of the British male was as much to do with the attitude towards knowing India, as much as it was a physical experience (Collingham 2001: 14).

Plate 7.1 Muslim Lady Reclining by Francesco Renaldi

Source: Yale Center for British Art, Paul Mellon Collection.

These everyday interactions between the British early colonialists and the 'natives' became more layered when carried to the intimate space. When we start looking at the interpersonal relationship that was conjured up between the British men and the 'native' women, we realise that it was not merely sexual, but also a relationship between the coloniser and the colonised – the modern law and the native one. These relationships flourished (as many would say) as necessity and were brought under the purview of the modern law by being a part of the British physical space – a household consisting mostly of Indian servants, a native mistress and the British man. Many scholars see these relationships, which were not homogenous, as a part of the British social life or as just their Indian experience. Some just enumerate the cases to prove the vast number of such liaisons in Warren Hasting's time, which ebbed as Cornwallis was at the helm of the political affairs.

A more nuanced way to look at it would be to emphasise that when Europe came face to face with the East, the 'local' women proved to be useful keys to the new language and other mysteries of the local society.

Their medical and cultural know-how was credited with keeping many European men alive in their initial, precarious confrontation with tropical life (Stoler 2002: 49). When we start looking at these relationships in isolation, rather than as a facet of colonial rule, we also tend to notice the different ways they unfolded, something that one finds frequently in the legal documents and the court cases at Calcutta High Court.

Apart from some cultural artefacts such as diaries, letters and paintings, most of the references to these inter-racial connections are made in legal documents. A number of them form an important archive that facilitates the study of the details of the domestic set-up that the British men who came to early colonial Bengal had entered into with the native women. Such domestic set-ups established by the British men with the women of native origins were not particular to Bengal, but existed in all areas where the British established their administration and residence. The term 'native' is quite politically charged, although it was used in the legal papers all the time. Here it would indicate women who were Indian or Indo-European by descent. We focus on Bengal though such native connections were aplenty even in the mofussil. In areas farther from the presidency towns, it was even more difficult for Europeans to congregate and socialise in large numbers among themselves.

The wills were written by British men and rarely by the native women, which also means we get to know of these relationships and the sphere of domesticity from strictly one perspective. In that sense we get an insight into how the British male perceived this relationship and the native female, her body and the progeny of their native 'connection'. The term 'domestic' literally means the setting up of a household; it also indicates different things depending on the time and place where it is used. Nineteenth- and early-twentieth-century treatments of mediaeval domestic life usually linked it to 'home' and focused on everyday activities, such as the structure of houses and the objects found therein (Kowaleski and Goldberg 2008: 2). What is clear is that 'domestic' refers to the private sphere, and it denotes the confines and comforts of home, not necessarily linked to the family. Felicity Riddy argues that 'domesticity' – even in its nineteenth-century form – was a 'state of mind' defined by privacy and comfort within the physical structure of a house wherein the occupation of a domestic space by members of the family evolved into the concept of home (Kowaleski, Jeremy and Goldberg 2008: 4). The concept of domesticity may be defined as a 'state of mind' that expressed comfort and privacy.

The usage of the word 'home' is more clearly linked to the 'family' as we understand in 'modern' usage of the word. Even the word 'household' is polysemic, glossing often conflicting concepts at many different conceptual levels (Netting, Wilk and Arnould 1984: 1). Therefore both the terms 'domestic' and 'household' are used here and would denote co-residence and cohabitation. They will also mean a familial set-up, not necessarily based on marriage, but denoting an acceptable social unit in late-eighteenth- to early-nineteenth-century Bengal (as also in the other parts of India).

One of the problems in studying these wills is that they give only the perspective of the British man – his role and his understanding of this domesticity. So while studying the nature of these 'households' one is struck by the relative absence of the voices of the native women, who are often not even mentioned by their original names. It becomes almost impossible to read their presence, let alone to know their views as they are silent and absent by virtue of being addressed by European names like Polly, Betty, Mary, Sarah or Nancy, along with other words like 'my girl', 'my housekeeper', 'the mother of my children', 'my female companion', 'female friend' and 'slave girl'. These terms are indicative of the relationship shared between two individuals, perhaps even of a domestic arrangement. They make the woman disappear as a part of history. Even the court cases that do have the 'natives' speaking were transcribed by the British officials as records. We do not even know the language in which the native defendants or witnesses spoke, as all of it is archived as legal records in English.

Major John Williams of the Bengal establishment in the year 1797 talked about his two 'natural' children in his will, leaving them well provided for. He then added that if more children were born to him, during his life or '10 months after his decease', the child/children should also be taken care of. But there is no reference to his mistress even as the mother of his children (IOR L/AG/34/29/13). But as his children are mentioned to be 'natural', it is clear that the mother of the future child was a native-born woman, to whom he was not married. Captain Peter Cullen, stationed at Futty Ghur Bengal, went to the extent of directing the executioners of his will to assist his mistress, so she received 'assistance and subsistence' after his death. But with regard to her identity all he had to say was that she was a native woman who was living with him at that time (IOR L/AG/34/29/8).

There are few such wills where the native women exist only as mothers of the children born of these relationships, without any other detail about them. There were certain typical English names given to these 'kept' women. The English names by which these women were commonly known may have been easy to pronounce or even easy to remember for these men, because of familiarity: Thomas Breton, for example left 14,000 rupees on trust to be divided between his sons Thomas, John and Peter and his daughter Mary and adds 'my faithful house keeper Hissen Knar (Khissen Khan?) commonly called and known by the name of Polly' (IOR L/AG/34/29/4). Another interesting and exceptional case is that of

Lieutenant Pierce Cassady of the Bengal establishment, who bequeathed 1,000 rupees to the woman who lived with him. He went on to inform 'This woman I call Polly, but her real or country name is Saib Jaun' (IOR L/AG/34/29/11). This phenomenon, however, certainly renders it rather difficult to know about the origins of the female counterparts of these relationships, since these wills do not spell out the details about the native women, who are regularly mentioned, until about the first quarter of the nineteenth century.

However, the wills do, occasionally, talk about how these relationships came to be established. Many times these native women were bought. It was surely a fairly common mode to offer money for the girl child and later take her up as a bibi, as was in the case of General Claude Martin. His will carried elaborate details of how he acquired a mistress (IOR L/AG/34/29/12). According to him, the native women were bought, for he mentions having 'paid' money, but he very clearly differentiates it from slavery. According to him he bought them so that no one from her previous family or anyone else could lay any claims on the girls. There is also clear reference to a conjugal relationship between him and his 'bought' women.

Otherwise we also get to know that a native mistress could be taken in by another British master. The will of Samuel Mageough of Behrampore mentions a certain Nancy, who was one of the two of his kept women. He adds for the executors of his will, 'I hope the mother of the child, from her youth and good disposition may be provided for by getting a good master' (L/AG/34/29/7). In the diary of Richard Blechynden, a civil engineer and building contractor and an official assistant to Calcutta's surveyor of roads, we get the reference to how he acquired his bibis. He got his bibi in the 1790s in a fairly typical manner, 'Luteeb came', he wrote, 'and told me that a very pretty Bebe was . . . in great Distress so much so that she would actually sell herself to anyone that would pay her Debts' (Robb 1998: 41). Blechynden was prevailed upon to meet the lady, Nancy, who 'laid such a scene of distress open' to him that he landed up paying all her debts off, took her to be his bibi and let her live at his garden-house. Next day he sent a palanquin for her and she came in that to live with him.

A native girl's physical presence or living in a largely European area too was taken to point towards her being a potential sexual/conjugal partner. In a case of sexual violence that involved the rape of a native girl, Mary Serraun aged 10, by a Frenchman Peter Bouton, a merchant in the EIC's service (Hyde: Reel 5, 12 December 1793), Bouton allegedly went up to her and offered to take her as his conjugal partner. There is also a reference to Bibi Kitty as the native woman who helped organise the 'arrangement' by offering Mary to him and telling him that she was twelve years of age. The girl being a maid could not be established, nor could the fact whether or not the Frenchman had the right information about the girl's correct age. However, the claim by Bouton that the girl was not a maid at the time of their sexual contact seemed to have sealed the case in his favour.

Another aspect of this connection that the wills sometimes mention is the issue of money or emoluments, though it is difficult to ascertain the amount of wages, as these women were also paid in kind at times. If some matters became contentious, they were sometimes taken to the court and were fought as court cases. Even such cases became a mirror of the various aspects of these relationships. There was a case involving Henry Pyne, a company merchant of Chittagong, who allegedly broke into the house of Peerun, who had previously been his bibi, for stealing jewellery as well as money (Hyde: Reel 11, 15 December 1789). The case established that Peerun was the breadwinner of their family. Peerun's sister, while giving the account of how Peerun acquired all that money and jewellery, mentioned that Peerun was first kept by Mr Jeffery and then by Mr Creighton. Thus, Peerun's sister testified that the contentious jewellery and money were Peerun's in the first place. Though this case resulted in acquittal, it established, just as numerous wills do, that it was not a taboo for a native woman to have been kept by more than one man in her lifetime. Nor was concubinage ever officially banned. At no point did the law condemn or question the presence of native women in the British households in India because these women in various ways did provide the British male populace with the comforts and confines of domestic structure. As Stoler explained,

> Concubinage could be banned by colonial administrations . . . but the quotidian comforts of colonial life created by the constant presence of native nursemaids and housekeepers, washerwomen and watchmen, [female] cooks and gardeners – who serviced and nurtured these European selves – could not.
>
> (Stoler 2002: 6)

These relationships certainly had various facets, including clandestine and temporary 'affairs' between the native women and British officials, but the domestic arrangements forged between the native women and the British men were certainly more complex than that. The set-up of this domain of domesticity was, mostly, without marriage but did have certain features of most formal marital households. The household set-up with a native woman was definitely a legal space, as we see the rule of law trying to settle domestic discords rather than punishing their perpetuation. One of the court cases, *Rex v. William Orby Hunter*, had a discussion as to whether concubinage was a legal contract in contemporary Britain or not (Hyde: Reel 17, 23 December 1796 to 12 January 1797).

There are many wills that mention 'slave/servant girls' who appear to have had conjugal relations with their masters and at times also mothered their children, bringing us to another angle of these relationships. The fact that 'washerwoman' or 'housekeeper' became a popular euphemism for a sexual partner gives another insight into the workings of this connection. At times men do refer, while bequeathing money or goods in kind, to these women for their 'care during illness' (or similar), making it difficult to ascertain the relationships between the master and female slaves/servants. These women were definitely being bought as slaves in many cases and thus blurring the lines between a housekeeper (mistress) and a servant girl. Lieutenant Francis Forde in the Royal Navy of Chittagong mentions his 'faithful servant Balinda' (IOR L/AG/34/29/5), whom he left an interest of 4,000 rupees and the house she was staying in. John Herbert of Dacca, writing his will in 1795, mentions his daughter who was married. He then goes on to talk about his 'true and faithful servant Sameeda' (IOR L/AG/34/29/11), leaving her a considerable amount of property, land, furniture and jewellery. He in fact declares that she had purchased herself by having paid him money for the house she was residing in. The usage of the term 'servant' interchangeably with 'housekeeper' (mistress) makes it impossible to view these relationships without trying to understand the details of these domestic set-ups. At times men do refer while bequeathing money or goods in kind to these women for their 'care during illness' etc. along with being the mother of their children, pointing to the layered nature of these relationships between the master and female slaves/servants. There was an overlap in a native woman's being a mistress and the servant of her British keeper, as often it was one and the same. This difference between the two terms 'bibi' and the female 'servant' rarely gets established, but it does in the aforementioned *Rex v. William Orby Hunter* case.

William Orby Hunter, along with his Bibi Baugwan Konwar, was tried at the Calcutta Supreme Court for wounding and ill-treating their two native female servants at the Hunter household (Hyde: Reel 17, 23 December 1796 to 12 January 1797). This case is important for various reasons, not only for the legal viewpoint of the relationship, but also because here the natives talked about the relationship – the wages he paid her and the relationship they shared. The role of Baugwan Konwar in Hunter's household became clear and also the difference between the bibi and the servant girl as well as the sexual relations between the master and the female slaves/servants. Most important, there is a discussion on concubinage within the court over this matter. Mr Lewison, who was Baugwan Konwar's attorney, said that she could not come under the court's jurisdiction as she was only his concubine and not under his services for any work. He said that under the terms of the charter of the Queen, concubinage was not a service as it was not a 'legal contract'. During the debate, Hunter's advocate held that concubinage in fact was known to the law of England as a species of employment only.

The reason given that Hunter was to be held responsible for the crimes was that they happened in his domestic life. There was much discussion on whether British men ought to be held responsible for their native concubines. The verdict of the court answered the question; Hunter was sentenced as the crimes took place in his household unit, over which he lacked authority to put a check on to such crimes. Baugwan Konwar, it emerged, was the mistress of Hunter, with an authority over other servants. The female servants established that Hunter did have carnal relations with them as well, though it does not seem to be an issue that he established sexual relations with Baugwan Konwar's servants who were living in his household.

One of the points raised by Hunter's advocate while making a statement in his favour is worth considering. He says,

> In considering who is most likely to have committed those [violent] acts, let it be remembered that William Hunter was born in a country of humanity, and educated in the habits of an English Gentleman; that Baugwan Konawar has been bred up in vice and habituated to it.
>
> (Hyde: Reel 17, 23 December 1796 to 12 January 1797)

Though both Hunter and his bibi were declared guilty, it was Baugwan Konwar who was pronounced guilty for having ordered a servant to cut off parts of Ajanassi's (another servant's) nose and ears and imprisoning the two servants. William Hunter was given only a fine, mainly due to his role as the master of household where such an incident had taken place.

The range of aspects these wills and the court cases reflect regarding the conjugal cohabitation of this sort is too many to enumerate here – how these 'connections' were formed, their various kinds, biases, polygamy, monogamy, long-term households, intimacy, master–servant relationship, acts of violence and others. But one of the most important aspects of these relationships mentioned in these wills was the progeny of these conjugal relationships. Many of them leave the children provided for: in the late eighteenth century many of them were sent back to Europe, to the 'family' of the British man. Later on they were to be kept in the orphanages, made especially for the children of mixed race.

Lieutenant Natheniel Leonald of artillery mentioned his three children, without referring to them as either 'natural' or illegitimate, were 'born of the body of a Native woman of Hindostan' who he calls Winifred. This will is almost like a letter to all his relatives whom he had not left anything from his property. In an attempt to be fair he writes,

> The mother of my children would be destitute of support and my own mother be in embarrced [embarrassed] circumstances in the decline of life should I omit to appropriate what property I am now possessed of towards their support – It is therefore my will that whatever I am possessed of to the amount of three thousand sicca rupees and no more, be put at interest.
>
> (L/AG/34/29/8)

He then wanted the interest to be paid to both of them equally. He seems further aware that 'probably my relations will blame me for putting my mother and female companion on a footing', and that he did not left anything to them. But he went on in that same tone about his children too and is deeply regretful that they would have to be sent to an orphanage. This will definitely establish a sense of domesticity, as the native connection seems more like a 'family' for him, as he speaks very warmly about them. Robert Nairne, a mariner of Chittagong, resided in Calcutta at the time of his will being written in 1788, leaves his natural daughter Anna Nairne all his real and personal estate upon her turning 21. He mentions that she resides in a seminary for the education of young ladies in Calcutta; he mentions about her passage to Britain as well. He does not mention the mistress, who could have moved to another master. In any case, these children born mostly out of wedlock were usually not given to the mothers.

The increasing social distancing of the early nineteenth century becomes very clear in the way Anglo-Indian or mixed-race children are mentioned. Charles Nicholson dictates terms to his legitimate British children, in a will written as late as 1819. This brings up the widening social distance between the Europeans and Indians, even the 'mixed' race children,

> I recommend to my children to conduct themselves prudently, pay proper respect and attention to their mother in all things proper and do nothing of importance without previously consulting two or three honest, prudent respectable people respecting the propriety of the measure. I like wise recommend them not to associate with or form a family connection with black or dark brown native Portigees or any other low description of people – but with honest industrious Europeans of respectable character education and connexion or their children being moderately white and in a situation to maintain them comfortably.
>
> (Wills Index Book: 8784)

These are legal sources, of course, but we need to read them keeping in mind the early colonial, racial as well as personal contexts (as each case could also be different from the others). If this archive highlights different facets of these relationships, it also points out biases against the natives, the racial physical distancing of the early nineteenth century as well as the position of the native woman as the 'colonised' female who was also the sexual partner of the 'coloniser'. As we read these documents, beyond just enumerating the cases of domesticity between the British man and the native women, we realise that they represent the modern law affecting the lives of colonised women. Although they were not given any rights over the man's property nor over the children she bore him, in almost all cases, the women were given the right to use the property during her lifetime, but without any absolute rights over it. It was to go to the man's family or the mixed-race child/children.

As we look closely at these legal documents, we can observe how the early colonial law influenced the native women and the workings of these shared domestic spaces. The native women coming under its purview by being a part of the British household did not in any way gain any rights. However, we do see these women negotiating with the modern law ushered by the EIC, by appealing over issues such as rape, emoluments and property being bequeathed to them, as witnesses and so on. The relationship was not only personal but also translated into a relationship between the colonising male and the colonised woman, where we catch the glimpse of the shared space from only one perspective, that of the British male.

All the relationships discussed here had a sexual element; the native women who were taken on as concubines were definitely a part of the 'household' of the British men in various ways. So in sharing the confined space of 'house' in terms of co-residence all the concubinage was conjugal as well as domestic. But we need to look at domesticity as a more fluid space, which develops over a certain duration, and in terms of constant sharing of space that was not 'unchanging'. The numerous relationships mentioned developed quite differently from each other, but all within the framework of domesticity, though only a few were formalised as conjugal.

References

Manuscript

Bengal Wills Series: various years beginning 1780. IOR L/AG/34/29.

Hyde Papers and reports: various years beginning 1789. Rare Book division, the National Library, Calcutta.

Wills Index Book. Old Records Department, Original Side, High Court. Kolkata.

Print

Bayly, C. A. 1988. *The New Cambridge History of India, Vol. 2, No. 1: Indian Society and the Making of the British Empire.* Cambridge: Cambridge University Press.

Bowen, H. V. 1989. 'Investment and Empire in the Later Eighteenth Century: East India Stockholding', *The Economic History Review* 42 (2): 186–206.

Cassels, N. G. 1988. 'Social Legislation Under the Company RAJ: The Abolition of Slavery Act V 1843', *South Asia: Journal of South Asian Studies* 11(1): 59–87.

Collingham, E. M. 2001. *Imperial Bodies: The Physical Experience of the Raj. c. 1800–1947.* London: Wiley.

Dyson, K. K. 1978, rpt. 2002. *A Various Universe: A Study of the Journals and Memoirs of British Men and Women in the Indian Subcontinent, 1765–1856.* New Delhi: Oxford University Press.

Hyam, Ronald. 1999. 'The Primacy of Geopolitics: The Dynamics of British Imperial Policy, 1763–1963,' in Robert King and Robin Wilson (eds.), *The Statecraft of British Imperialism: Essays in Honour of WM. Roger Louis.* London: Frank Cass

Khan, A. M. 1969. *The Transition in Bengal, 1756–1775: A Study of Saiyid Muhammad Reza Khan.* New York: Cambridge University Press.

Kowaleski, Maryanne, Peter Jeremy and Piers Goldberg. 2008. *Medieval Domesticity: Home, Housing and Household in Medieval England.* Cambridge: Cambridge University Press.

Leask, Nigel. 1992. *British Romantic Writers and the East: Anxieties of Empire.* Cambridge: Cambridge University Press.

Marshall, P. J. 1987. *Bengal: the British Bridgehead, Eastern India 1740–1828.* Cambridge: Cambridge University Press.

Mukherjee, S. N. 1968. *Sir William Jones: A Study in 18th Century British Attitudes to India.* Cambridge: Cambridge University Press.

Netting, R. M., R. R. Wilk and E. J. Arnould. 1984. *Households: Comparative and Historical Studies of the Domestic Group.* California: University of California Press.

Prakash, Om. 2002. 'The English East India Company and India', in H. V. Bowen, M. Lincoln and N. Rigby (eds.) *The Worlds of the East India Company*, pp. 1–18. Suffolk: Boydell & Brewer.

Robb, Peter. 1998. 'Clash of Cultures? An Englishman in Calcutta in the 1790s', School of Oriental and African Studies, Inaugural Lecture, 12 March.

Stoler, A. L. 2002. *Carnal Knowledge and Imperial Power: Race and the Intimate in Colonial Rule.* Berkeley: University of California Press.

Wilkinson, Theon. 1976. *Two Monsoons, with Drawings by Bill Smith.* London: Duckworth.

Wilson, Jon E. 2008. *The Domination of Strangers: Modern Governance in Eastern India, 1780–1835.* New York: Palgrave Macmillan.

8 The travellers' tales

The travel writings of Itesamuddin and Abu Taleb Khan

Jeena Sarah Jacob

Travel writing does more than merely chronicle places and events; it also contains an understanding of the self that goes along with the exploration of a new place and a new culture. The travelogues of Mirza Abu Taleb Khan, the *Masir-i-Talibi*, and Sheikh Itesamuddin's account of his travel from the Indian subcontinent to England in the late eighteenth century, the *Shigurf Namah-i-Velaet*, manage to capture these multiple layers. This chapter will attempt to understand the travel writing of these travellers, considering what inspired their writing and their perceptions of the lands they visited. In so doing, it ruminates on the connections between new spaces and cultures and alterations to the self.

Mary Louise Pratt analyses the nature of travel writing in her book *Imperial Eyes, Travel Writing and Transculturation.* Pratt uses the theory of the 'contact zone', which refers to the colonial frontier. For Pratt the asymmetry between the cultures that come in contact with each other in the 'contact zone' is what provides the spark for the travelogue to be written. Pratt's idea can be reconsidered on two levels. First, if we invert the contact zone, where someone is moving from the periphery to the metropolis, the dynamics of this power relation change. In this kind of travel, though the power relations may remain asymmetrical, there is no conflict or coercion. What in this case is the spark for the travelogue? Second, if we agree with Pratt that the 'contact zone' and the relations formed therein may provide the impetus for the travelogue, it needs to be considered that this contact between the periphery and the metropolis had been taking place long before the advent of colonialism, and that it is colonialism that brings in the dimension of power relations. In this case it needs to be considered whether power relations are as absolutely imperative in the writing of travel literature as Pratt's argument suggests.

Travelogues from Persia and the Indian subcontinent have received attention only in the recent past. Prior to this, most of the travelogues that captured the interest of readers were from Europe, travelling to various parts of Asia or to the New World. Muzaffar Alam and Sanjay Subrahmanyam, in their book *Indo-Persian Travels in the Age of Discovery*, explain that any reader of modern-day scholarship on travel literature would find that books dealing with travel literature are primarily 'occidental' in their leaning (2006: 2). They look at a variety of Indo-Persian texts that counter this idea. Alam and Subrahmanyam point out that the kind of Indo-Persian texts that gained ground in Europe were those that found the Indo-Persian world lacking in many ways compared to Europe, or were an entertaining text like the *Thousand and One Nights* (2006: 8). A counter argument to this assertion can be seen in the reasons Charles Stewart, the translator of the travelogue of Mirza Abu Taleb Khan, gave for wanting to translate this work. He wrote that Abu Taleb was an intelligent man from Asia whose observations on the institutions of Europe would be interesting and important for Europeans to know.

Michael Fisher, in his *Counterflows to Colonialism*, deals with the nature of interactions between the British and people from India. He writes that since the time the British had been coming to India, Indians have been going to Britain and settling there and as the power of the English East India Company grew, more people travelled to England, which also complicated the way in which they were received there (2004: 1–3). Fisher, drawing on Partha Chatterjee's work, opines that in the 1600s no Indian had clear knowledge of what Britain was and their travel was to an unknown land. The information they brought back helped, both to supplement and contradict British self-representations in India. However due to limited circulation and publication these accounts remained restricted to being passed on orally or in manuscript form (Fisher 2004: 4). This allowed, in Fisher's opinion, fresh insights, though it put the Indians at a disadvantage as the British understanding of India was increasing (2004: 5). The Mughals, Fisher notes, showed only a limited interest in exploring European cultures with which they were extensively associated both politically and economically. Therefore Europe remained an unknown place to the Indians till about the end of the eighteenth century (Fisher 2004: 7). Juan Cole is also of the opinion that the reaction of Muslims to the changes taking place in Europe was very tepid. Cole is sceptical about finding, in texts of travellers from the subcontinent to Europe, 'a mirror image of "Orientalism" and a systematic critique of colonialism and European culture' (1992: 3).

One major concern that arises here from Cole's argument is whether, in studying texts of travellers from the Indian subcontinent to Europe, we are really looking for a 'mirror of Orientalism'? The texts reveal the originality of the writers and the fact that they are unhindered by such notions of homogeneity of culture. This is particularly evident in the fact that though, for example Itesamuddin visited only France and England, he wrote about the various countries of Europe and defined their differences very clearly in terms of religious practices and forms of government. Mirza Abu Taleb, in a manner that chimes with other travelogues, also points to the fact that these travellers were cognisant of the differences between the countries of Europe. A brief background of the circumstances that led to the journeys of the two travellers should provide a window into understanding the way in which they wrote and what they chose to represent.

I

Sheikh Itesamuddin travelled from the subcontinent to England in 1767. His travelogue, titled *Shigurf Namah-i-Velaet* or *Excellent Intelligence Concerning Europe Being the Travels of Mirza Itesamuddin in Great Britain and France* (henceforth *Shigurf Namah*), was originally translated into English by James Edward Alexander in 1825. Having been defeated in the battle of Buxar, Shah Alam II, the Mughal emperor, signed the Treaty of Allahabad. The right to collect the *diwani* of Bengal, Bihar and Orissa was given to the company and the official transfer took place on 12 August 1765. Itesamuddin was involved in writing the text of the Treaty of Allahabad with another *munshi*. He reported that Shah Alam with tears in his eyes told Clive and Carnac, who were getting ready to leave after the signing of the treaty, that they were abandoning him among his enemies without a thought for his safety (*Shigurf Namah* 1827: 5).

Itesamuddin noted that a shamed Clive and Carnac told the emperor that they would be unable to leave a regiment behind to take care of him without the consent of the British monarch. It was for this request to be placed before King George III of England that Sheikh Itesamuddin was sent to England. It was also decided that gifts worth a lakh of rupees would also accompany the letter. The letter having been written, Captain Archibald Swinton was chosen to present it and the gifts to the British monarch. Itesamuddin was informed by Captain Swinton, a week into the journey, that the gifts meant for the king had still not come from Benares and that Clive had decided to hold back the letter due to this. Itesamuddin was shocked at these developments and realised that there was some plot afoot, in spite of which he decided to go ahead with the journey. The unravelling of this plot occurs suddenly at the end of Itesamuddin's travelogue. He described the way in which Clive manipulated the letter and gifts, hiding the letter and presenting only the gifts to the king in his own name. He did not mention his return journey and concluded quickly that he had no want of any temporal gains and that he was only looking to be reunited with his loved ones after two years and nine months. An overarching theme that Itesamuddin's text reflected was his adherence to Islam. Through reading the text one gets the sense that religion and his religious identity were crucial to him. The *Shigurf Namah* carried with it an air of lamentation. The text gives us the feeling of the uncertainty that existed in the lives of those who were witnessing the declining power of the Mughal state. The comparisons he makes between the British and the Mughals and of the upper classes in both England and back home are particularly telling.

The other travelogue for discussion here, the *Masir-i-Talibi*, was written by Mirza Abu Taleb Khan who travelled to Europe in the last decade of the eighteenth century. He provided a long description of his work and the problems he faced that made him desperate for a change that prompted him to travel to Europe with his friend Captain David Richardson (Khan 1887: 1.18–19). The story of Abu Taleb's life can be read from the descriptions of his circumstances in his introduction to his travelogue. In 1775 Asaf-ud-daula became the *Nawab* of Awadh. Abu Taleb, having been employed by the Nawab of Awadh, was instrumental in safeguarding him against the attacks of the Rajputs led by Balbadhar Singh. However intrigued by Haider Beg, the deputy of the Nawab, who wanted Taleb on his side, and the return of the resident in Lucknow back to England made it difficult to continue working there. His autobiographical details in the text describe a period of oscillation between Lucknow and Bengal looking for employment. With promises of help and support Abu Taleb tried gaining employment, but was unsuccessful and suffered great financial crisis. At this time Abu Taleb wrote that some of his children and employees of his father left him. It was at this time that he met Captain David Richardson and decided to travel to England.

Having decided to travel to Europe, Abu Taleb took passage on one of the ships of the English East India Company, the *Charlotte*, which burnt down a few days later. He then went and secured for himself passage on the *Christiana*, a Dutch ship (Khan 1887: 1.19). He undertook a spectacular journey, half by sea and the other half by land. His return journey was via a land route where he crossed modern-day France, Turkey, Iraq and then proceeded to Bombay by sea. The diversity that he encountered, the new things that he saw, even when he reached back to the subcontinent all of the observations he made suggest that he wanted his readers to be fully informed about all the details of his travels.

II. Encountering state and polity in eighteenth-century England

Looking in particular at the text and the descriptions of England provided by the two travellers, we sometimes see convergences and divergences of views between the two travellers. It is important to keep in mind the disposition of the two travellers, Itesamuddin with his extremely specific religious ideas and Abu Taleb with his flair and open approach to experiences.

Regarding the political organisation of England Itesamuddin wrote that at the time he travelled to England it was being ruled by the brave and wise King George III who was the father of sons. The king of England, unlike the Mughal emperor, could not make unilateral decisions without the consent of his ministers, nobles and a few elected members of the middle class (*Shigurf Namah* 1827: 136–7). He noted that if there was discord among the rulers, as was the case in Hindustan, wealth and government would not be theirs any longer. He quoted a poem to drive his point.

> All wealth is acquired by concord:
> Discord begets poverty.
> Many kings (from not advising with their ministers)
> have lost their dignity,
> And their sovereign rule hath departed from them.
> (*Shigurf Namah* 1827: 138)

Gulfishan Khan is of the opinion that in his praise for the British monarchy Itesamuddin is echoing the thoughts of John Locke and J. J. Rousseau of 'popular sovereignty' and 'social contract', without using these words as these ideas were prevalent among the middle classes with whom Itesamuddin interacted during his stay in London (Khan 1998: 339). While these may have been ideas that were popular, it needs to be considered whether Itesamuddin was in fact aware of them at all. It can be reasonably assumed that since it was something new and interesting that Itesamuddin would have written about it; however, the fact that he did not mention these concepts or make allusions to ideas of this nature in the course of his descriptions in the travelogue makes it difficult to accept that he was influenced by them.

Abu Taleb offered the most detailed discussion on the British administrative system. George III was the ruler of Britain at that time. Gulfishan Khan points out that though neither Taleb nor Itesamuddin had a word for 'constitutional monarchy' in their vocabulary they had done a reasonable job explaining the system (Khan 1998: 337). Taleb noted that he was a king like none other, intelligent and with a scientific temperament (Khan 1887: 1.276). King George III was, in the eyes of Itesamuddin as well as Abu Taleb, a ruler interested in the good of his people. Taleb extolling his virtues wrote,

> It would be an endless task to recite all the praise-worthy and disinterested acts of his Majesty; but how shall we sufficiently appreciate the

> merits of a monarch, who could divest himself of all authority over the Judges, by conferring upon them *their offices for life*; thus relinquishing all those powers which stimulate and bias the actions of mankind, whether of hope, or of fear?
>
> (Khan 1887: 1.276)

Both Taleb and Itesamuddin had met the monarch, but only Abu Taleb provided his readers with a description of the meetings. Taleb discussed the question of primogeniture and inheritance and explained that the throne was to go to the son and if there was no son it was to go to the daughter. Only someone duly qualified by law could come to the throne, minimising chances for confusing (Khan 1887: 1.278). While discussing the throne in Hindustan a British gentleman shuddered at the degree of cruelty involved in Aurangzeb killing his brothers and confining his father as well as the war that had taken place between Bahadur Shah and his brothers. Abu Taleb retort was that if the choices facing the English princes were war or the coffin, things would have been very different (Khan 1887: 1.279).

Both Taleb and Itesamuddin were of the opinion that the government was a mixture of monarchy, aristocracy and democracy. Taleb felt that such a well-rounded representational system was the best system human intelligence could have come up with (Khan 1887: 1.273). Taleb provided an anecdote about the time of William Pitt, the prime minister who was removed from his office, along with five ministers by the king. When this took place, Britain was at war with France and the king was very unwell; however, the existence of rules helped in averting crises in the country (Khan 1887: 1.275).

In discussing the administration, both the travellers observed that the British had a strong military and naval presence. The British presence on the seas could be understood from the fact that Abu Taleb was advised, a suggestion he shared with his readers as well, to travel only by a British ship as the ships of other countries and their crew were not as well equipped and didn't know enough about navigation. Abu Taleb noted their naval strength was such that if they succeeded it was good for the empire, if not they only suffered minimal loss. Taleb also provided a description of a war where the kings of Prussia, Russia, Denmark and Sweden wanted to get back at England to search their ships for French goods. They ordered all the British merchant and naval ships in their ports to be seized. When this information reached England, Lord Nelson was sent with fifty ships of varying sizes to sink, burn or seize the ships of the countries who dared to confront the British ships (Khan 1887: 1.227).

Itesamuddin's primary observation regarding the British navy was that they were always ready for war and had their ships constantly prepared.

Their natural genius in naval aspects made other European nations cautious about launching hostilities towards the British (*Shigurf Namah* 1827: 140). During peace time the ships were unrigged and the masts were pulled down, but could be reassembled at the shortest notice. Itesamuddin may have exaggerated the nature of the British soldier, who was known, according to him, for their bravery, skill and military tactics but noted that the commander-in-chief's word was treated as gospel by the soldier (*Shigurf Namah* 1827: 140).

While discussing military prowess, Abu Taleb made observations regarding how conquests were carried out. In chapter twenty-nine, in the second volume of the travelogue, Taleb, while noting the vices of the British, suggested that one vice was the amount of luxury that they were used to. He gave the example of the Tartars and the Arabs who he claimed did not conquer extensive territory through large numbers or superior weapons, as they had only bows and arrows and swords. Their success was due to limited wants and the ability to subsist on limited food and meagre salaries. People were, in Taleb's opinion, willing to have these conquerors come as they reduced tax burdens due to their limited need of money and were excellent administrators, due to which they managed to conquer a large part of the world in such short time (Khan 1887: 2.36–7). Taleb's observation is an interesting point that can be read to understand how he looked at the relationship between the conquered and the conqueror. It also raises the question as to whether Abu Taleb was subliminally mentioning the burden the company rule had on the people under them.

Itesamuddin described the British army in rich detail. He noted that the royal army was distributed in different cantonments. He offered a vivid description of the army men.

> Those persons selected (for it) who are robust and of a proper height, and they are disciplined as dragoons or foot soldiers. They are dressed in clean clothes and of one colour, and are instructed in the drill and martial exercises. (Each of the cavalry regiments consist of) seven hundred horses, and every regiment is of one colour; as one is black, (and another) white or bay. For this reason, at the time of exercise, the hearts of beholders are gladdened, for (the horsemen) are splendid to look on, the men get their rations and uniform from the government.
> (*Shigurf Namah* 1827: 139)

The precise manner in which the British army was conducted caught Itesamuddin's attention. Deviation from the rules or retreat in battle was met with the death penalty. Officers received portions of war booty according to their ranks to ensure that their troops remain valiant (*Shigurf Namah*

1827: 141–2). The epitome of desirable qualities, the British soldier, Itesamuddin wrote, was brave and did not appreciate flattery compared with the sepoys and officers of Hindustan who considered flattery as very important (*Shigurf Namah* 1827: 142–3).

In their discussions on governments and military systems, Gulfishan Khan points out that the travellers like Abu Taleb and Itesamuddin did not see the legal system as being separate from the administrative system. She points out that Itesamuddin particularly equated the word 'parliament' with the *khana-i-adalat* or House of Justice, which she says would explain why Itesamuddin's discussion of the judicial system of England was brought in with his description of the administration and military departments (Khan 1998: 343). Abu Taleb on the other hand spent a chapter dealing with the legal system of England, adding details of personal experiences as well as throwing some light on the system of English courts in Hindustan.

Abu Taleb emphasised the fact that the laws of the country were laid down by the Parliament, which had control over the judiciary. Abu Taleb noted that the *shariat* or divine ordinance was not the basis for the penal code; rather it was based on past judicial decision that could be modified by the legislators. Having been afforded the opportunity to witness some hearings, he was impressed by the jury system. The jurors were twelve people of the city who were asked to give a ruling based on the hearing they attended. Taleb, however, felt that though this was what was generally portrayed as the brilliance of the British legal system, a judge could persuade a jury to interpret the case in a particular way. In such cases the jury was kept locked away in an apartment, or other coercive measures were used, until they reconsidered their decision. Taleb admitted that eventually it seemed that the verdict on the case depended more on the judge than it did on the jury. Taleb observed that the judges, being wealthy, were not tempted to try making extra money in the court. However the lawyers, whose only income came from the plaintiff or the defendant, tried to draw out the cases in order to keep charging their clients (Khan 1887: 2.4–6).

Taleb took the description of the British legal systems as an opportunity to also share his feelings about the English courts that had been set up in Hindustan, which he felt needed a serious overhauling (Khan 1887: 2.9). The ambiguity of the English law in the way in which it was implemented in Hindustan was one problem, Abu Taleb wrote, but the bigger trouble would be for those who were forced to use the system, as he had observed in England. The corrective he suggested was that lawyers be paid out of the public funds to keep them from extorting money from their clients (Khan 1887: 2.15–17).

Itesamuddin too compared the judicial system in Calcutta with that in England and was very impressed with England, because he observed that in these courts the law could not be circumvented and that people could not attempt to bribe the judge (*Shigurf Namah* 1827: 145). However, he felt that there was an incongruity between the punishment and the crime. Using an example from Muslim law he pointed out that for theft the robbers' hands would be cut off. He also mentioned that most highway robbers were generally sons of wealthy parents who had squandered away their inheritance and taken to robbery (*Shigurf Namah* 1827: 147–8). This offers a very interesting insight into the class of bandits in England. Other legal issues that he brought up pertained to women. Rape, he wrote, was also punishable by death. In the case of cohabitation, if two people chose to live together, they were not harassed by the police unlike in Hindustan. If a man caught his wife cheating on him and was in possession of a sword he could kill the man and the woman without being charged with murder. On the other hand if he went to find a weapon and in the meanwhile the two adulterers left the premises and claimed not to know one another, then the husband would be helpless, unless there was a witness. If without a witness he killed the woman or man he would be then charged with murder (*Shigurf Namah* 1827: 149–50).

III. The counter gaze: impressions of women and society in England

The most interesting divergences in attitude can be seen in the attitude and approach of the two travellers can be observed in the way in which they represented women, religion and the functioning of society. Abu Taleb, it appears from his writing, was a man who enjoyed the company of women and through the course of his travelogue focused on the various women he managed to meet and described those interactions very vividly. Itesamuddin noticed the people around him and made some very pertinent comparisons between England and Hindustan. He did not enjoy the company of women as much as Taleb did and noticed and used them as pivots to support his arguments pertaining to matters of law, justice and so on. Itesamuddin's main focus seemed to be to provide a detailed explanation of Islam.

The reaction of the people of England to seeing Itesamuddin interested him. He was aware of the fact that he looked and dressed differently. He mentioned that he was treated kindly as he was a foreigner but that he was always met by a crowd of people who were curious about him. He narrated an incident where he was taken to a gathering. He wrote that

> As soon as we arrived there, a stop was put to the dancing and the music, and they all began to stare at me, and having examined my robe, turban, shawl, and other parts of my costume, they thought that

> it was a dress for dancing or acting in. I endeavoured to persuade them to the contrary, but they would not believe me; and everyone in the assembly continued to gaze at my dress and appearance, and I continued observing their excellent entertainment: and it is singular that I, who went to see a spectacle became myself a sight to others.
>
> (*Shigurf Namah* 1827: 36–37)

Itesamuddin, however, admired the behaviour of the British towards foreigners and felt that they went to great lengths to make him feel comfortable. He noted that until his arrival the British only knew of lascars from Chittagong and Jahangirnagar and were unfamiliar with the manners and conduct of a Hindustani and so considered him to be at least the brother of a Nawab of Bengal if not one himself (*Shigurf Namah* 1827: 39–40). The locals peered at him through their windows as he passed by in the market and children kept away from him calling him the 'black devil'. In the summer he was dressed in a long garment, with a sash around his waist, a turban on his head and a dagger tucked into his sash. While his appearance was appreciated by many, others thought of it as the 'dress of the Harem' and of 'delicate females'. A few months into his stay the people stopped fearing him and would stop him in the market and ask him for a kiss (*Shigurf Namah* 1827: 40–41). Itesamuddin believed that Captain Swinton wanted to use him, as he looked different to prove that he had gone to Bengal and had become so important that he was accompanied back to Europe with the brother of a Nawab (*Shigurf Namah* 1827: 195–6). Abu Taleb too was seen as a unique individual in England. He was called the Persian Prince, a title he chose not to correct, presumably because he enjoyed the attention or the chance at being considered a prince. He was asked to attend many charity events, and it was advertised in the papers that 'Prince Abu Taleb' would be in attendance for the event (Khan 1887: 1.222).

The sense one gets from reading these descriptions is that on the one hand these travellers really enjoyed the attention that they received for looking different and that they did this on purpose. In choosing to maintain the way in which they dressed it is almost as if they were returning the 'gaze' firmly establishing their identities and creating for themselves a safe space to help themselves deal with the unfamiliar.

The observations of the two travellers regarding women are very insightful. Itesamuddin provided his reader with a general understanding of how marriages were conducted in Europe. The consent of both the parties was required and the man had to be good looking, of a good temperament, skilled in business and well employed. The lady also had to be good looking, with wealth from either her father or a previous husband, of good temperament and versed in some of the fine arts (Khan 1887: 1.76). Some, he also noted, married only for money and if a woman was ugly and poor she would remain single because Europe being the 'emporium of beauty, and women exceeding in loveliness are very common; also wealthy and virtuous ones [abound]' (Khan 1887: 1.76).

The classes of people that Abu Taleb interacted with in England were what have been described as 'the leisured classes of Hanoverian England' (Khan 1998: 179). He moved in this society because a large number of his acquaintances were those who held high positions in the administration in the subcontinent, like former governor-generals and officials of the company.

Taleb, who was invited to many parties, wrote that his 'society was courted'. He met many women in these gatherings and found them and their dancing very charming (Khan 1887: 1.162). Abu Taleb wrote an 'Ode to London' of which some selected verses read:

> Henceforward we will devote our lives to London
> and its heart alluring Damsels;
> Our hearts are satiated with viewing fields, gardens,
> rivers and palaces.
> Fill the goblet with wine! If by this I am pre-
> vented from returning
> To my old religion, I care not; nay, I am the
> better pleased.
> If the prime of my life has been spent in the
> service of an Indian Cupid,
> It matters not: I am now rewarded by the smiles
> of the British Fair.
> These wounds of Cupid, on your heart, Taleba,
> are not accidental:
> They were engendered by Nature, like the streaks
> on the leaf of a tulip.
>
> (Khan 1887: 1.179–80)

He did not just write about women and their beauty, though. Regarding the employment of women and legislation pertaining to their social lives, Abu Taleb noted that to keep women out of trouble it was best to involve them in 'whatever business can be effected without any great exertion of mental abilities or corporeal strength, is assigned to the women' (Khan 1887: 1.259).

Though homemaking was the woman's duty, Taleb noted that they were also allowed to tend shops because they would be able to attract customers with their grace and beauty. The men on the other hand had jobs waiting tables and taking care of cattle and farms. This clear division of labour, Taleb felt, did not lead to confusion (Khan 1887: 1.259).

Taleb also noted the 'salutary restraints' women were placed under by the English legislators so that they would not misuse the liberties they had in mixing with male company. A woman was never introduced to strangers, nor was a woman allowed to visit a bachelor who was not a relative. A woman was never allowed to walk outside other than in the company of her husband, relative or a trustworthy servant. She was never allowed to go out after dark nor could she stay at another house, even at her own parents' house unless her husband was there. This ensured that women did not get the opportunity to act in an 'unbecoming manner'. If a woman acted inappropriately, the shame, Taleb mentioned, fell on the whole family. The law also allowed a man to beat his wife with a stick as long as he did not break her bones, or he could lock her in her room as punishment. If caught, the woman chose to continue to behave in an 'unbecoming manner', she was shunned by all her relatives, acquaintances and every lady of high social standing. The husband was also allowed to take away the woman's ornaments and property, keep their children away from her and even turn her out of the house. If he could find reasonable proof of her misconduct, he was also entitled to file for divorce, which would leave her without any right over anything she had previously owned (Khan 1887: 1.260–1).

The women of England, though they appeared to have many liberties, were confined to strict bondage by the law, while Muslim women, though believed to be kept behind the curtain and not allowed to mix in society, could go out, wearing a veil and stay at their parents' or friends' houses without any trouble. Regarding liberties, Taleb definitely maintained that Hindustani women or 'Asiatic' women had more liberties than Europeans did (Khan 1887: 1.261–2).

On this matter Abu Taleb wrote a tract entitled *The Vindication of the Liberties of Asiatic Women* while in London, in which he justified the conduct and being of the women of Hindustan. Though he wrote the *Vindication*, Michael Fisher (2000: 230) brings to our notice that later, back from his trip, under the pseudonym *Londoni*, Taleb attempted to introduce ideas to provide correctives to some practices from his own culture. He wanted to selectively emulate certain ideas from the British and altered some of the assertions that he had made in the *Vindication*. He was aware of who his audience was and tempered his writing accordingly. For example, he wrote that polygamy destroyed family life, whereas in the *Vindication* he had maintained that instances of polygamy were minimal.

Fisher also shows how Abu Taleb, at the time of his travels in Europe, was a man in his mid-forties, married with a family and exotic to the women he met in England. This took him out of being considered for any conventional marriage with the women with whom he spent time. Therefore all the poetry that he wrote was also taken in a much lighter vein, rather than it being considered an insult to the woman or the honour of her family. The graphic descriptions made by Taleb only helped increase his popularity as the women saw it as being flattered in exotic ways (Fisher 2000: 224). While he could do this in England and get away with it, Fisher noted that Taleb knew that British men would never have similar access to women of his society or family.

Taleb observed the high incidence of sexual intercourse outside marriage, which could be observed in all classes of British society, through prostitution, pre-marital and adulterous sex (Fisher 2000: 217). His observations included the incidence of elopement and cohabitation before marriage. He was alarmed by the number of prostitutes who lived on almost every street; however, his main grievance, and the reason he believed that their choice of way of life was more condemnable, was because they lived on streets with names like 'Providence Street' and 'Modest Court', the former being an a moniker of God and the latter indicating a desirable virtue, as well as 'St. Martin's Lane', 'St. James's Street' and 'St. Paul's Churchyard' which were all named after the Apostles of Christ. He also added that those who rented out such places were more reprehensible than the women (Khan 1887: 2.45).

IV. Debating religion in eighteenth-century England: Islam and Christianity

Taleb's observations on religion, compared to his views on other matters, were rather limited. Taleb explained that the clergy was meant only to guide the flock in spiritual matters and that in England law and religion were separate matters (Khan 1887: 1.289–90). Taleb had the opportunity of meeting a few bishops with whom he debated. His narrative is peppered with anecdotes that he primarily used to establish his religious prowess.

For Itesamuddin religion was one of the main topics that he engaged with through his travelogue. His views on Judaism, Christianity, the different versions of Christianity and his understanding of Hinduism were described in great detail. He describes in detail the debates that he had with certain British people regarding Islam, the Prophet and practices in Islam. Beyond that, religion seems to be one of the focal points for him when he analyses European society.

Itesamuddin believed that he was very well read especially regarding religion and that he had a good understanding of the subject. He was well acquainted with the New Testament of which he had a Persian translation. His understanding of Christianity was informed by a traditional Islamic view of Christianity. His comments on Christianity were, in short, a comparison of the different ways in which it helped him identify between the British and the French. It is interesting to note that he did not once refer to the two sects as Anglican or Catholic. The analysis that he provided suggested that he saw the two as different religions as they differed on a number of issues.

Itesamuddin was far more sympathetic to the British form of Christianity. While this could be part of his overall appreciation of the British, he also considered the Anglicans more rational. He held this opinion because the English people did not accept that Christ was born of a virgin, but that there was only one God who, by his divine favour, allowed Jesus to call him his father. This honour having been given to him made him the most important of all the prophets (*Shigurf Namah* 1827: 96). Itesamuddin felt that the English, being a peaceful people, managed to coexist with those of other faiths like the Muslims and the Jews. He mentioned that a Muslim could build a mosque and give the call for prayer without any trouble in England (*Shigurf Namah* 1827: 101). Itesamuddin noted that the British were of the opinion that God had created the universe for man's comfort and it was man's duty to maximise this comfort. The British, he mentioned, believed that excessive praying and fasting would distract the people from other duties and render their constitutions too weak to deal with crises like foreign attacks.

In a debate regarding heaven, Itesamuddin's British friends argued that the Muslims believed that it was only those who recited the confession of the faith would go to heaven. Given the limited number of Muslims in the world they asked him whether they actually believed that God created the rest of the world to have them suffer in hell. To this Itesamuddin replied that that was indeed God's intention and the reason that hell was four times the size of paradise (*Shigurf Namah* 1827: 128–9).

Even with regard to food Itesamuddin was a stickler and refused to partake of wine or eat meat that was not prepared according to the Muslim way. As he couldn't take his servant with him to prepare food, during a journey Itesamuddin did not eat the food given to him and subsisted on a few dried fruits; though Captain Swinton tried to convince him to have food with him, assuring him that there was no pork on the table, Itesamuddin refused on the grounds that it was not prepared according to the prescribed Islamic law (*Shigurf Namah* 1827: 199).

Itesamuddin's dealing with his British friends' questions was rather pointed and portrayed the anxiety of a person far removed from what he knew and found comfortable. A reading of the text gives us the feeling that this was a man who was defending his religion to the hilt, which for him was also a way of life and a major marker of his identity. One gets the sense that for him Christianity in its various forms was not just a religion, but an intrinsic part of the identity of the people of Europe. In a sense he used religion as a platform over which he constructed his idea of 'Western civilisation'.

Conclusion

The observations of the travellers about the governments, society, gender relations in particular and religion lead us to ask questions such as why they chose to describe these in the way in which they did. Michael Fisher argues, as we have seen earlier, that Abu Taleb, in representing women the way he did, was providing a corrective to the kind of ideas pertaining to women that were prevalent in Europe. It was not just women; Fisher argues that all of Asian society was made effeminate by the Europeans so that they would have a sense of superiority and access to it. Taleb in this regard was trying to break through that notion. In providing extensive details of his interactions with women of various social classes there, he was trying to prove a difference about the easy access that he had to their society, not just women, which they would not be given in Hindustan. Gulfishan Khan argues that they were not able to compare the societies of Europe with that of Hindustan and points out that beyond light references to home such as a comparison of the Thames and Ganga, or the comparison of St. Paul's Cathedral and the mausoleum of Mahmud Shah, there was no real comparison that the two travellers made.

I would argue that in the case of society, as Fisher has pointed out, the comparisons made and the points that were to be proved were done in a subtle manner. Taleb realised that there were things lacking in his society, so later wrote about improving it, but when travelling and writing his narrative he was representing his background and his people. Itesamuddin too did provide subtle (and not so subtle) references to his homeland, especially when he debated about religion and comportment. The basic point is that they used themselves as a yardstick to understand the society they were visiting. It is precisely for this reason that the both of them also mentioned how they were being received and perceived in the places they visited. Their notions of what was expected from their hosts and their behaviour were contingent on how they expected them to behave, based on what they knew in their own contexts. In reflecting on the different cultures they witnessed in London, both authors could not help but connect their selves to these reflections.

References

Alam, Muzaffar and Sanjay Subrahmanyam. 2006. *Indo-Persain Travels in the Age of Discovery.* New Delhi: Oxford University Press.

Cole, Juan R. I. 1992. 'Invisible Occidentalism: Eighteenth-Century Indo-Persian Constructions of the West', *Iranian Studies* 25(3/4): 3–16.

Fisher, Michael. 2000. 'Representing "His" Women: Mirza Abu Taleb Khan's 1801, "Vindication of the Liberties of Asiatic Women"', *The Indian Economic and Social History Review* 37(2): 215–239.

———. 2004. *Counterflows to Colonialism, Indian Travellers and Settlers in Britain 1600–1857.* New Delhi: Permanent Black.

Itesamuddin, Mirza. 1827. *Shigurf Namah-i-Velaet*, Translated from Persian to English by James Edward Alexander. London: Purbury, Allen and Co.

Khan, Gulfishan. 1998. *Indian Muslim Perceptions of the West during the Eighteenth Century.* Karachi: Oxford University Press.

Khan, Mirza Abu Taleb. 1887. *The Travels of Mirza Abu Taleb Khan through Asia, Africa and Europe during the years 1799, 1800, 1801, 1802 and 1803*, Translated from Persian by Charles Stewart. London: R. Watts.

Part III

Diplomacy, power and the company state

9 Jahangir's paintings

Liam D. Haydon

During the first British embassy to the court of Jahangir, a series of paintings were offered to the Mughal emperor by Thomas Roe and the East India Company (EIC). While in some ways this was a standard part of diplomatic protocol and a normal procedure for those separated by distance, the paintings provided by Roe and the company reveal much about the strategies they employed at the Mughal court. These gifts demonstrate the ways in which the company wished to use visual signals to cement cross-cultural connections.

Recent historiography of Roe's time in India has revised the classic interpretation of the embassy as an early, if faltering or misguided, sign of incipient empire (Cohn 1996; Singh 1996). The revisionist historiography has had two strands: the practical reconsideration of Roe's two masters, the Crown and the company (as well as his own ambitions); and a theoretical revaluation of the nature of the exchanges and power struggles, which is more alert to the strategies employed by both Roe and the Mughal court, and the effects of the resultant clash of the ideological, representational and power structures of the European and Asian worlds.

The first strand requires a vigilant awareness of the fact Roe 'juggled two competing claims on his time and energy in India' (Games 2008: 158). Understanding the limitations that each role placed on the other has helped not just to explain the success or failure of Roe's embassy but to reconceptualise what is meant by 'success' in this context, when a diplomatic success came at significant economic cost, and supplicating for commercial privilege reduced the pomp and dignity of the ambassadorial state.

Alison Games places Roe in a historical context as one of the 'cosmopolitans' helping to push forward English expansion. As part of this, she views his embassy as a carefully balanced exercise in which the need to maintain a dignified position as the proxy of the sovereign alternated with the need to 'creepe and sue', in Roe's words (Foster 1899: 358), for the commercial needs of the company. Roe, she argues, spent his embassy in a state of 'constant vigilance from a gauntlet of what he viewed as petty assaults and gratuitous offences' (Games 2008: 156). Jealously guarded privileges ensured Roe's status at court and were, in Games's reading, his only recourse against his distance from the 'financial networks, patronage, employers, supplies, information, [and] military support' of England (Games 2008: 159).

Rupali Mishra, likewise, has recently argued that Roe served not two, but three masters, seeing a conflict between what 'he hoped to gain for himself, for James, and for the East India Company in the 1610s' (2014: 8). As Games does, Mishra stresses the difficulties in squaring the need for royal and national honour and the commercial requirements of the company who was, after all, paying his wages and supplying his gifts, though Mishra does nuance this slightly by noting the ways in which these aims might interlock. Moreover, by a study of Roe's correspondence, Mishra notes the way in which his self-presentation differs according to whether Roe is serving the Crown or company, as well as some less guarded moments in which Roe seems to reveal his desire 'to serve time abroad and return to a better – and more regularly paid – position in England' (2014: 13). These letters requesting patronage were, Mishra argues, part of a wider system of information exchange: Roe's desire for usable information stems not from an ambition to better inform the company, but to ensure that he has a vendible commodity to translate to influence and patronage on his return home. His observations of the governmental systems, culture and society of India are, therefore, born out of a desire for advancement in England, not India.

More significantly, scholars have increasingly stressed that these meetings were what Miles Ogborn (2007: 32) calls 'attempts at exchange, shaped by the interests and understandings of each side, and moments when either party might seek to dominate the encounter, in words or deeds'. Ogborn's consideration of the 'writing that travels' brought by Roe to India is a useful model for the paintings given to the emperor; perhaps even more than writing, these existed as material signs that were valuable as objects to be interpreted; in the processes of gifting and explanation, we can see a struggle for domination in the different interpretations given to these material artefacts by Jahangir and the company's servants.

Richmond Barbour has also seen the embassy as a clash of interpretative systems, in this case, representation. He argues that Roe's embassy was in fact a series of challenges met by theatrical self-representation, ranging from his initial arrival with huge ceremony at a beach near Surat to the difficulties of presenting himself well at the Mughal court. This highly self-conscious attempt at portraying himself as a dignified ambassador was, Barbour argues, a response to his weakness and unimportance at the court of the emperor: 'The discursive hegemony that he strives to sustain – a frame in which many critics have seen intimations of empire – he cultivates in compensation for his relative impotence at the scene of negotiation' (2003: 147).

Like Barbour, Sanjay Subrahmanyam has argued that Roe's journal and other written records (official letters and commissions) are important not as an authoritative archive of India, but as a deliberate attempt at self-fashioning, an attempt, however small, to control the encounters and representational contests at the court of Jahangir. Subrahmanyam (2012) sees the embassy of Roe as a moment of conflict, albeit a contained conflict, not one in which the signs of two cultures are made intelligible to each other, but one in which they are in competition. Yet they do not have to be, as the journals of other travellers to India testify; his analysis of the journals of Mutribi Samarqandi, from Persia, and the European Jesuits at the court of Jahangir, demonstrates the potential for positive engagement and cross-cultural interaction at the Mughal court.

Though Roe does observe some of the culture of the Mughal Empire, for Subrahmanyam he can never quite get past his initial prejudices and preconceived beliefs about the nature of the power structures in India:

> Here then is a key to understanding Roe's presentation of the Mughal to the English reader, an understanding which I would contend is far less subtle than that of the Spanish and Portuguese Jesuits at the Mughal court, and far more apt to drift towards the topoi of Oriental Despotism: absence of laws, arbitrary royal power and a penchant for blood-lust, absence of private property.
>
> (2002: 77)

Roe, in this reading, does not write the journal to learn, but to present his largely irrelevant embassy as a success, and to confirm European ideas of Oriental despotism.

Without wishing to fundamentally challenge these two modes of interpreting Roe's embassy, in this chapter I would like to nuance both, by considering the deployment of the particular material goods of paintings. Paintings were, I argue, used by Roe to unite the two disparate goals of his embassy; they were an economically viable way of offering the gifts required by the court, as well as serving a diplomatic and cultural purpose. Roe (and the company more generally) placed importance on the gifting of paintings precisely because they represent a way of generating surplus value, as one of the few types of goods that are more valuable in India than in Europe. Moreover, Roe uses paintings as a way of inserting himself into the complex power and representational networks of Jahangir's court; more precisely, they are attempts to impose a representational or symbolic order onto India that is favourable to the goals of the company, and by extension the English state. As Lisa Jardine and Jerry Brotton have pointed out with reference to similar material exchanges with the Ottoman Empire, presenting goods like paintings and carpets that could be made to signify in particular ways 'showed an astute understanding of the shared imperial and iconographic preoccupations of the courts' (2000: 120). Though this strategy may well have had some early success, Roe soon lost his ability to control the interpretation of paintings, opening the gifts from a one-way imposition to a moment of exchange containing the sort of power dynamics outlined by Ogborn and Barbour.

A close examination of the moments of gifting, and the reaction to them, on both sides, can thus help us see the power struggles and ideological representations involved in early cross-cultural connections in India more clearly. Moreover, these gifts reveal themselves to be a series of individual moments of interaction; rather than a continuum from weak beginnings to imperial masters, the gifting of paintings demonstrates the variety, and variability, of political strategies and positionings employed by the company and its servants. Considering these moments precisely as a series of moments (instead of a grander strategy, or a teleologically inflected first step to mastery and empire) shows us something of the contingencies of early encounters and the variety of strategies employed (with varied success) to meet them.

I

Members of the EIC who arrived in India before Roe soon discovered that paintings were useful gifts, and potentially even a valuable commodity. The company tried a range of gifts for the emperor and other local potentates, as Thomas Mitford records:

> Mr. Edwardes delivered our King's Majesty's letter with these presents, viz. our King's Majesty's picture, the Queen's and Lady Elizabeth's, the rich cloak, the rich case of strong waters, one great black glass set in an ebony frame, and a case of knives.
>
> (Foster 1896–1902: III:85)

Though this is, in many ways, a fairly standard list of gifts, the paintings stand out not simply as being the first listed, but as objects of representation, perhaps even 'representation in its pure form', as Foucault (2001: 18) puts it in his discussion of *Las Meninas*, also, of course, a 'King's Majesty's picture'. That is the other gifts offered to Jahangir derive their value from their status as curiosities, but the curiosity they arouse is limited, largely, to the object itself, though the power of the mirror to speak to a world where the emperor is the 'master of all originals and replicas' (Barbour 2003: 175), to reflect back the face of power upon itself, should not go unnoticed. Paintings, however, have value in two ways (and, as we will see, the servants of the EIC were well aware of this distinction). The object itself may be valued for its workmanship, or the skill of the painter. Perhaps a greater value, though, comes from the paintings' potential to exist as signs, to point beyond themselves to ideas of political and social organisation or cultural practice. They can, in short, present something, even just a glimpse, of the ideology of the gifting party; I will argue it is in this role that the company deploys them as presents, though the complexity of the networks of signs they open out ultimately weakens the direct political strategy of gift-giving.

Unlike many of the English (or European) products that were brought to India but found to be not vendible, paintings seem to have aroused much interest in the local population. The EIC merchant William Edwards, based in Surat, wrote to the company that

> pictures of all sorts are much requested for presents but not for sale, but those on boards will be defaced by the heat of the weather, as these now sent, in warping and splitting, but for their workmanship are much esteemed.
>
> (Foster 1896–1902: III:16)

Edwards had himself been involved in giving paintings as diplomatic gifts, though not without some scandal. Asaph Chan, a nobleman and minister of the emperor, had taken one of the paintings Edwards proposed to present to Jahangir as his own gift, meaning that Edwards had to present one of his own collection, by all accounts an inferior specimen. Nonetheless, regardless of the workmanship, his attempts to ingratiate himself with Jahangir were doomed, since 'the title of a merchant is of them much despised' (Foster 1896–1902: III:18). Still, the value of paintings was recognised through this incident, and Edwards requests more pictures later in the same letter:

> Among other pictures, if you send any, it would do well to appoint a dozen of those small creased pictures which show, some two faces or persons, and some three, according as you stand to look upon them. They were esteemed in England when they first were devised, but since are little regarded. They are cheap there and would be much esteemed here, for having never been seen in these parts. . . . The fight of '88 and our Saviour's passion would do well.
>
> (Foster 1896–1902: III:19)

Edwards has grasped the novelty value of European paintings, or rather the particular style of the triptych, which he claims will be useful precisely because they have 'never been seen in these parts'. He does grasp that there is surplus value to the paintings in India but only seems to conceptualise this in economic terms: it is fortunate that they are out of fashion in England because that makes them cheap. The floating opposites of 'cheap there' and 'much esteemed here' does suggest a link between the economic and the fashionable (i.e. exchanges between economic and non-economic value), but Edwards does not develop that thought any further. Similarly, the suggested subjects (the Armada and the Crucifixion) point towards an awareness that English or European culture and history can be exoticised and commodified in the East, though here, too, Edwards does not develop the point.

The same commodification of European history can be seen in Edwards's contemporary in Surat, the chief factor Thomas Kerridge. In a letter just a few weeks after Edwards, Kerridge offers a fuller consideration of the policy of offering pictures as gifts:

> The Mogoll's picture drawn in England is nothing like him; so will serve for no use at all. The rest of the pictures brought up hither, most of them are given for presents and the rest reserved for like uses. Divers have been earnest to buy of them, but none have been sold; wherefore if five or six dozen were appointed for that purpose I think they would sell. They may be of several sizes and being well wrought, those of France, Germany, Flanders, etc., are fittest for that purpose; for they esteem not of the ladies' pictures according to their value, except only for the rarity of the workmanship ; so a few extraordinary of them for presents will suffice. The rest may be of different fictions of feigned gods, histories, gardens, banquets and the like, with some two or three hundred pictures, which are cheaper. Black hair or brown is most esteemed here, agreeing with their complexions.
>
> (Foster 1896–1902: III:67–68)

On the surface, this is simply a 'shopping list' from Kerridge back to the company, a simple piece of information exchange that updates their preconceptions about Indian or Mughal desires. However, Kerridge cannot escape either the materiality or the significance of the pictures, and so his almost-forcedly neutral and polished account cannot fully obscure the troubling and difficult questions raised by the process of artistic gift-giving.

On an economic level, Kerridge acknowledges the need for the company to bend itself to the realities of the market as it is in India; we may read 'agreeing with their complexions' not just as a statement of anthropological fact, but a tacit acknowledgement that it is necessary for the company's goods to accord with the desires of the Indian population. That is Kerridge could not create a market for European artwork, but could only recommend appropriate supplies of art to meet more or less pre-existing demand.

Perhaps most interesting is Kerridge's concept of 'value'. Although Kerridge is a touch vague, the 'value' of the portraits of the ladies is clearly not based on their purchase price, or (as Kerridge seems to mean) the social rank of the ladies, but on the 'rarity' of the workmanship – presumably either an especially high-quality work or one exhibiting new and unusual forms of representation. Conversely, in the case of the 'Mogoll's picture', the value (the 'use') is entirely reliant upon the accuracy of the representation. There is, then, a disjunction in types of value, one at the level of the object (workmanship) and one at the level of the sign (representation). Yet Kerridge states that only a 'few' of the first sort are required – as with the other presents, the curiosity value of objects is limited. Instead, he seeks increasingly symbolic paintings ('fictions', 'feigned gods', etc.) for 'the rest', revealing something of his understanding of the importance of paintings-as-symbols to the company's diplomatic activity in Asia.

Though we might imagine the company attempting to commission a painting of Jahangir 'drawn in England', in fact the representational problem they encountered was not one of distance, but time. The painting was in fact a painting of Tamburlaine, supposedly the origin of the Mughal emperors. Thomas Aldworthe, the chief factor at Surat, wrote to Kerridge in 1614 regarding William Edwards's mission to Jahangir. He noted that '[Edwards] brings one picture that we think will content [Jahangir] above all, which is the picture of Tamburlaine, from whence he derives himself' (Foster 1896–1902: II:138). Sadly, the painting looked nothing like Jahangir, or his father, and so it was rejected. Curiously, the Jesuits had tried a similar gambit:

> Mukarrib Khan sent me a picture, stating that the Portuguese believed it to be the portrait of Tímúr. . . . If this had been true, in my opinion there could not have been a more valuable curiosity in my possession; but as it bore no resemblance to his royal descendants, I was not at all satisfied of the truth of the statement.
>
> (Jahángir 2013: 320)

Jahangir's refutation of the painting's accuracy depends on the immutability of his own lineage: to accept a painting of an ancestor that looks nothing like the current ruler is to put all the iconography of the emperors into question, undermining their claims to an unbroken lineage back to Tamburlaine.

The picture, however ill-received, was clearly meant as flattery to Jahangir. What does it mean for the company to attempt to transmute the Tamburlaine of the European imagination into an honoured and celebrated ancestor? The key image of Tamburlaine for the English was Marlowe's eponymous play, first presented in 1590, which went through a number of reprints in the decades that followed. Marlowe's Tamburlaine is a cruel and iconoclastic ruler who, by the end of the play, feels able to threaten the security of heaven itself: 'Jove, viewing me in arms, looks pale and wan, / Fearing my power should pull him from his throne' (Marlowe 1966: V.i). Of course, an alternative reading of Tamburlaine as a powerful and triumphant ruler was also available to early modern English audiences (Levin 1984); indeed, much of the early part of Marlowe's *Tamburlaine* stresses the valour and military brilliance of the Scythian shepherd, and presumably it is this referent the company is trying to activate in its gift. If so, the picture of the 'Great Mogull' becomes, rather than a coded insult, an attempt to sublimate the ambiguous morality of the 'European' Tamburlaine to the glory of the 'Asian' Timur, founder of the Mughal dynasty; in effect, the painting acknowledges that Western ideas, rather than being imposed on the natives, must bend to accommodate the ideological structure of their hosts.

The questions raised by Kerridge's request thus lead to one larger question: how far are images of England and Englishness valuable at all? Kerridge's request seems to reflect a reality in which the English must subordinate themselves to Oriental desires, systems of representation and, by extension, agency.

However, in the same letter, Kerridge asks the company to send

> some courtlike pictures, as the running at tilt, the King and nobility spectators, the King sitting in Parliament, and suchlike will be graceful and give content, being done curiously, that his own people may come short in imitation, of whom he hath and some skilful.
>
> (Foster 1896–1902: III:68)

Kerridge's request shows even more clearly than Edwards's that these paintings ought to be particular representations of Englishness. Yet, since Kerridge has seemingly acknowledged the impossibility of forcing Englishness onto the Indian mass market, we must speculate that these pictures were for quite another purpose entirely, as political gifts rather than objects for sale. Like the paintings for sale, there is a nod to the value of the workmanship in the request for them to be 'done curiously', but the specificity of the settings is suggestive. Perhaps they were designed to implicitly counter the splendour of the Mughal court, where these pictures of the English court might serve as markers of European power and organisation.

The internal wars of Europe gestured towards directly in the armada painting, as well as the religious wars obliquely referenced by the crucifixion, can be transmuted in India to a unified show of European power and splendour. As Anthony Milton has demonstrated (Milton 1994: 113), Protestant self-representation often came with a rhetoric of conciliation, in which the goal (however unlikely) of reuniting the Protestant churches surmounted national or even regional politics: 'Domestic problems might dwindle when placed in an international context and in the midst of a suitably irenical atmosphere.' We can perhaps see something of this goal of unification in India, where a painting of a European war is designed to show not division (except in a latent anti-Catholicism), but a triumphant, powerful and divinely supported Protestantism.

The presence of the Parliament offers a slight rebuke, perhaps, to the Mughal court, with its focus on the absolute will of the emperor. Indeed, as Joan-Pau Rubiés has shown, 'European concerns about the nature of monarchy were actually affected by observation of non-European cultures' (Rubiés 2005: 112), so it should be no surprise to see reflections upon constitutional matters within the gifts offered by the company. Kerridge's choice of subject, demonstrating the performative yet collaborative nature of English kingship, offers an alternative constitutional model, with sovereignty rooted in overlapping and interlinked legal polities, domestic and international (Halliday 2010; Withington 2010; Benton and Ross 2013).

However, the political motivation behind the choice of subject may very well have been not Jahangir but the European competitors at his court. Kerridge had written in an earlier report of the Jesuits strategy of denigrating the political system of England to gain favour with Jahangir:

> Those Jesuits . . . shame not to say, we are a people rebelled subjects to their king, and make us and the Hollanders as one, they allege further our country and prince of no respect nor force, having only one city wherein a few merchants, and that our king hath no hand in this business, which they instanced upon an answer made by Paul Canning to the king at the delivery of the present: The king demanded of him from whom the letter was sent, he answered the letter was from his king and the present from the merchants which the Jesuits, noting his haughtiness to mislike, they furthered his disesteeming thereof, saying, our king sent him nothing, it was the merchants only through desire of traffic.
>
> (Foster 1896–1902: I:280)

The presentation of the Parliament makes much more sense as a response to this Portuguese strategy. It is commonplace that early modern European rulers developed spectacular displays as a strategy of power; the painting would, presumably, be of this tradition, placing a stress on the wealth and power of the king (and state) by showing this ritual occasion – the symbolism of the king, with all the trappings of royalty, addressing a respectful collection of his subjects, would be the perfect rejoinder to any renewal of Jesuit claims (now that a statesman was present at court) of a weak king presiding over a poor and fractured state. Moreover, as Timon Screech (2005: 64–65) has shown, EIC factors in Japan also presented pictures of James I in the Parliament, with particular reference to the gunpowder plot, as a way to distance themselves from the Jesuits and disparage the Dutch.

The company's strategy therefore becomes one of political triangulation, using the interpretative capacities of the emperor as a check on Portuguese power. Of course, for this strategy to be effective, Jahangir must be able both to interpret the political message behind the painting and to compare it to the verbal reports of the Jesuits at his court. This requires a certain symbolic sophistication, not least in Jahangir's presumed ability to interpret and finesse representations of a form of power alien to him.

For both of these company men, it is clear that the material value of the paintings is far surpassed by their use value in India. In part this is because they offer an exotic view to Jahangir, who was, as contemporary reports attests, curious about civilisations outside India. But their choice of scenes reveals that these pictures are to be viewed not as exclusively material objects, but as signs that can, potentially, be deployed and manipulated.

The submissive gesture of present-offering thus becomes an opportunity for the rituals of the Mughal court to be appropriated to English semiotics, a chance to demonstrate either English superiority (political and/or technical) or the ability to understand and thus categorise the Mughal court, even if that understanding involved a recognition that the English need to submit themselves to Mughal power. Such a categorisation was an established part of the toolkit of travel writers – organising and taxonomising the Other was one way in which those writers 'performed rhetorically the processes of decontextualisation whereby Europeans extracted objects from their New World environments and gave them new values that were desirable and meaningful to European audiences' (Wisecup 2013: 265). Wisecup usefully complicates this description by noting the ways in which the objects described by Europeans could never be fully separated from their context; nonetheless, the attempts to place Mughal art appreciation in direct relation to hair or skin colour clearly fit with the desire to classify the world, even as it reveals the accommodation and mutability required of the Europeans in Asia.

Though I largely concur with Subrahmanyam's readings of the embassy as an implicit conflict, I hope to reconsider a little of his formulation of the relationship between power and knowledge:

> [W]e might say that the problem we are dealing with here is not one where knowledge is shaped by actual power (for the English had very little power in India, whether at the time of Roe or that of Norris); rather, it is of a will to power where a form of political ethnography, in which various political systems are compared and ranked, has become the standard framework for the ambassadorial account.
>
> (2002: 95)

To draw a distinction between 'actual' power and the 'will to power' (presumably the difference between a martial presence and the dream of empire), Subrahamanyam relegates knowledge to being an outcropping, or function of power, whereby different types of power produce different forms of knowledge; the desire to impose a new form of government on India naturally leads to an interest in the existing political economy, and how it compares to the European model.

Though this does help us understand some of Roe's goals at the Mughal court, it cannot fully explain the motivation to give pictures as gifts – what purpose would they serve in this economy of power? It is only by understanding paintings as a site of conflict over representation – that is knowledge that produces power – that the company's (and Roe's) strategies can be fully understood:

> [T]here is no power relation without the correlative constitution of a field of knowledge, nor any knowledge that does not presuppose and constitute at the same time power relations.
>
> (Foucault 1979: 27)

That is there is also an inherent inversion of Subrahmanyam's formulation of the ethnographic will-to-power, in which knowledge creates and modifies power structures. In this Foucauldian sense, the gifting of paintings becomes an attempt to circumvent political realities. The company attempts to impose, through these objects, a system of understanding that can be deployed to produce new knowledge without the need for physical power to support or create it: it is, in effect, a form of 'soft power' through the art of resemblances. This was not, as we have seen, the case in every gift, nor was it always (or ever) successful. Nonetheless, it is apparent in these early gifts that thought has been given to the symbolic knowledge contained in art and its effects on the power relations at the Mughal court, whether direct Anglo-Indian relations or a competitive triangulation in which European diplomats jostle for favour. This is not to say, of course, that the strategy is the same in every gift; in fact, the series of paintings suggests something of the way in which strategies of European accommodation, and fantasies of power, have been adapted by negotiation with locals.

In what remains of this chapter, I will follow these company men in assuming that a picture has the capacity to represent far more than is on its surface. The practice of gifting these objects interrupts the unity of the sign; in their existence between two owners, two cultures and two modes of interpretation, the gift-paintings become loose signifiers, pointing to a whole range of potential signifiers. The ultimate meaning of these objects, and the right to arbitrate that meaning, remains open to question and challenge. Moreover, those contests and challenges make visible the usually elided systems of representation on which the paintings are based or in which they might take part: the semiotic questions they leave unanswered call attention to the 'purpose' of representation, the validity of representative and interpretative systems and the cultural contests inherent in the transmission of one representative model into, or onto, another.

II

With this culture of pictures as presents in mind, then, let us turn to the embassy of Sir Thomas Roe to Jahangir (1615–1618). Roe's embassy has been well-covered, of course, by scholars across a wide range of disciplines: despite the fact that other merchants (including Edwards and Kerridge) had presented themselves to Jahangir, Roe's status as the first official ambassador gives the cross-cultural interaction more weight and prominence in cultural and historical studies. Though I, too, will prioritise the exchanges between Roe and Jahangir, I want to stress the importance of the corporate setting and commercial interests in Roe's behaviour; his gifting of paintings comes, at least in part, from the company's own wishes (and funding), as its minutes report: '[I]t is thought he should not have power to make presents without advice . . . Roe is not to intermeddle with their business and merchandise' (*CSPC* October 7–14, 1614).

As such, through the gifting of paintings we can see him try to reconcile commercial and diplomatic aims by making one object serve both needs. However, because he is an explicitly cultural liaison, in a way that merchants are not, the gifting of paintings also offers an opportunity for a conflict between types of representations, in which Roe first attempts to write English norms on to the Mughal court, and eventually is reduced to fighting a rearguard battle against the imposition of a 'Mughal' reading by Jahangir.

Roe and Jahangir spoke directly on the matter of paintings on a few occasions. In fact, Jahangir considered himself something of a connoisseur of artworks, noting in his memoirs that

> I am very fond of pictures, and have such discrimination in judging them, that I can tell the name of the artist, whether living or dead. If there were similar portraits finished by several artists, I could point out the painter of each. Even if one portrait were finished by several painters, I could mention the names of those who had drawn the different portions of that single picture. In fact, I could declare without fail by whom the brow and by whom the eye-lashes were drawn, or if any one had touched up the portrait after it was drawn by the first painter.
>
> (Jahángir 2013: 360)

Notably, Jahangir's expertise extends only to the manner of construction of the painting, not the aesthetic qualities or meaning. There is, in fact, nothing here to suggest Jahangir's skill as an *interpreter* of meaning, since his focus was exclusively on the skills of the painters: or, more accurately, his own skills in identifying the origin of the painting or parts of the painting. Aesthetic considerations are secondary to identification; indeed, the only sense of the picture-as-representation comes in the assumption that he will be looking at a 'portrait', rather than any other kind of scene or image.

Moreover, in accordance with Jahangir's own estimation of his skills, Roe notes that he required many 'judgements' of them, suggesting a shared appreciation of the skill of the artists put before the emperor. On one occasion Jahangir presented Roe with a selection of miniatures, copied from an English model, and challenged him to discern which was the original and which the copies.

> [T]hat I was by candle-light troubled to discerne which was which, I confesse, beyond all expectation: yet I shewed mine owne, and the differences, which were in arte apparant, but not to be judged by a common eye. But for that at first sight I knew it not, he was very merry and joyfull, and craked like a Northerne man: I gave him way and content, praising his mans art. Now, saith he, what say you? I replyed, I saw his Majestie needed no Picture from our Countrey.
>
> (Roe 1625: 547)

Roe notes some amazement at the skill of the Mughal artists, despite adding the caveats of poor lighting and subtle differences in quality. Here again the focus falls on workmanship, and duplication, not on the creation of representations. Nonetheless, even with an acceptance of Mughal skill, Roe's admission that no further English gifts are required is a strange one; it is made more strange by the fact that Roe offers (once his offer of money has been refused) a gift for the painter from his house, perhaps 'a good Sword, a Pistall, a Picture' (Roe 1625: 547). It may be that English workmanship cannot fully eclipse Mughal efforts at duplication, but Roe's insistence on offering an English painting from his collection suggests that the symbolic value of paintings remains current.

This sort of test seems to have been common practice with Jahangir; Subrahmanyam (2002: 82) notes a similarly constructed scene in which Jahangir shows copies of Persian works to Mutribi, who carefully corrects some of the details:

> [T]he significance of the incident lies in the fact that while Mutribi is concerned to show the meticulous nature of Mughal portraiture and the confidence that was vested in him as a judge of its quality, Roe's is a grudging acceptance of the painter's skills, framed as a story in which the skills that are brought to the fore are his own, for he tells the reader he does not have a 'common eye'.

Here, too, Roe subtly emphasises his own skills while revealing those of the Other, since though Jahangir's requests for his 'judgements' flatter the ambassador, they also demonstrate the emperor's curiosity about, and understanding of, artistic techniques. That 'Mughal artists deftly and selectively coopted European subjects as well as stylistic conventions and pictorial realism' has been made clear in recent scholarship, from Bailey and others (Bailey 1998: 25; Keller 2013: 344–7). Nor was this a one-way process since, as Subrahmanyam (2012: 180) has recently demonstrated, from the middle of the seventeenth century, 'vastly greater numbers of Indian paintings began to arrive in Europe, mainly in the Netherlands'. Curiosity developed into artistic experimentation on both sides of the Indo-European exchange.

Yet Jahangir was capable, perhaps even more capable than Roe, of manipulating the representative schema of a picture. In his journal, Roe recalls an occasion on which he was forced to open a cargo of presents in the presence of the emperor:

> Then next he demanded whose the Pictures were. I answered, sent to me to use on occasions, and dispose as my businesse required: so hee called for them, and caused them to be opened, examined me of the women, and other little questions, requiring many judgements of them. (Roe 1625: 564)

Jahangir examines all the pictures closely, including a discussion with Roe about the women featured in them, which perhaps suggests Kerridge was right to assign 'value' based on the social status of the sitter of a portrait; although, of course, this examination reveals that is not an inherent value of the painting, but one that requires an additional explanation to make manifest.

However, once Roe and Jahangir are discussing a scene, rather than a portrait, any sense of shared judgement, or mutual artistic techniques, soon dissipates:

> of the third Picture of *Venus* and a Satyre: he commanded my Interpreter not to tell me what he said: But asked his Lords what they conceived should be the interpretation or morall of that, he shewed the Satyres hornes, his skinne which was swart, and pointed to many particulars: every man replyed according to his fancie; but in the end hee concluded they were all deceived: and seeing they could judge no better, hee would keepe his conceit to himselfe, iterating his command to conceale this passage from me: But bade him aske me what it meant: I answered, an Invention of the Painter to shew his arte, which was Poeticall, but the interpretation was New to mee that had not seene it. Then he called Master *Terry*, to give his judgement, who replying, hee knew not. The King demanded why hee brought vp to him an inuention wherein hee was ignorant.
>
> (Roe 1625: 564)

Roe refuses to offer an interpretation, but attempts to move into the territory that Jahangir claims to occupy in his memoirs, refusing interpretation for a consideration of artistic skill. It is curious that Terry, too, fails to offer an interpretation – and that Jahangir is surprised by this, wondering why the English have presented a painting they cannot explain.

This moment is a triumph of what Greenblatt calls 'improvisation', 'the ability both to capitalize on the unseen, and to transform given materials into one's own scenario' (1980: 227). Indeed, what could be more improvisational than deciphering an unseen painting to gain political-cultural advantage? This, though, is not a Greenblattian imposition of a cultural system onto an external culture (specifically a European mode onto a non-European world), but rather improvisation as contest between two well-developed ideological and semiotic systems.

Although both men claim in their writings to be skilled at interpreting paintings, this moment seems to be about the ability to impose a meaning rather than discern one. (Roe, after all, is as capable as Jahangir at producing the anti-Oriental reading, since he later surmises what Jahangir meant.)

Faced by a non-European with the capacity to improvise, Roe retreats and resorts to stereotypical warnings about untrustworthiness:

> This I repeate for instruction, to warne the company and him that shall succeed me to be very wary what they send, may be subiect to ill Interpretation: for in that point this King and people are very pregnant and scrupulous, full of jealousie and trickes, for that notwithstanding the King conceited himselfe, yet by the passages I will deliver my opinion of this conceit, which (knowing, I had never seene the Picture, and by Ignorance was guiltlesse) hee would not presse hard upon me. But, I suppose, he understood the Morall to be a scorne of *Asiatiques* whom the naked Satyre represented, and was of the same complexion and not unlike; who being held by *Venus* a white woman by the Nose, it seemed that shee led him Captive. Yet he revealed no discontent, but rould them up, and told me he would accept him also as a Present.
>
> (Roe 1625: 565)

As ever, we must be cautious about the actual truth of Roe's words – the idea that Jahangir takes 'no discontent' seems unlikely, even based on Roe's own relation of the scene. But at the heart of that relation is the emperor's unwillingness to be led, and Roe's own powerlessness to lead – he is literally unable to offer any interpretation of the painting, and so Jahangir is left to 'conceit himself', that is develop his own interpretation.

Perhaps we can see, behind the stereotypes, a fear of the Other who is as skilled as the Europeans, able to easily insert himself into European systems and in doing so reveal them as systems, as things that can be exploited and turned back against the visitors to the court. Roe's comments suggest a failure of European agency, unable to perform power as they do in Europe, and unable to enforce a representative or interpretative schema on the new locations in which they find themselves. Jahangir's challenge to the projected fantasy of European power produces no satisfactory answer from Roe, whose base denial and attempts to move the discussion to a more neutral territory of artistic skill are clearly unsuccessful.

These gifts of paintings show us the moves that the company's agents were making towards translatability, whether that came in the form of imposing European ideals, or, more frequently, as accommodation to Indian markets and desires. But this is not to suggest that these were first steps on a smooth path to mutual understanding; rather, they show us the 'process' of intercultural translation, with its difficulties, missteps and misunderstandings. The range of strategies involved in the gifting of paintings reveals the difficulty of constructing a single idea of 'Englishness' or

'Europeanness' in India and the ways in which the EIC was forced to adopt its self-presentation in the face of an Indian market it could neither control nor predict.

References

Bailey, Gauvin Alexander. 1998. 'The Indian Conquest of Catholic Art: The Mughals, the Jesuits, and Imperial Mural Painting', *Art Journal* 57(1): 24–30.

Barbour, Richmond. 2003. *Before Orientalism: London's Theatre of the East, 1576–1626.* Cambridge: Cambridge University Press.

Benton, Lauren, and Richard J. Ross. 2013. 'Jurisdiction, Sovereignty and Political Imagination in the Early Modern World', in Lauren Benton and Richard J. Ross (eds.), *Empires and Legal Pluralism*, pp. 1–21. New York and London: New York University Press.

Cohn, Bernard S. 1996. *Colonialism and Its Forms of Knowledge: The British in India.* Princeton; Chichester: Princeton University Press.

Foster, William, ed. 1896–1902. *Letters Received by the East India Company from Its Servants in the East.* 6 vols. London: S. Low, Marston & Company.

———, ed. 1899. *The Embassy of Sir Thomas Roe.* London: Hakluyt Society.

Foucault, Michel. 1979. *Discipline and Punish: The Birth of the Prison.* Translated by Alan Sheridan. Harmondsworth: Penguin.

———. 2001. *The Order of Things: An Archaeology of the Human Sciences.* London: Routledge.

Games, Alison. 2008. *The Web of Empire: English Cosmopolitans in an Age of Expansion 1560–1660.* Oxford: Oxford University Press.

Greenblatt, Stephen. 1980. *Renaissance Self-Fashioning.* Chicago: University of Chicago Press.

Halliday, Paul D. 2010. *Habeas Corpus: From England to Empire.* Cambridge, MA: Belknap.

Jahángir. 2013. 'Dwásda-Sála-i Jahángírí; Wáki'át Jahángírí', in Henry Miers Elliott and John Dowson (eds.), *The History of India, as Told by Its Own Historians*, Vol VI, pp. 276–391. Cambridge: Cambridge University Press.

Jardine, Lisa, and Jerry Brotton. 2000. *Global Interests: Renaissance Art between East and West.* London: Reaktion.

Keller, Vera. 2013. 'Air Conditioning Jahangir: The 1622 English Great Design, Climate, and the Nature of Global Projects', *Configurations* 21: 331–67.

Levin, Richard. 1984. 'The Contemporary Perception of Marlowe's *Tamburlaine*', in J. Leeds Barroll (ed.), *Medieval and Renaissance Drama in England*, pp. 51–70. New York: AMS Press.

Marlowe, Christopher. 1966. 'Tamburlaine the Great, Part I', in Havelock Ellis (ed.), *Five Plays.* New York: Hill and Wang.

Milton, Anthony. 1994. 'The Unchanged Peacemaker'? John Dury and the Politics of Irenicism in England, 1628–1643', in Mark Greengrass, Michael

Leslie and Timothy Raylor (eds.), *Samuel Hartlib and Universal Reformation*, pp. 95–117. Cambridge: Cambridge University Press.

Mishra, Rupali. 2014. 'Diplomacy at the Edge: Split Interests in the Roe Embassy to the Mughal Court', *Journal of British Studies* 53(1): 5–28.

Ogborn, Miles. 2007. *Indian Ink: Script and Print in the Making of the East India Company*. Chicago: University of Chicago Press.

Roe, Thomas. 1625. 'Obseruations Collected Out of the Iournall of Sir THOMAS ROE, Knight, Lord Embassadour from His MAIESTIE of Great Britaine, to the Great Mogol', in Samuel Purchas (ed.), *Hakluytus Posthumus, or Purchas, His Pilgrimmes*, pp. 536–78. London.

Rubiés, Joan-Pau. 2005. 'Oriental Despotism and European Orientalism: Botero to Montesquieu', *Journal of Early Modern History* 9(1): 109–80.

Sainsbury, W. Noel (ed.). 1862. *Calendar of State Papers: Colonial: East Indies, 1513–1616*. London: HMSO.

Screech, Timon. 2005. '"Pictures (the Most Part Bawdy)": The Anglo-Japanese Painting Trade in the Early 1600s', *The Art Bulletin* 87(1): 50–72.

Singh, Jyotsna G. 1996. *Colonial Narrative/Cultural Dialogues: 'Discoveries' of India in the Language of Colonialism*. New York: Routledge.

Subrahmanyam, Sanjay. 2002. 'Frank Submissions: The Company and the Mughals between Sir Thomas Roe and Sir William Norris', in H. V. Bowen, Margarette Lincoln and Nigel Rigby (eds.), *The Worlds of the East India Company*, pp. 69–96. Woodbridge: Boydell.

———. 2012. *Courtly Encounters: Translating Courtliness and Violence in Early Modern Eurasia*. Cambridge, MA: Harvard University Press.

Wisecup, Kelly. 2013. 'Encounters, Objects and Commodity Lists in Early English Travel Narratives', *Studies in Travel Writing* 17(3): 264–80.

Withington, Phil. 2010. *Society in Early Modern England: The Vernacular Origins of Some Powerful Ideas*. Cambridge: Polity.

10 The contested state

Political authority and the decentred foundations of the early modern colonial state in Asia

David Veevers

In recent years, there has been a shift in the direction of the historiography of the English East India Company, both in terms of the period studied and in terms of the focus of the historian. Up until the past few years, the field was proliferate with research on the commercial activities of the company and its servants in eighteenth-century India. The company was, after all, a corporation, and the eighteenth century represents the most visible period of its expansion. Such research traces its heritage back to Holden Furber's pioneering study *John Company at Work* (1948) and arguably culminated in the works of eminent historians P. J. Marshall (1976) and the late C. A. Bayly, especially the latter's most definitive monograph, *Rulers, Townsmen and Bazaars* (1983). These studies revealed the breadth and depth of connections between the company's European servants and the Indian societies they interacted with and lived among. There was little of the coloniser-and-colonised dynamic of traditional early twentieth-century histories of the British in Asia, but rather a culture and practicality of cooperation and interdependence. Indeed, some historians describe the relationship between company servants and Indians in the eighteenth century as creating an 'Age of Partnership' (Kling and Pearson 1986), while Bayly revealed how European expansion relied entirely on the pre-existing networks of Indian capital and credit made available to them by certain groups of Indian elites.

The recent shift has been two fold. The corpus of research on the commercial nature of the company and the cross-cultural activities of its servants revealed the longer 'pre-colonial' history of the company in Asia, a period that has often been described in relation to the company as the 'Dark Age' (Keay 1991: 220–1). Thus new and innovative research is shedding light on the company's seventeenth-century engagement with Asian commerce, significantly from a – most welcomed – social perspective (Mentz 2005; Erikson 2014). Such research has helped to provide glimpses of an earlier history of the company that is far less a sedate precursor to the rampaging imperialisms of the eighteenth century, and far more of an expansive, dynamic and complex foundation for an emerging colonial polity. Indeed, the emphasis on the company as a state in its own right is perhaps the most exciting new thread to emerge from this tapestry of cutting-edge research. With the publication of Philip J. Stern's groundbreaking book *The Company-State* in 2011, historians have been forced to reinterpret the traditionally accepted 'trade-to-empire' narrative of the company in Asia. The company was a 'body politic', capable of waging war, planting colonies, raising taxes and exercising sovereignty. According to Stern, while often contested by other commercial groups and even the British state itself, the company's chartered rights as granted by the Crown allowed it to construct a colonial polity beyond the Cape of Good Hope, which largely determined the political foundations of the company in Asia well into the eighteenth century. It has therefore become more appropriate to recognise Europe's overseas corporations as early as the seventeenth century as 'company states', and not just 'mere merchants' (Weststejin 2014).

We therefore stand on the threshold of a new historiographical direction in the study of the company and of the British Empire in Asia more widely, one that focuses on the political character of the company before the late eighteenth century. As we move forward, however, it is important that political understandings of the company as an institution capable of projecting sovereign power and building state structures do not erase an earlier generation of historiography. The complex, fluid and private relationships between company servants and Indians that largely determined the political landscape in India – often against the metropole's wishes – must continue to have a role in our understandings of the development of the British Empire in Asia (Veevers 2013). Indeed, as Anna Winterbottom concluded when studying the networks of knowledge within the company in the seventeenth century, the actual practice of the company in Asia, beyond East India House, its Crown charters and the metropole, proved 'a far more chaotic reality' (2010: 8). The trend towards perceiving the company as a monolithic institution in which social relationships and political authority in Asia could be sufficiently regulated is in danger of papering over the cracks, fissures and the generally eclectic nature of early modern colonial state formation (Ogborn 2007: 69–70).

This chapter seeks to explore the decentred and contested nature of the English East India Company's emerging colonial state in Asia in the seventeenth century. It argues that the processes of state formation evolved around a shifting nexus of interpersonal relationships forged between Europeans and non-Europeans in the service of the company. Such relationships allowed company servants to acquire political authority, often beyond the limits imposed upon them by East India House and their highly coveted royal charters. In turn, Asian allies and partners could exercise political agency by directly engaging with the company, shaping the political landscape around them in places such as Madras in an often transformative manner. Whether through financial opportunity, social elevation or political influence, Europeans and Asians joined together to determine the development of the company for their own advantage.

In the late seventeenth century, it became apparent that the fluid and unregulated nature of political authority within the company facilitated struggles for political power within its Asian settlements. This naturally created a contested dynamic between company servants, especially when new arrivals from London attempted to enforce their authority according to their mandate from East India House, rather than integrating themselves into the local political landscape by establishing profitable and influential relationships with non-Europeans. In the contest over power, conflict between company servants became endemic and, at times, destructive, as Europeans and non-Europeans resorted to physical force, murder and even rebellion to acquire or increase their political authority. This chapter will present a case study of Madras in the 1660s, a turbulent phase of the company's development in India when the contest over political authority revealed the formative role played by Anglo-Indian 'connections' in decentring the emerging colonial polity. It will then place this within the context of the growth of the company's community in Asia and analyse the links established between Europeans and non-Europeans in the form of interracial families, business partnerships and political factions.

'Wee are the companys servants': Anglo-Indian connections in Asia

On 16 September 1665, Sir Edward Winter, a deposed agent of Madras, launched a 'coup' and seized by force Fort St. George, the English East India Company's most important possession on the Coromandel Coast, if not in all of Asia. Sir Edward, accompanied by a gang of armed accomplices, burst into the council chambers and, in a hail of gunfire, injured the new agent of Madras, Sir George Foxcroft, and his son Nathaniel Foxcroft, and shot dead William Dawes, a member of the council. After this attack, Sir George and his son were imprisoned and, according to the agent himself, Sir Edward 'became possessed of the Fort by rebellion, blood and murder' (Love 1913: 1.230–9). For the next three years, Sir Edward ruled Madras through a regime of terror and violence. According to one witness, he 'did burne the faces, drub and otherwise punish' any who refused to 'comply' with his new regime and 'justifie his usupration' (Love 1913: 1.242). Further bloodletting was to follow, and it was soon widely known that within Madras those who opposed the usurper were 'cruelly and barbarously burnt and mangled', and many left to languish in the cells of Fort St. George (IOR G/40/3, Captain Hutchins, Surat, 15 March 1666). In fact, the cells became so full of prisoners that Sir Edward was forced to convert the 'godowns' into makeshift prisons (Love 1913: 1.242).

The cause of this seemingly unprecedented and exceptional event, known to Sir Edward as a 'revolution' and to his masters at East India House in London as a 'rebellion', seemed simple enough. According to Sir Edward and his supporters, Sir George and his son Nathaniel had publically used 'severall seditious and treasonable words . . . against his now Majestie Charles the Second, King of England'. They therefore justified their 'revolution' as a defence of the Crown's sovereignty and, in letters to East India House, charged the Foxcrofts with the 'weight of treason against his Majestie' (Love 1913: 1.225–7). Yet there was nothing unprecedented or exceptional about Sir Edward Winter's rebellion at Madras, let alone the way in which his supporters attempted to justify it. Rebellion was a frequent recourse for company servants seeking to contest political authority, either with their masters at East India House or with their rivals in Asia. In fact, there were seven rebellions throughout the company's settlements between 1665 and 1713. On the island of Bombay in 1683, for example Richard Keigwin, a commander of the company's cavalry, led a rebellion that established a new regime claiming legitimacy directly from the Crown and refusing to acknowledge the authority of the company (Stern 2011: 64–65). While constitutional tensions undoubtedly provided a common undercurrent to rebellions within the company, they acted more as a retrospective justification of violent seizures of power than a direct cause of the willingness of company servants to contest political authority, and in doing so provided such acts with a thin veil of legitimacy. This was certainly the case at Madras, where the claim of treason to the Crown was made over a month after the supposed offence had transpired.

Beyond the superficial notion of royal duty and the charges of treason, the causes of Sir Edward Winter's rebellion were more complex and entrenched, revealing the way in which non-European agency could engage with and reshape the dynamic of political authority within the company in Asia in the seventeenth century. During his own period as agent of Madras between 1662 and 1665, Sir Edward had been under investigation by East India House for corruption, especially in using company funds for his own private trade and for monopolising provisions and commercial goods at Madras (IOR E/3/86, Court of Committees to Madras, London, 16 December 1663). In 1664 Nicholas Buckeridge arrived from London to investigate these claims and within a year had compiled an extensive list of frauds and crimes committed by Sir Edward. The latter was outraged that the supervisor had dared to contest his authority as governor, let alone 'to prescribe mee rules and Orders' (IOR E/3/86, Court of Committees to Madras, London, 21 December 1664). He proceeded to rail to East India House that he was now an 'Agent of Wax', shaped by others. 'The world is now come to that passe that all are Councellors', he continued, 'and there's scarcely any left to bee Commanded, and less that will obey any thing that is ordered hence' (IOR G/40/3, Madras to Court of Committees, Madras, 12 January 1665). Despite his protestations, Sir Edward was superseded as agent in June 1665 when Sir George Foxcroft arrived at Madras.

The new agent had been appointed specifically to reform the political corruption facilitated by Sir Edward (IOR E/3/86, Court of Committees to Madras, London, 21 December 1664). The latter was immediately demoted to second of council, and Sir George set about investigating his predecessor's frauds, embezzlements, favouritism and monopolisation of trade. However, Sir Edward did not intend to acquiesce in the formal structures of power created by East India House and the corporate hierarchies that were projected from London. As the new agent's rigorous audit of Sir Edward's accounts began to uncover the extent of the latter's corruption, he decided to reject Sir George's authority over Madras and usurp East India House's legitimately appointed agent and the delegated power he exercised on behalf of his masters in London. As Sir George informed East India House through correspondence smuggled out of his gaol shortly after being imprisoned, Sir Edward had launched his coup quite simply 'to nest himself in this Fort and not to obey any of your Commands' (IOR G/40/3, George Foxcroft to Court of Committees, Madras, 8 September 1666). The superseded agent resented the loss of his authority and believed that the use of force was an acceptable way in which to contest his threatened position.

Through their alliance and collaboration with non-European groups, company servants like Sir Edward Winter and his supporters were able to contest political authority within Asia and even subvert and refashion the corporate framework imposed upon them by East India House. For their part, prominent Indians at Madras were able to exploit the contested dynamic of company power relations to elevate their own standing within the Indian community and to enrich their business interests. Indeed, the longevity of Sir Edward's regime at Madras was made possible through his alliance with two of the most powerful individuals at Madras: Beri Timmanna and Kasi Viranna, known, respectively, to company servants as the 'black' merchants 'Timothy' and 'Verona'. Although they were appointed as the company's chief merchants at Madras – later to be known as *dubash* – Timmanna and Viranna were more than just mere 'merchants'. They were also governors, diplomats, patrons and caste leaders. Take Beri Timmana, for example. He had become a prominent figure in Madras barely more than a decade after the settlement was founded. He was crucial in provisioning the fledgling settlement with vital goods, and his control of the rice trade made him a powerful figure, both to Madras's growing Indian population and to the company's establishment (Mukund 1999: 70). For this reason, Timmanna was privately employed by the early agents of Madras, providing them with credit and managing their private trade (Mukund 2005: 137). Meanwhile, Timmanna's brothers, Pedda Venkatadri and Chinna Venkatadri, were leaders of the right-hand castes of Madras and could thus command the loyalty and support of tens of thousands within the city (Mukund 1999: 149). Timmanna also wielded considerable religious power. As a major city patron, he constructed Madras's two Hindu temples, a project he financed by levying a tax on the town's inhabitants (Mukund 1999: 70). Furthermore, along with Viranna, Timmanna constructed the city's granary warehouse, jointly oversaw the city's mint and coinage and, perhaps most important, managed the *choultry*, an institution that acted as a combination of customs house, law court and town hall, before the reforms of Streynsham Master in the 1680s (Madras Diary: 1.90). Prominent Indian elites such as Timmanna and Viranna could thus become so integrated into the everyday workings of the fledgling polity at Madras that they considered themselves no less part of the company than their European partners. 'Wee are the Companys Servants', declared two long-serving Brahmins to the agent of Madras in 1654 (Love 1913: 1.142). And as company servants, they too could shape the political landscape of Madras.

The heights of power and influence Timmanna had reached by the 1660s meant that he was often distrusted by company servants at Madras, and he was frequently accused of various crimes. One early accusation was that he had met disaffected company servants in secret and encouraged them to launch a coup against the agent in 1654 (Love 1913: 1.142). However, when Sir Edward Winter was appointed agent in 1663, Timmanna's stature was such that he was entrusted with handling all of the company's investment at Madras, he being 'the Company's ancient broker, a person only experienced and trusted at present in the extremity of time' (Mukund 2005: 137). Although Timmanna was frequently described as Sir Edward's 'creature', his willingness to serve the latter's interests was the result of a violent struggle between both of them. Sir Edward feared Timmanna's influence over Madras and wrote to his brother that he believed Timmanna had 'employed people to bewitch me to death' (Mukund 2005: 138). The agent's ability to conduct the company's trade was also hostage to Timmanna's control of commerce at Madras. Again to his brother, Sir Edward anxiously wrote that should Timmanna have refused to manage the company's investment, 'we could not possibly send home full returns annually' (Mukund 2005: 137). Aware of his vulnerability and dependence, Sir Edward exercised his authority as agent and used force to subordinate Timmanna to his interests. The latter was presently imprisoned, and Sir Edward had a gallows erected in the middle of Fort St. George, threatening to hang him. After this demonstration of violence, Timmanna was released upon payment of 20,000 pagodas to Sir Edward and from then on agreed to become both his and the company's agent (Mukund 2005: 137).

'Usurpers of your power': the struggle for political mastery in Madras

The triumvirate of Sir Edward Winter, Beri Timmanna and Kasi Viranna achieved a staggering hold over Madras from 1663, reaping substantial financial, social and political rewards. Just one example that Sir George Foxcroft quickly uncovered during his investigation was the way in which Sir Edward had arranged the company's cotton investment exclusively through Timmanna and Viranna. They in turn charged an excessive rate and split the profits with Sir Edward. In this manner, as Sir George reported to East India House, the triumvirate 'joyned to defraud you' (IOR G/40/3, George Foxcroft to Court of Committees, Madras, 26 September 1665). Beyond the financial incentives, their alliance with Sir Edward allowed Timmanna and Viranna to engage with the company politically and exercise a form of agency that enabled them to shape the foundations of the emerging colonial state at Madras. After shortly arriving as the new agent, Sir George discovered that Timmanna and Viranna 'had the Government of your Towne of Madrass-Patna . . . the people had such a feare of those persons . . . that no man durst adventure to come to make any proposals to deale with us' (IOR G/40/3, George Foxcroft to Court of Committees, Madras, 26 September 1665). Sir George echoed a host of company servants who complained about the political power gathered up in the hands of those they contemptuously perceived to be two 'black' merchants, virtually governing as they did the city through their alliance with Sir Edward. In 1659 Reverend William Isaacson, who had been stationed at Madras, informed East India House upon his return to London that 'onely the Agent and Timana, a blacke servant, are privy to all passages, and those that were appointed by the Hon[ourab]le Company to be of the Councell cold never be calld to advise with them' (Love 1913: 1.179–80). Timmanna and Viranna acquired and exercised as much political authority at Madras as the agent, perhaps even more so. This was reflected in the custom of *tashreef*. When a new agent was appointed at Madras, the neighbouring Naik of Poonamalee would dispatch a dress of honour to the agent as a diplomatic gesture. Significantly, however, Naik also sent one to the chief merchant, as the Naik Mahmud Ibrahim did to Viranna when Streynsham Master was appointed agent in 1678 (Madras Diary: 2.77).

The political landscape Sir George Foxcroft found himself in upon his arrival at Madras in 1665 was therefore one that had largely been engineered by the Anglo-Indian triumvirate. The new agent's policy of systematically reshaping this landscape was ultimately what provoked a fierce reaction from those who benefitted from the regime of Sir Edward, Timmanna and Viranna. Indeed, Sir George began his government by demoting Sir Edward to second of council for six months, after which time he was to be removed from the company's service. Timmanna and Viranna were also stripped of their authority when Sir George removed them from managing the *choultry*, replacing them with William Dawes, secretary to the council. Yet despite thoroughly undermining the triumvirate's hold over Madras, Sir George discovered that the Anglo-Indian alliance was entrenched throughout Madras. 'What influence Sir Edward on the one hand, and Timana and Verona had on the other', the agent complained to East India House, 'hold up a combination against us'. Only when Sir George divested Timmanna and Viranna of managing the company's investment as chief merchants in July, and then had them seized and imprisoned, did he finally believe that 'at length we broke the combination' (IOR G/40/3, George Foxcroft to Court of Committees, Madras, 26 September 1665). In doing so, however, Sir George threatened the fabric of cooperation, dependence and alliance between company servants and Indian elites that early colonial Madras had been raised upon and subsequently shaped by.

Before the coup that deposed him, Sir George was exposed to a taste of the forces stirring against his policy of undermining the Anglo-Indian alliance at Madras. In early September, Sir Edward marched into the council chambers with an armed 'confederacy' that included a mixture of European officers from the garrison and company servants. Significantly, however, they were also joined by a retinue of 'black attendants', comprising Indian elites similar to the imprisoned Timmanna and Viranna. Despite this, Sir Edward failed to intimidate the agent and after exchanging 'hot words' was forced to retire rather humiliatingly. However, when Sir George ordered the garrison to arrest Sir Edward, they hesitated, and although 'after long demurr' eventually imprisoned him, after forty-eight hours they released him against the agent's orders (IOR G/40/3, George Foxcroft to Court of Committees, Madras, 26 September 1665). Shortly afterwards, on 16 September, the confederacy regrouped and once again stormed the council chambers but this time, as related earlier, succeeded in their endeavour to remove Sir George.

Once power had been seized by Sir Edward and his confederacy, the authority and legitimacy of the regime they established continued to be contested. Over the course of its three-year existence, it had to contend with a range of opposition groups within and outside the city. Two attempts were made to retake Madras by force, one in 1666 from the crew of the company's ship *Greyhound*, and the other by an expedition launched from the neighbouring company settlement of Masulipatnam in 1667; both failed miserably and swelled Madras's prison population further (IOR G/40/3, Madras to Court of Committees, Madras, 29 October 1667). One such captive, Benjamin Brond, wrote shortly after to East India House that he hoped they would not fail to punish 'such murderers and usurpers of your power' (IOR G/40/3, Benjamin Brond to Court of Committees, Madras, 14 October 1666). Opposition to Sir Edward's political authority was more serious within the walls of the city, however. Alongside the endless stream of Europeans imprisoned, those Indian elites who opposed the new regime were also confined to gaol, many of whom shared cells with company servants (IOR G/40/3, George Foxcroft to Court of Committees, Madras, 8 September 1666). Sir Edward defended his seizure of power and tightened his grip on Madras by utilising the resources and support of the settlement's culturally diverse community. Support to enforce Sir Edward's rule came from two prominent groups: Indians and Indo-Portuguese. As so many European soldiers had to be purged due to suspected disloyalty or outright opposition, Sir Edward relied on a greatly expanded personal bodyguard to carry out his policies, made up entirely of Indian soldiers, or peons. As far away as Surat, the governor, Sir George Oxenden, heard reports of how Sir Edward had expelled his English garrison, 'confiding altogether in his black Guards' (IOR G/40/3, Surat to Court of Committees, Surat, 26 March 1667). Alongside these, however, Sir Edward relied heavily on Madras's substantial mixed-race Indo-Portuguese community, also known as *topasses*. Dominic Navarette, a Spanish priest who visited Madras around 1670 in the wake of what he described as 'a great contest betwixt two English governors', related how 'the Portugueses were divided, some favour'd the one, and others the other. One got the better, and banish'd many of the Portugueses that oppose'd him, together with the French Capuchins' (Love 1913: 1.278–9). After purging those European soldiers who refused to 'justifie his usurpation', Sir Edward recruited the loyal *topasses* to take their place. As Sir George related to East India House, Sir Edward 'fills the Fort with Portingalls in Liew of the English that are gone and in prison and dead' (IOR G/40/3, George Foxcroft to Court of Committees, Madras, 8 September 1666).

Despite gaining firm control of Madras, Sir Edward's confederacy of disaffected company officers and servants, Indian elites, lowly peons and loyal topasses could not resist a further contest over their political authority which materialised in 1668 when a flotilla of warships sailed into the

Madras road. They had been despatched from London by East India House to seize back control of the city. The threat of overwhelming military force was enough to force Sir Edward's regime to capitulate peacefully, conceding power to the expedition's leader, who presently released and restored Sir George Foxcroft as agent (IOR G/40/3, Joseph Hall to Court of Committees, Madras, 8 December 1668). Remarkably, there were no punishments for the three years of what many deemed to have been a regime of terror and violence. Sir Edward Winter himself was allowed to continue to live at Madras, where he remained until returning to Britain in 1672, while Timmanna and Viranna were restored to all of their offices and power. Only Sir George Foxcroft found this astonishing, observing that in allowing his captor to not only walk free, but remain a resident of Madras, would further 'begot troble to us and prejudice to you' (G/40/3, Madras to Court of Committees, Madras, 8 October 1668). However, Sir George, who had never previously been to India and had little knowledge or experience of the company's presence there, failed to realise that such contests over power were part of the fluid and shifting dynamic of political authority within the company in Asia. But as one company servant observed of Sir George's unfortunate situation, 'I looke upon the company as having bin especially [guilty] . . . in sending an Agent out that was never in India' (Love 1913: 1.224). And although they were rarely as violent as Sir Edward's regime, frequent rebellions and day-to-day factionalism and struggles for mastery throughout the company's settlements served to shape and constantly reshape the way in which the company functioned in Asia. East India House did not fail to prosecute Sir Edward, but rather chose not to as it accepted such contests as inherent within a disparate and complex global community. In fact, the contest for mastery in Asia was so endemic, and the power dynamic within their settlements in such constant flux, that in 1681 East India House ordered that whenever their ships arrived at one of their settlements, before they could dock and land their cargo or passengers, they first had to verify that those in charge of the settlement were those who had been appointed by East India House, and had not themselves seized power. This would, they argued, 'prevent ye worst that Mad men may do in disobedience or rebellion to our Authority' (IOR E/3/99, Court of Committees to Bengal, London, 8 November 1681).

'A mixt nation': the company's polyglot communities in Asia

The connections between Europeans and non-Europeans in India were not merely opportunistic or expedient. There was an organic growth of long-term relationships between the two groups, a process that produced interracial and cross-cultural communities right across the subcontinent in the seventeenth century, facilitating the emergence of a far more amorphous polity than historians have previously accepted. The blending of Europeans and non-Europeans served to decentre the contested dynamic of the colonial polity even further, as political authority dissipated throughout the thickening web of interpersonal and even familial connections which increasingly bound the company's colonial communities together. Significantly, this process increased the agency of non-Europeans within the company.

The new judiciary established at Madras in 1687 encapsulates the way in which private cross-cultural ties served to decentre the formal frameworks of the company. Before 1687, legal matters were dealt with in the town *choultry* or, as was more often common among Europeans, settled privately through petitions to the agent or even by duelling in the streets. However, the new law courts were intended to provide a legal regulatory framework in which company servants would have to operate. However, as described by the historian Mattison Mines, the new judiciary was 'highly personalized, antagonisms were rife, and relationships constantly in flux, a product of personal competition and opportunistic alliances between individuals rather than of company hegemony or even local social hierarchy' (2001: 37). The new courts were rapidly manipulated and controlled by powerful factions within Madras who used them to exercise their influence or contest political authority. Indians played a major role in this. One of the new courts, the Mayor's Court, consisted of twelve judges, half of whom were usually non-European (Brimnes 2003). Indian elites frequently utilised the Mayor's Court to prosecute political enemies and commercial rivals. As one disparaging company servant observed, Indians in the Mayor's Court deployed all 'manner of villany, for swearing, lying, forging, or any other vile action to gain their end' (Wheeler 1861: 43–44). In the early eighteenth century, Chitteramah Chittee, son of a former *dubash* (chief merchant), even brought a case against the governor of Madras himself, James Macrae. Chittee brought in a number of Indian allies as witnesses to testify against Macrae, and the case was successful (Mines 2001: 46–51).

The undermining and refashioning of the newly established judiciary at Madras, an institution which was supposed to formalise and regulate the social lives of the company's servants and subjects, serves to illustrate the extent to which the company's communities had themselves been reshaped by decades of interracial relationships, alliances and, increasingly, family ties. The formation of mixed-race families had particularly served to blur and negate the company's formal chartered boundaries through the porous and shifting social, cultural, commercial and political exchanges which took place within such familial networks, connecting company servants into regional and even global Asian societies (Veevers 2015). Historians have seldom looked at the interracial family dynamic of the company's settlements before the late eighteenth century. However, 'company families', as I term these interracial formations, became increasingly important as early as the seventeenth century, and were themselves a product of the increasingly cross-cultural makeup of the company's communities in Asia, their unregulated and rapid growth having become strongly evident to East India House in the late seventeenth century.

Following Sir Edward Winter's rebellion at Madras, East India House became increasingly concerned that the growth of the company in Asia was serving to destabilise their authority over their servants and settlements. Shortly after regaining control of Madras in 1668, the court of committees temporarily halted employment to the company's service, declaring that further growth would cause their 'affaires not to bee well manadged' (IOR E/3/87, Court of Committees to Madras, London, 20 November 1668). However, the Madras agency continued to expand at an unsettling rate, which the committees acknowledged in 1675, observing 'how numerous the people grow' (IOR E/3/87, 24 December 1675). The committees were not referring to their European servants alone, of course. Less than a hundred company servants across an area the size of the Madras agency presents a modest, or even microscopic, community. Yet the unofficial, even unacknowledged, servants of the company – soldiers, sailors, commercial brokers, diplomats, apprentices, wives, children, kin, all of whom engaged and shaped the company to an extent – made this a far more amorphous community: hard to measure, difficult to record and impossible to regulate, especially from London. For example, alongside the 200–300 European soldiers maintained at Madras were the vast number of auxiliary forces, raised locally and maintained often contrary to the orders of the committees in London, who were constantly ordering their servants to affect a retrenchment and stop 'indulging their ambition in setting up one petty Prince or putting down another' (IOR E/3/98, Court of Directors to Bencoolen, London, 13 January 1713). On the west coast of Sumatra, for example the deputy-governor commanded a garrison of 100 Europeans, but also recruited the same number again of Indo-Portuguese *topasses*, as well as native Malay troops from the surrounding villages (IOR G/35/8, A List of Covenanted Servants Now at York Fort, Bencoolen, 25 August 1713). In addition to this, they raised a unit of fifty Madagascan slaves whom they found particularly suited to quelling discontent in the hinterland (Allen 2014: 81).

The polyglot make-up of the company's military garrisons was reflected in its civil establishment, too. The company's covenanted servants included men like Thomas Clarke, a favourite of Sir Edward Winter. Clarke was the son of Thomas Clarke senior, the first agent of Masulipatnam, and his Indian wife, whose name is unknown. Sir George Foxcroft noted Clarke's interracial heritage when he observed that he had been 'borne in the Countrie and never out of it' (IOR G/40/3, George Foxcroft to Court of Committees, Madras, 26 September 1665). He was fluent in Persian, Hindi, Portuguese and Dutch, and for that reason was appointed by Sir George to the *choultry*, which dealt predominantly with non-European affairs (IOR G/40/3, Madras to Court of Committees, Madras, 6 September 1671). Clarke's wife was also of mixed-race, having married an Indo-Portuguese lady named Elizabeth Hartley (Love 1913: 1.466). The establishment of such families was the norm in places such as Madras. Of the estimated 80,000 people living there by the turn of the eighteenth century, there were approximately 300 British and 3,000 Indo-Portuguese, while the rest were predominantly Indian. It is little wonder that Sir Edward Winter described Madras as a 'mixt Nation' (IOR G/40/3, Madras to Court of Committees, Madras, 9 January 1666). In fact, of the thirty-eight wives recorded among company servants at Madras in 1700, twenty-one were non-European (Love 1913: 2.64–6). What is clear, however, is that the majority of European men in India in this period would have maintained extra-marital relations with non-European women, perhaps even multiple ones, and often maintained the mixed-race families which were a product of such unions. Indeed, when figures became available later in the eighteenth century, over half of all children baptised at St. John's Church in Calcutta, for example, were described as 'natural children', meaning that they were both illegitimate and of mixed-race (Ghosh 2006: 39–40).

Even before Calcutta had become a bastion of company power in Asia, the company's settlements across Bengal in the seventeenth century reflected the proliferation of 'Company families' and revealed the extent to which colonial communities had established a hybridised polity. Two years after the company acquired a farman in 1698 for the settlement that became known as Calcutta, Edward Littleton remarked how numerous the population of the fledgling community had grown. In writing to East India House, he was particularly interested in the fact that so many 'servants should intermarry with any of the people of the Country or those of mixed Race'. Edward Littleton curiously observed that this custom did not exist in the settlements of the Danish East India Company, 'they being all suplyed with Europe Women' (Yule 1888: 2.264). This in itself fails to explain why company servants chose to marry, cohabit and raise families with non-European women in the seventeenth century. For European women were present in Asia, often following their sons, brothers, fathers or husbands out with them in the service, frequently marrying European men operating in places such as Bengal (Veevers 2015: 119). Rather, beyond the obvious factors of sexual opportunity and romantic attraction, interracial family formations allowed company servants to draw on powerful local sources of political, economic, social and cultural authority in their attempts to refashion the political landscape in which the company's settlements were situated.

William Hedges, newly appointed agent of Bengal, arrived in India in 1682. Much like Sir George Foxcroft at Madras, Hedges had no previous experience in Asia, and his policies for governing the Bengal agency had been formulated in the distant courts of East India House in London, from where he had been plucked and charged with reforming the agency. His most important instruction was to remove the incumbent agent, Matthias Vincent, who had been accused of a host of corrupt practices, including fraud, supporting interlopers and even murder (Yule 1888: 2.15–9). Unfortunately for Hedges, the political landscape of the company's settlements in Bengal was alien to him and, because Vincent had been tipped off shortly before Hedges' arrival that he was to be deposed and taken back to London as a prisoner, visibly hostile as well. Vincent had been in Bengal for twenty years and, while being chief of Kasimbazar, had married an Indo-Portuguese woman. Beyond the social and cultural implications of such a union, there were also religious consequences which similarly muddled the Anglicanism enshrined in the company's charters. 'We are informed that Our Factory of Cassambazar', declared the court of committees to Bengal in 1675, 'is frequently visited by Jesuits and Romish Priests, that goe up and downe to Mr. Vincents wife and family'. If Vincent wished to remain as chief, the practice had to be 'wholly refrayned' (IOR E/3/87, Court of Committees to Madras, London, 24 December 1675). But as more company servants married Indo-Portuguese women, Catholicism spread throughout the company's settlements. On a tour of Bengal in 1693, Sir John Goldsborough observed the disregard the 'agent had for our Religion, and by the Incouragement [his] wife had putt into the Papists, by whose Example severall of English men's black wives turned Papist that were not soe before' (Yule 1888: 2.122–3).

Vincent frequently utilised his interracial family to extend his de facto control over the company's settlements in Bengal. The year before Hedges's arrival in 1682, another company servant who opposed Vincent had felt the full force of his power and influence in Bengal. John Thomas, a member of Vincent's council at Hugli, related to East India House his harrowing suffering at the hands of Vincent and his allies. The latter, so Thomas claimed, had 'practised Diabolicall arts with the Braminees' which included 'bewitching' Thomas, so as to allow Vincent to 'better fulfil his lustfull desires with his Wife'. To East India House's horror, they were told how Vincent had used 'charmes' and 'poyson' against his victims in Bengal, chaining Thomas to a 'Stake' and subjecting him to 'inhuman cruelty' with the help of 'Witches or other Natives'. That Thomas suffered from mental illness was clear to see, but the court refused to consider it a natural affliction, choosing rather to believe that his 'distemper' had been caused by Vincent's 'barbarities' (Yule 1888: 2.345). Although it is nonsense to believe that Vincent resorted to witchcraft in his contest for power with Thomas, the colourful story serves to highlight the private connections Vincent had established in Bengal, with both Indian and Indo-Portuguese groups.

This was most visible when Hedges landed at Hugli to capture Vincent and take him back to London in chains. Having been forewarned, Vincent issued out of the company's factory at Hugli with what amounted to a small army of Indian and Indo-Portuguese soldiers 'well armed' (Yule 1888: 1.32–3). Gravely outmatched by this show of force, Hedges was unable to seize Vincent, who proceeded to evacuate his family, papers and goods from Hugli to the Dutch settlement of Chinsurah further upstream. In the meantime, Vincent sent forty soldiers to capture the flotilla Hedges arrived. Cut-off, he attempted to pursue Vincent by land, but was soon overtaken by a small Mughal force sent to by the governor of Hugli to the assistance of Vincent (Yule 1888: 1.32–3). Shortly after, Vincent's nephew, the interloper Thomas Pitt, landed at Hugli 'with 4 or 5 files of soldiers in red coats, well armed, and great attendance of Native Soldiers and Trumpeters' (Dalton 1915: 36). Vincent was now effectively impervious to arrest, surrounded by a vast force, supported by the resources of his family, sheltering beyond the company's jurisdiction, and protected by the Mughal governor. Beyond the reach of Hedges, Vincent and his family built new warehouses, gained a farman from the Mughal governor of Hugli to begin a new commerce and 'by Vincents influence' managed to engage 'the Companys black Merchants', to the horror of Hedges and his masters in London (Yule 1888: 3.11).

Hedges spent two more years engaged in conflict with Vincent in Bengal, but to little effect. After attempting to contest the growing power of Job Charnock at Kasimbazar, who had married a Rajput 'princess' named 'Maria' and was described as reigning 'more absolute than a Rajah', Hedges had become a spent force: undermined, defeated and excluded from government (Hamilton 1930: 1.8–9). In 1683 he fled Bengal on an interloping vessel bound for Persia (Dalton 1915: 46). It was little wonder that one former agent of Bengal believed that the success of company servants in contesting the corporate and chartered authority of the company in Asia was due entirely to their utilisation of interracial family networks. The solution was clear: 'A Standing Rule that none Doe Rise in your Service . . . that shall marry with any of the Country not of Europe parents, but immediately bee Discharged from being either Factor, Merchant or higher quality' (Yule 1888: 2.264).

Conclusion

The struggle for power at Madras in the 1660s challenges previously held notions about the early colonial polity in Asia, and more specifically about the nature of the English East India Company in the seventeenth century. Principally, it betrays how political authority was not a static, defined and formal asset, monopolised by a powerful metropolitan centre which regulated its delegation to distant subordinate agents. Rather, it was a fluid, dynamic and amorphous currency, one that was frequently contested, often through spectacular violence. As the sociologist Pierre Bourdieu defined it, in the early modern period political authority remained 'diffuse' and was not 'institutionally guaranteed. It can only be lastingly maintained through actions whose conformity to the values recognised by the group is a practical reaffirmation of that authority' (1994: 188). This was very much the case within the contested interracial communities of the early modern colonial polity in Asia. Even more revealing is the way in which political authority could be shaped and reshaped through non-European agency, transforming the company itself by, for example pulling down or raising up regimes such as that of Sir Edward Winter. Indian elites, as political leviathans in their own right, facilitated the flow of political authority within Madras, and acquired and exercised it for their own ends, becoming just as powerful, or more so, than the company's European agents and servants.

The political landscape of places such as early colonial Bengal similarly reveals a more complex and shifting understanding of the company's communities in Asia than traditional narratives of 'White town' and 'Black town' or 'English' and 'Indian' suggest. Rather, it was a landscape peopled by Anglo-Indian confederacies, mixed-raced families, violent rebellions and the never-ending refashioning of the political dynamic within the company. Only those who came to Asia with no prior experience and little knowledge of the company's engagement there, men such as Sir George Foxcroft and William Hedges, dared to transform this landscape, and their ultimate failures reveal how proliferate and entrenched the cross-cultural nature of the early colonial polity proved to be. In conclusion, it may therefore be more accurate to consider the company in the seventeenth century as less of a 'company state', and more of a 'Contested-State'.

References

Manuscript

EIC Factory Records, Miscellaneous: 1664–1681. IOR G/40/3.
EIC Factory Records, Sumatra: 1711–1737. IOR G/35/8.
EIC Letter Books: various years beginning 1661. IOR E/3/86–99.

Print

Allen, Richard. 2014. *European Slave Trading in the Indian Ocean, 1500–1850*. Athens, OH: Ohio University Press.

Bayly, C. A. 1983. *Rulers, Townsmen and Bazaars: North Indian Society in the Age of British Expansion, 1770–1870*. Cambridge: Cambridge University Press.

Bourdieu, Pierre. 1994. 'Structure, Habitus, Power: Basis for a Theory of Symbolic Power', in Nicholas Dirks, Geoff Eley and Sherry B. Ortner (eds.), *Culture/Power/History: A Reader in Contemporary Social Theory*, pp. 155–99. Princeton: Princeton University Press.

Brimnes, Niels. 2003. 'Beyond Colonial Law: Indigenous Litigation and the Contestation of Property in the Mayor's Court in Late Eighteenth-Century Madras', *Modern Asian Studies*, 37(3): 513–50.

Dalton, Cornelius. 1915. *The Life of Thomas Pitt*. Cambridge: Cambridge University Press.

Erikson, Emily. 2014. *Between Monopoly and Free Trade: The English East India Company, 1600–1757*. Oxford: Oxford University Press.

Furber, Holden. 1948. *John Company at Work: A Study of European Expansion in India in the Late Eighteenth Century*. Cambridge, MA: Harvard University Press.

Ghosh, Durba. 2006. *Sex and the Family in Colonial India: The Making of Empire*. Cambridge: Cambridge University Press.

Hamilton, Alexander. 1930. *A New Account of the East Indies*. 2 vols. London: Argonaut.

Keay, John. 1991. *The Honourable Company: A History of the English East India Company*. London: HarperCollins.

Kling, Blair B and M. N. Pearson (eds.). 1986. *The Age of Partnership: Europeans in Asia before Dominion*. Honolulu: University Press of Hawaii.

Love, Henry Davison. 1913. *Vestiges of Old Madras 1640–1800*. 2 vols. London: Murray.

Marshall, P. J. 1976. *East India Fortunes: The British in Bengal in the Eighteenth Century*. Oxford: Clarendon.

Mentz, Soren. 2005. *The English Gentleman Merchant at Work: Madras and the City of London, 1660–1740*. Copenhagen: Museum Tusculanum Press.

Mines, Mattison. 2001. 'Courts of Law and Styles of Self in Eighteenth-Century Madras: From Hybrid to Colonial Self', *Modern Asian Studies*, 35(1): 33–74.

Mukund, Kanakalatha. 1999. *The Trading World of the Tamil Merchant: Evolution of Merchant Capitalism in the Coromandel*. Chennai: Orient Blackswan.

———. 2005. *The View from Below: Indigenous Society, Temples, and the Early Colonial State in Tamilnadu, 1700–1835*. New Delhi: Orient Longman.

Ogborn, Miles. 2007. *Indian Ink: Script and Print in the Making of the English East India Company*. Chicago: University of Chicago Press.

Stern, Philip J. 2011. *The Company State: Corporate Sovereignty and the Early Modern Foundations of the British Empire in India*. Oxford: Oxford University Press.

Veevers, David. 2013. 'The Company as Their Lords and the Deputy as a Great Rajah': Imperial Expansion and the English East India Company on the West Coast of Sumatra, 1685–1730', *Journal of Imperial and Commonwealth History*, 41(5): 687–709.

———. 2015. '"Inhabitants of the Universe": Global Families, Kinship Networks, and the Formation of the Early Modern Colonial State in Asia', *Journal of Global History*, 10(1): 99–121.

Weststejin, Arthur. 2014. 'The VOC as a Company-State: Debating Seventeenth-Century Dutch Colonial Expansion', *Itinerario*, 38(1): 13–34.

Wheeler, James Tolboys. 1861. *Madras in the Olden Time: Being a History of the Presidency.* 2 vols. Madras: Graves and Co.

Winterbottom, Anna. 2010. 'Company Culture: Information, Scholarship, and the East India Company Settlements, 1660–1720s'. Unpublished PhD dissertation, University of London.

Yule, Henry (ed.). 1888. *Diary of William Hedges, esq., during His Agency in Bengal as Well as His Voyage Out and Return Overland, 1681–1687.* 3 vols. London: Hakluyt Society.

11 Messing, caste and resistance

The production of 'jail-scapes' and penal regimes in the early 1840s

Rachna Singh

The English East India Company had originally arrived in South Asia as a trading body, but by the mid-nineteenth century it presided over a mammoth Anglo-Indian empire. Historians differ in their interpretations of this metamorphosis, but almost invariably acknowledge the complex role of the company state in organizing the realms of social and economic life, political thought, law, governance and punishment (Marshall 1976; Bayly 1983, 1988, 1999; Cohn 1987; Marshall 1987; Subrahmanyam and Bayly 1990; Alavi 1995; Alam and Subrahmanyam 1998; Singha 1998; Travers 2007; Stern 2011). Jails and dungeons had existed as places of detention and confinement under pre-colonial regimes also, mostly for persons awaiting trial or execution and sometimes for political prisoners. But by and large, these regimes preferred less capital-intensive modes of punishment such as fines, flogging, branding, mutilation, *tashir*, impaling, stocks, blowing from a gun, hanging and drowning (Bannerjee 1963; Singha 1998; Sen 2007). As the English East India Company consolidated its empire in South Asia, the nature and scope of imprisonment was completely transformed. Imprisonment emerged as the punishment of first resort. As T. B. Macaulay, the key figure in the first Prison Discipline Committee (1836–1838), aptly stated, imprisonment was to be 'the punishment to which one must chiefly trust', to be 'resorted to in ninety-nine cases out of every hundred', and therefore it had to be made a 'terror for wrongdoers' (Sen 2007: 40).

I argue that during this process, company jails were produced as a distinct kind of social space through new spatial practices of inhabiting jail-scapes constituted by various actors including prisoners and jail administrators (Lefebvre 1991). Within these jail spaces, modules of colonial power/knowledge were formulated, tested, contested and redefined in complex ways that cannot be reduced to 'a simple story of either epistemic domination or of elite collaboration' (Dirks 2001: 8), or even of subaltern resistance (Yang 2004). In this chapter, I analyse the role of spatial practices in producing jail-spaces by examining an early moment in the history of the imposition of messing in British Indian jails in 1841–1842, with special reference to the spatial practices in the jails of Chuprah, Gyah and Bhaugulpore. I use a spectrum of responses, from the almost quiescent enforcement of messing in some jails to near-violent resistance against it in others, in order to unravel the complex rhythms of the everyday within the lived space of these jails.

I. Early company jails

The English East India Company acquired the *diwani* or revenue collection rights of the provinces of Bihar, Bengal and Orissa in 1765. However, it could exert indirect influence only upon the Nizamat (department of military administration and criminal justice) until 1772, when the company under Warren Hastings was granted the powers of the Nizamat. The Regulating Act of 1773 passed by the British Parliament established the Supreme Court at Calcutta. In the same year, imprisonment was introduced as a distinct form of punishment in India. During the early period of company dominion in the 1770s, jails were usually placed under the immediate charge of the Faujdar heading the police establishment and the overall supervision of the Nizamat Adalat and the Naib Nazim. In keeping with the prevailing Orientalist ethos of ruling in an Indian idiom rather than acting as innovators, the intervention with respect to prisoners and prisons was minimal. With the arrival of Lord Cornwallis (governor-general 1786–1793), there was a greater Anglicization of the company's administration and the imposition of Whig principles of governance like the idea of 'improvement', protection of individual rights and private property, separation of the judiciary from the executive and rule of law. In this changing climate, the running of prisons and the fate of prisoners became matters of far greater concern for the company state. For example, the Regulation of 1787 required the magistrate was to inspect the jails at least once a month and to report cases of ill-treatment of prisoners, if any, to the government. By the turn of the eighteenth century, new ideologies of rule and apparatuses for administration were being fashioned, which necessarily had to offer a philosophy of punishment and a blueprint for the organization of jails (Bannerjee 1963; Fisher 1993; Metcalf 1994; Sen 2007).

During the late eighteenth century jails in Bengal were mostly temporary structures, congested, poorly ventilated and ill-located, with mud-walls and straw-thatched roofs. These jails were frequently ravaged by disease, storms or fire. Prisoners' escapes were common. After the company assumed direct charge of the Nizamat in that year, the Regulations of 3 December 1790 vested the magistrate of every district with powers of management and control over the jail in his jurisdiction. The conditions within jails, however, continued to remain abysmal. Preliminary attempts at the classification of prisoners made in 1790 and 1793, respectively, were largely frustrated by the architectural limitations of jail buildings. When Cornwallis abolished the punishment of mutilation in 1790 and substituted it with imprisonment, the government of Bengal resolved to rebuild its jails as permanent, brick-built structures (Bannerjee 1963; Sen 2007).

As jails came into sharper administrative definition by the early nineteenth century, the degree of control over prisoners' lives, bodies, work and behaviour became more decisively interventionist. In 1816, the judges of circuit were especially directed to inspect the jails at each jail delivery and to receive and pass orders on the petitions presented by convicts. General rules for the superintendence and management of jails throughout the company's dominion were framed under Regulation XIV of 1816. The magistrates were vested with the authority to punish specified offences upon a summary enquiry. The punishments prescribed for such offences were solitary confinement, use of the rattan, substitution of heavy fetters for those in ordinary use and temporary addition of neckchains of moderate weight or handcuffs and reduction of diet allowance. The magistrates were enjoined to prevent the maltreatment of prisoners by native officers employed in the jails, to enquire immediately into prisoners' complaints and to punish the offenders suitably when required. The superintending surgeons were also required to report on the state of the jails and the treatment of prisoners during their periodical tours of inspection. Corporal punishment and penal strategies directed explicitly at the prisoner's body, including regulation of his diet, were routinized. It was reiterated in 1830 that corporal punishment could be inflicted upon a convict under sentence of labour in irons, in extreme cases of 'breach of jail discipline' (Bannerjee 1963: 325–6; Sen 2007: 29). The offence-linked calibration of punishment within the jail appears to have been governed by two criteria: the original sentence passed upon the prisoner determined the first order of penal strategies; and this was modified in view of his subsequent (mis-) behaviour once lodged inside the jail, especially with regard to the performance of labour and obedience to jail rules and administrators.

In addition to these, certain other criteria had always shaped punishment under company rule. The overall quantum and texture of punishment as experienced by prisoners was almost invariably shaped by their gender, age, rank and social status inside and outside the jail. Radhika Singha has shown that certain pre-colonial forms of punishment such as public execution, gibbeting, tashir, public flogging and labour in fetters on roads were retained in the earlier phase of company rule and were even seen as a 'crucial component of deterrence'. By the 1830s, there was a wide-ranging discussion on the 'forms and symbols of rule'. The ending of the company's trade monopoly, the elaboration of paramountcy and the closer association of the company's government with the British Parliament imbued its actions in the colony with the 'sense of an "age of reform"' (1998: xvi–vii, 230–2).

In light of such shifts, the Prison Discipline Committee of 1838 called for a radical overhaul of Indian prisons. Among its most significant recommendations were: extramural labour to give way to work tasks within the prison; a more systematic division of prisoners into classes; increased use of solitary confinement and transportation and less resort to fetters and chains; urgent improvement in prison health and sanitation; recruitment of more dependable prison guards; the construction of central prisons or penitentiaries where troublesome prisoners could be kept under close surveillance; and the replacement of food allowances by common messing (Arnold 2007). Historians like Anand Yang suggest that the 1838 committee epitomized a 'new "science" of punishment' in the colonial period emanating from Britain, wherein punishment was directed no longer at the body but at the mind (even though the body remained an important site in the operationalization of new penal strategies). The 'centrepiece' of this 'new "science" of punishment' was the prison, with its 'new regimen of diet, work and solitary confinement' (1987: 29–30).

However, it is difficult to sustain the argument that during the 1830s and 1840s, the body itself became increasingly irrelevant in the logic of punishment. Rather, a distinct, new, powerful emphasis on the prisoner's body emerged within penal strategies and was reflected in the formulation of jail regulations pertaining to bathing, shaving, clothing, dietary practices and corporal punishment. As Singha has shown, the 1838 report provided a roadmap for 'sharpening the rigours of a jail sentence through a regime of "negative severities", one that would maintain the offender in health, but would deprive him of all the pleasures of the social and the familiar' (1998: 256–7).

Such complex penal strategies had to be carried out by investing designated offices with appropriate powers of superintendence over jails. This was an issue that had long divided administrative opinion and produced a layered distribution of authority with respect to jails. Eventually, the government repealed all previous enactments regarding the superintendence of jails and vested these powers in the hands of the magistrate and joint magistrates, acting under the sessions judges. Though the sessions judge could communicate directly with the magistrate on matters pertaining to jails, he could not interfere with the latter's management of these institutions. Instead, he was obliged to make a representation to the government direct if he felt the need for intervention. The management of district jails remained the responsibility of the magistrate till 1860 (Mouat

1862; Bannerjee 1963). It thus transpired that it fell to the magistrate to implement various orders pertaining to the running of jails, including the messing orders issued by the Nizamat Adalat through circular letters dated 9 July 1841 and 17 December 1841, respectively.

II. Diet and discipline; health, economy and punishment: issues in the move towards messing

From the 1830s onwards, within the limits of the self-avowedly liberal and humane creed of the colonial regime, penal technologies were exerted to reconstitute prisoners' bodies, to discipline and refashion prisoners into, if not penitent, then at least compliant and productive subjects. One such penal technology, shaped alike by the discourses of economy labour, medicine, health, humanitarianism and punishment, was the regulation of jail dietaries. The company state had not concerned itself much with such matters earlier in its rule. In the Lower Provinces of Bengal presidency, it was customary to allow prisoners a daily money allowance (generally nine piece per head per day, ranging between five pice and one *anna* a day) with which they could purchase their own food from one or more of the shopkeepers who were allowed access to the prison. The money allowance varied with fluctuations in the prevailing market price of grain. There were special allowances for European prisoners. Prisoners could buy and cook their own food at a designated place within the jail yard. Prevailing strategies of punishment by and large excluded the manipulation of jail dietaries (Mouat 1862; Bannerjee 1963).

Nevertheless, as Singha has argued, imprisonment 'as confinement alone' was very much a 'subsidiary category' (1998: 253). Even in the late eighteenth century, there were voices that argued for the introduction of more punitive elements that would render the imprisonment more onerous and therefore more deterrent. In 1795, the 2nd Judge of the Calcutta Court of Circuit mooted the idea to the Nizamat Adalat that it was necessary to deprive prisoners of the 'luxuries of smoking and cooking for themselves' (an argument to be advanced decades later by the Prison Discipline Committee of 1838). This was brought into effect by the Nizamat Adalat with respect to prisoners sentenced to imprisonment for life or for a term of seven years or upwards through a circular to all magistrates dated 23 April 1795. It was further decided that the victuals of all Hindu prisoners would be dressed by a Brahmin cook and that of all Muslim prisoners by a Muhammedan cook. This early attempt to introduce messing into jails on a limited scale was jettisoned when prisoners in several jails refused to eat their food and threatened to go on a hunger-strike. The magistrate of Dacca went so far as to complain about the 'numerous female connections, wives, mother and children' of the prisoners, who were supposedly 'incapable of providing for themselves', and were supported by remittances made by prisoners from their 'jail allowance and other trifling profits of their industry in jail'. Upon the stoppage of diet money, these dependants were 'reduced to the most deplorable state of distress' and were on the brink of death (Bannerjee 1963: 336). When the magistrate of Behar district imposed cooked food in 1796, he encountered resistance among the prisoners; the prisoners informed him that they preferred a reduced allowance of 2 piece provided they could dispose of it at will. Such pressures were powerful and, on the whole, widely perceived as legitimate since the Nizamat Adalat repealed its previous orders. On 6 July 1796, it directed all magistrates to discontinue all restraints and to discharge the cooks employed by them for preparing food for the prisoners.

During the late 1830s, there developed a multi-pronged critique of such dietary practices within jails. The collection of statistical data on jails by the colonial state, particularly with regard to sickness and mortality, raised uncomfortable questions about the existing arrangements for the dieting of prisoners. These fears were confirmed by the medical specialist who was increasingly associated with the running of jails. In 1836 Lord Auckland (governor-general, 1836–1842) set up an enquiry into the manner in which prisoners were furnished with food in the Bengal jails: the findings severely indicted the money allowance system (IOR/F/4/1897/80599). A more detailed critique was developed by the Committee on Prison Discipline of 1838, which vehemently objected to the fact that all over Bengal prisoners were kept better and with more comfort than agricultural labourers. The 1838 report pointed out that prisoners were able to save a large portion of their money allowance in order to remit it to their friends or family, or to bribe the guards, or to form a hoard of savings that they carried away upon release. Prisoners also had a free hand in procuring articles of diet, often ones not conducive to health. The Committee recommended that urgent provision be made in each district for the purchase of 'the coarsest grain on which the mass of the people of that district live(d)' as the 'staple article' of prisoners' food. It recommended a switch to cooked rations distributed through messes with suitable regulations ensuring a proper variety of food and a sufficient quantity of stimulating condiments to assist digestion. No convicted prisoner was to be allowed to cook his own victuals, but instead, a Brahman and a Muhammedan cook was to be provided for each jail. The Committee further suggested that all convicted persons sentenced to hard labour ought to be completely deprived of every indulgence not absolutely necessary to their health (Mouat 1862:186; Bannerjee 1963: 336–7; Sen 2007: 47).

In keeping with the recommendations of the Prison Discipline Committee, a ration system was introduced in all the jails of Bengal presidency in 1838. The rations consisted per prisoner of one *seer* of rice, one seer and a half of wood and one *kucha* of tobacco. In addition one pice per week was to be allowed to each man for shaving and washing. In April 1839, the government decided to adopt the contract system for providing the food at a fixed rate all the year round, when this was found to be practicable. Matters of detail, such as inducing prisoners to form themselves into messes, appointing one man to cook for them and making arrangements for employment of cooks, were left to the discretion of the district authorities. A few months later, these provisions were simplified. Every prisoner was to be allowed the quantity and description of food that a working prisoner of the agricultural class ordinarily had, irrespective of the price of commodities. The government undertook to keep the prisoners healthy and fit for labour irrespective of financial costs. The magistrate was to determine the daily scale of rations after consulting the wishes and habits of the prisoners as far as reasonably possible, always keeping in mind that no prisoner was to be allowed when in jail luxuries not usually accessible to free persons of his class, and not necessary to keep a working man in a state of health. The food was examined by the medical officers in charge of the prisons, who could sanction a small increase in the diet of specific prisoners for reasons of health (Mouat 1862: 186–7; Bannerjee 1963: 337–8; Yang 1987).

The ration system was 'imperfectly understood, and not fully carried out': not surprisingly, it did not work well. Medical officers alleged that the inadequacies of the jail dietary were a major cause for high levels of sickness and mortality among prisoners. A further enquiry instituted in 1840 revealed that while the ration system had 'very generally superseded the money allowances', and no prisoners were exempt from it, the plan of messing had 'not been so generally introduced' (Mouat 1862: 187). At the behest of the government of Bengal, the Suddur Nizamat Court's issued Circular Orders dated 9 July 1841 and 17 December 1841, directing that all criminal prisoners be formed into messes. Each mess was to consist of twenty men as the standard number with one cook assigned to it. The civil surgeon of each station was to see the prisoners at a meal, at least once a week. His visits were to be at irregular intervals and unannounced. Members of a mess were to eat according to the principle of *ek rikabi*, which some zealous officials like the magistrate of Tirhoot interpreted as meaning 'literally out of one dish', but that actually appeared to have meant 'at the same time' (Bannerjee 1963; IOR F/4/2150/102999).

It is important to understand the ideological and administrative dimensions of the introduction of the ration and messing system between 1838 and 1841. Anand Yang argues that the 1838 Prison Discipline Committee drew heavily on the 'Benthamite "rule of severity"', a rule that also underpinned the Poor Law Report of 1834 in Britain. The latter stated 'that no prisoner should enjoy a lifestyle better than that of the poorest of free persons' (1987: 32). The Poor Law of 1834 was designed to prevent the idle poor from battening off state resources by insisting that poor relief be provided only in workhouses, where conditions were kept so bad as to deter all but the genuinely destitute from entering. In British Indian jails, however, the thrust of utilitarian reform was punitive, yet enabling: the prisoner had to be kept healthy enough to be as productive as he would have been when free. As argued later by the first Inspector of Jails in the Lower Provinces, F. J. Mouat, even at this 'early period of inquiry into the matter', it was certainly difficult if not impossible to work out a dietary for the prisoner that would 'keep him in health', but not allow him to 'fare better' than the 'class to which he belonged in a state of freedom from crime' (1862: 187).

An intervention in the dietary regime of prisoners of the order being called for by the Prison Discipline Committee required critical inputs from medical experts. Radhika Singha argues that the medical officer was in effect being asked to 'suggest ways in which the prisoner could be kept alive, and, by implication, fit for work under the new strategies for enhancing jail severities'. However, the concerns of health and discipline were 'not always easily reconciled'. The withdrawal of prisoner choice in the matter of food was justified on grounds of health and better discipline. But medical intervention also made it necessary that the substitute diet be varied and its quantity increased for labouring prisoners. Some officials went to the extent of arguing that such medical interventions had 'diluted the disciplinary intent of cooked food altogether'. In fact, Singha suggests that the medical discourse on prisoner's health stood in for the voice of humanitarianism in jail reforms, otherwise missing in the utilitarian language of that context and that period (1998: 232–4). She also points to a curious anomaly in the calibration of caste-linked status and punishment. On the one hand, the 1838 report argued that the introduction of trades or crafts in jail would shame a man of high caste, extend the punishment to his family and create resentment against the law. On the other hand, it did not express any apprehensions about caste when advocating the messing system. In fact, the system of ration and messing was pushed through the Bengal presidency despite indications that it would lead to administrative difficulties, increased expenditure and considerable resistance from prisoners, while its effects on heath remained uncertain (1998: 257). Such optimism was bound to be belied. It is not surprising, therefore, that the imposition of messing in company jails in the early 1840s brought into existence a varied range of responses among various actors including prisoners, prison administrators and the general public and became the site for one of the most engaged discussions on colonial punishment in the first half of the nineteenth century.

III. Understanding messing: caste, commensality, punishment and colonialism

Messing was introduced in almost every district of Bengal and Orissa, but was not 'generally introduced' in the Bihar provinces (except for Monghyr and Bhaugulpore, where it was introduced successfully) owing to fears about 'opposition' by prisoners. The government of Bengal, the Nizamat Adalat and local officials were all taken aback by the intensity of anger provoked by the imposition of messing and unsure of their ability to contain protests. Various reasons were cited by the Nizamat Adalat in its report of October 1842 to account for the discontent with messing: some prisoners found the quantity of rations inadequate (Dinagepore); others complained of the pilferage of rations by the mess cooks (East Burdwan); yet other prisoners felt that messing deprived them of 'the pleasure of cooking' (Purnea, Northern Cuttack, Central Cuttack, 24 Pergunnahs, Baraset, Backergunge, Rungpore and Mymensingh); or that it led to an 'enhancement of punishment' (Bhaugulpore, West Burdwan and Dacca). Apart from the deprivation of the pleasure of cooking, the last grievance was linked to the popular perception, especially powerful in the Bihar provinces, that messing violated laws of commensality and led to loss of caste. For example, messing was said to be 'highly disliked' in Patna since the people believed that Brahmins and Rajpoots could only eat food 'cooked by themselves, their families or their *purohits* (priests)'. Even Muslim prisoners were said to be not impervious to caste distinctions, though the exact nature of these remained relatively unclear. For example, the Adalat pointed out that at Bogra, messing had been introduced among 'the Mussulman prisoners who formed the majority, but not among other castes', though the joint magistrate was taking measures to 'make the system general'. At all points, the colonial government remained deeply unsure of its ability to find satisfactory solutions to popular grievances and to put down popular uprisings. For example, the Nizamat Adalat stated that messing had not been introduced in Patna because any uprising would have been difficult to contain given the 'incommodious and insecure nature of the temporary buildings or *chalies* in which the prisoners were confined, and their distance from each other'. Overall, there appears to have been no holistic framework through which the norms of caste and commensality, and the modalities of messing and penal discipline were understood either by prisoners or by officials.

Resentment among prisoners simmered and spluttered, but was usually quashed either through exemplary punishment for the principal offenders or through persuasion by local officials. For example, in the district of Nuddea, the Mussulman convicts had been formed into messes of twenty each and so were the Hindus 'as far as prejudices of caste have allowed'. But the upcountrymen Brahmins and Rajpoot convicts proved to be the 'most difficult to deal with', as they would not feed with the Bengal Hindus. Some of these prisoners abstained from food when first ordered to mess together, but the opposition subsided after nine of them were 'transferred to the western provinces with the sanction of the western court'. Often corporal punishment was used against the 'ringleaders' to break the back of the anti-messing opposition. For example, in Purnea district, ten or twelve 'low caste Hindoos' were 'refractory', but when two prisoners especially noted for their insubordination were punished with '2 rattans a piece', all of them 'partook of the meal prepared for them'. Likewise, there was 'considerable dissatisfaction at first' in West Burdwan, and around fifty convicts 'obstinately refused to eat their dinner on the first day'. But they submitted after 'a slight corporal punishment' was inflicted on their leader. In yet other cases, a blend of firm and conciliatory policies appeared to have worked well. For example, in Dacca the prisoners initially 'offered some resistance, and on occasion assaulted their guards', but were 'speedily reduced to order'. Subsequently, 'attention was paid to the wishes of the prisoners in the formation of the messes, and the choice of the cooks'; as a result, the prisoners became 'in great degree reconciled to the system'. However, the most successful examples of the introduction of messing came from districts where force was almost entirely displaced by the use of conciliatory methods. In Bhaugulpore, for example messing was introduced 'without opposition and without the use of coercive means' through conferral with the local community to remove objections based on caste (IOR/F/4/2150/102999: 1–4, 71–77).

Some of the complex threads of the extremely textured public discussion in the early 1840s on caste and commensality, messing and penal discipline emerge through the official correspondence about the Gya jail in Behar district. Magistrate E. Drummond anticipated 'great difficulty' in implementing messing given the architectural limitations of existing jail buildings and the crowded state of the wards. He met with 'great opposition', and 'all sorts of threats were uttered by the convicts against their guards, etc'. The prisoners 'declared they would rather die than submit to what would deprive them of their castes'. Evidently, such protests dampened the magistrate's enthusiasm to implement messing because though he said he had initiated the process in March 1842, it was still not completed by the time he learnt of the Chuprah jail uprising in June 1842. News of the successful introduction of messing in districts like Tirhoot built pressure on magistrates like Drummond who had not managed to accomplish as much.

Luckily for Drummond, a 'demi-official' communication from the Bengal authorities arrived in the meantime. This letter laid down that messing was not to be carried into effect by force but through conciliation, and if this was not possible, it was to be abandoned altogether. Having at last found the pretext that he had so clearly desired all along, Drummond gave up the messing experiment stating that 'the convicts to a man' had declared that they would 'not submit to it except by force, and even then that they would rather die'. Even the people in general looked upon messing as 'an unnecessary interference with the prejudices of caste' and an 'infringement of rights which . . . [had] hitherto been held sacred'. Any attempt to persist would not only lead to a 'serious disturbance', but it would also disabuse the belief of the subjects of the colonial regime in 'the scrupulous non-interference of government in matters of religion'.

Magistrate Drummond identified what he called 'the grand obstacles to the introduction of messes' and explicated how the argument about loss of caste operated at various levels. The 'aversion' of prisoners to messing was so powerful that they declared their readiness to 'suffer a diminution in the quantity of their rations to the extent of one fourth', rather than be subject to it. Furthermore, Drummond noted that the prisoners were afraid of the reaction of their 'friends and connections' among whom they needed to validate their caste status during imprisonment and after release: such persons would never accept that messing in jails was enforced without violating caste. Rational persuasion may have convinced the prisoners themselves that 'interference with caste was by no means intended'. But it would never dispel prevailing perceptions in society at large arising from 'ignorance' about what went on within the walls of the prison, hidden from the public gaze. Drummond did not rest his case with the suggestion that popular fears about messing and loss of caste were based on native 'ignorance'. He also recognized the genuine difficulties confronting the government in composing appropriate caste-based messes. The 'subdivisions' of caste were 'very minute', and the colonial official's knowledge of such principles of social organization, very tenuous. If the laws of commensality governing all these 'numerous' subdivisions were to be respected, the convicts would get the necessary pretext to resist the introduction of messing, especially since they already saw it as an 'addition to their former quantum of punishment'. Drummond pointed out that even a Brahmin cook was not acceptable to all prisoners, even though Brahmins were the highest in the caste hierarchy and their touch, presumably, could not be defiling. While 'Rajwars, Dosadhs, Boonyas, Mooshurs, Kaits, Kahars, Dhanooks and other inferior castes' would not object to eating food cooked by a Brahmin, 'Babhuns, Rajpoots, Goalas and Koiries' only ate 'food cooked only by men of their own caste, and even these must be connected with them, however distantly by intermarriage'. Drummond confessed that he possessed 'but small means for the control of 1500 mutinous convicts'. And the concerns about messing extended to an audience far outside the walls of the jail (IOR F/4/2150/102999: 62–67). The Sessions Judge C. Garstin endorsed all the remarks of the magistrate of Behar and even went a step ahead to urge the Suddur Nizamat Adalat to abandon the plan of messing altogether (IOR F/4/2150/102999: 60–61).

Drummond's evidence suggests that in any given context, the laws of commensality and caste were not determined entirely by birth; other criteria like physical belonging to the same pool of marital partners and a certain immediacy of social contact were also important. These norms were not uniform across caste groups nor could they be encompassed within a monolithic set of principles or logic. Goala prisoners, not of very high caste ranking, could refuse to eat food cooked by a Brahmin. And yet Magistrate Drummond emphasized the usefulness of caste divisiveness in sustaining colonial rule. The magistrate of Behar was almost unique in his criticism of importing messing from what he described as alien contexts (no matter 'however usual in other countries'), since it was by 'no means adapted either to native habits or feelings'. With grim candour, he warned that any undermining of 'the exclusiveness of caste' would erode the social barriers that brought about the 'separation of interest and disunion' among native subjects, which in turn could create serious 'danger' for a colonial regime (IOR F/4/2150/102999: 62–67).

Some of the issues raised by Drummond featured in other contemporaneous discussions on the introduction of messing in company jails in 1841. I seek to do a close reading of two contrasting sites – the Chuprah jail where there was a popular if short-lived anti-messing uprising and the Bhaugulpore jail that saw a more or less quiet transmission to it – in order to understand how precisely the spatial practices and public discussions in the wake of messing shaped jail-scapes in the early 1840s.

IV. The anti-messing uprising in Chuprah: reading resistance, caste and the production of jail-scapes

The most spectacular example of prisoners' resistance against messing came from the Chuprah jail of Saran district, where around 700 prisoners supported by a 'mob' of three to four thousand townspeople rose in an uprising on 10 June 1842, forcing the authorities to suspend the implementation of messing altogether. Though the Nizamat Adalat underplayed the Chuprah uprising in its report of October 1842, it was actually serious enough to prompt local authorities to seek additional information regarding caste, commensality and prevailing religious mores regarding food.

The requisite processes of information-gathering and the production of colonial knowledge(s) had begun before the uprising itself. Upon the receipt of messing orders, in a staggering act of ethnographic reconnaissance, the magistrate of Saran district, G. D. Wilkins, had produced a detailed list delineating the caste identity of prisoners and clubbing them into caste-based messes. He modified this list after consultation with both his assistant Brodhurst and his Naib Nazir, a Hindu officer, who in turn were asked to confer with the prisoners, to allow them to nominate their own mess cooks and to even invite petitions regarding their concerns. These petitions were said to have been few in number: Wilkins reported passing orders on them but did not elaborate on their contents. The amended list submitted by Brodhurst showed significant changes from Wilkins's original line of thinking. This suggests that conversations with local interlocutors played a very important role in shaping colonial knowledge(s) pertaining to practices of caste and commensality (Bayly 1996). Eventually, 575 male prisoners sentenced to labour were identified by caste and subcaste and grouped into fifty-two messes of widely divergent sizes, ranging from 1 to 23. Wilkins sought to disguise the highly irregular size of the messes by emphasizing the statistical average of 12.5 prisoners per mess. The male prisoners without labour, much fewer in number, were also suitably divided. All eight women prisoners were clubbed into one 'caste' group, and a Rajpootni was appointed cook. Wilkins interpreted the orders for the messing of each gang as enjoined by Rule 8 of the Adalat's Circular, technically called 'ek rikabi', to mean the practice of eating out of one dish. He pointed out that this order was 'relaxed in favour of messes 1–43 and 57 on account of their numerous acknowledged sub-divisions'. A Panday from his rank was selected to cook for the first mess and one Panday (a Kunoujia Brahmin sentenced without labour) was allowed to eat alone.

After describing at great length his meticulous attention to details of caste in implementing the messing orders, Wilkins confessed that strict obedience to the instructions of the Adalat was not possible: 'the subdivisions of caste' were 'endless', and he had had to make relaxations, particularly in favour of Brahmins and women prisoners. With a sense of righteous surprise and anger, he narrated how, in spite of this circumspection and the general conciliatory methods used while composing messes, the prisoners still chose to resist the measure. On the first day itself, three of the designated mess cooks pretended to have fallen ill, and all but ten of them steadfastly refused to cook or even to receive the rations for their respective messes. After trying to reason with them unsuccessfully, Wilkins flogged six of the recalcitrant cooks, 'chiefly upper caste men', but they remained obdurate and had to be sent to the hospital while substitutes were found for them. The rest then consented to cook. Feeling the need to justify the use of violence, Wilkins described how, before flogging them, he had tried to explain to the six errant prisoner-cooks that no injury to their caste could arise if they ate food they had cooked themselves. He had even offered that the other members of the concerned messes could refuse food for that first day after giving their reasons for doing so.

When the prisoners labouring outside returned in the evening, they were asked to remain outside the jail till such time as their food was ready. Tremendously enraged, they turned upon the guard. It was only with the 'greatest difficulty' that they were prevented from attacking the Jail Darogah and the Subahdar of the jail *burkundauze*, whom they blamed for the flogging of the 'mutineer cooks'. By that time, a dense 'crowd' of three or four thousand townspeople, 'impossible to disperse', had surrounded the jail gate. Further emboldened, the prisoners attempted to 'get out of the front gate'. They threw opposite it 'all the cooking pots and food' and 'threatened violence to any one of the jail *omlah* who ventured to go near them'. Wilkins could not get the prisoners to 'keep silent or sit down', or the 'crowd to disperse or even to fall back from the threatening position they had taken'. The magistrate instructed the jail guard to keep their eyes on the prisoners alone and to use their weapons to force back any prisoner who tried to break loose. When he was leaving the jail to fetch the Collector Farquharson, his armed forces and the Sessions Judge Gough, the crowd was initially 'disinclined' to let Wilkins pass, but 'gradually gave away'. Even then, '6 or 8 of the number' kept throwing 'clods of earth' at him and abused him as he went past. One of these fellows was 'seized . . . in the act' by a *chuprassie* and 'kept hold of to the end'. When he returned accompanied by Gough and Farquharson, sentries were posted on the roads 'to prevent interruption from the crowd. Thereafter, the prisoners were forced back into one ward and locked up. When they showed a disturbing disposition to be violent, the burkundauze sepoys were ordered 'to make a show of forcing them in with their bayonets'. Yet, as Wilkins hastened to assure his superiors, 'not a single prisoner was touched even by a sword, stick, or bayonet'. He repeatedly insisted that due process had been observed both in implementing messing and in dealing with the uprising in its aftermath. And with hindsight, he vowed that had he known that the 'feeling was so universal and violent, and that people outside were so much excited against the measure', he would have deferred the implementation of messing and sought further instructions.

During the night of 10 June 1842, still shaken by the presence of the crowd, Wilkins posted thirty-two sentries around the inner walls of the jail, with orders to fire at anybody who tried to scale the wall. The crowd began to disperse, but he felt this was more due to an 'impending storm'. Curious about the composition of this crowd, Wilkins found out 'from several sources' that apart from the townspeople, 'numbers' had assembled 'from all parts of the district'. These persons were 'connected with the prisoners as relatives, friends or dependants' and had 'come in to assist them in resisting the enforcement of a measure' which they believed was 'aimed at their castes and families' and 'prejudicial both to the prisoners and to their own future positions and respectability'. At about 11PM, the Thannadar informed the magistrate that 'at several shops in the Nya Bazar there were groups of strangers putting up and discussing in loud terms what had occurred'. Wilkins even despatched a letter by express to the Commanding Officer at Dinapore asking for military aid. He realized that he could 'barely manage the prisoners' with 'the means at hand', but had 'no chance of doing so for an instant' if there was 'any combination outside to cooperate with them'.

Eventually, the magistrate of Sarun decided to defer the messing experiment in the Chuprah Jail, pending a reference to the Nizamat Adalat. Wilkins was 'convinced' that the 'measure' could not have been 'intended as a punishment, as which it would act so unequally'. He acknowledged the fact that the impact of messing upon various prisoners was mediated by caste, rank and possibly other factors. The ringleaders and other offenders in the Chuprah uprising were identified after the magistrate 'took evidence' of his 'jail people and others who were on the spot at the time'. The men 'in most authority' among the prisoners were 'chiefly Rajpoot and Bahmun Zemindars' of Sarun and Patna districts – persons 'of known violent characters', enormously influential both on account of their 'wealth, and the number and attachment of their relatives and ryots'. The magistrate was afraid that as long as these ringleaders continued to be housed within the Chuprah jail, their supporters would continue to try to rescue them. While minor offenders could be given summary punishment by the magistrate, Wilkins decreed that the 'ringleaders' would stand their trial in the Sessions Court. He also recommended that in addition to whatever punishment was awarded to them, the ringleaders ought to be banished to other jails as they were so influential. Even banishing these offenders would require 'either great assistance or successful stratagem', so great was 'their dislike to such a measure, and their power to resist it'.

Wilkins argued on the basis of his wide administrative experience in all but one of the Bihar Provinces that messing was an unworkable plan: the intricacies of subcastes were too complex; the 'feelings' of prisoners were 'sincere and genuine'; 'nothing, no force, restraint or punishment however sever and cogent' would ever induce all prisoners to act against these sentiments; and a 'collision with the populace' was always possible. The magistrate warned that the prisoners were 'nowhere so turbulently inclined themselves, so well cared for by their friends without, or so bigoted and sturdy in maintaining their castes and family connections' as in Sarun district. He urged that the evils of the money allowance system could be adequately addressed by returning to the system of giving rations in kind. If due regard was given to the caste sentiments of prisoners, they would argue for 'endless' subdivisions or subcastes among themselves, whether 'real' or 'pretended', and the point of messing would be lost altogether. Conversely, if these objections were largely ignored and the rules were enforced as they existed on paper, it would excite unrest.

To clinch his argument, the magistrate attached a 'sketch of the various subdivisions of castes said to prevail in this district', a perusal of that would have given the most inveterate supporter of messing pause. For example, there were two Brahmins, both enumerated as Surwurria Tewary but kept in separate sub-divisions as they declined to eat with each other because they were of the same subcaste, their families were not linked through inter-marriage. Some Brahmins ate meat and fish, others did not and one Panday prisoner subsisted on a diet devoid of grain. The division of the Lohar caste group into the subdivisions of Putunia and Casheea was based on the principle of 'nativity' alone, but this was considered sufficient grounds for composing distinct messes. The Mussulmans were pronounced to be 'Hindooized' and therefore also organized into subcaste groups such as the 'Sheicks, Doonias, Fuqeers, Byragees and Kisabs'. These groups also refused to eat together. Even among a caste group ascribed very low status such as Chumars, there was an individual prisoner who refused to eat with the rest. The Bengalee Koormes claimed that they had no objection to 'any arrangement', but had only protested at the suggestion of the others (IOR F/4/2150/102999: 15–49). Clearly, the hierarchy of castes and subcastes and the norms governing them remained extremely fluid, even when being systematized and organized through the exercise of colonial power. Pinning down this fluid system into precise principles that could guide state policy was an exercise bound to be fraught with tension, ambiguity, contestation and invention.

When forwarding Wilkins's report to the Nizamat Adalat, the Sessions Judge G. Gough added his voice to the magistrate's plea. Gough reiterated that the 'Bramen and Rajpoot classes' of Saran and Shahabad districts were more ferociously attached to their caste and ritual status as compared to Bengal Hindus. They 'would sooner undergo any extremity rather than relinquish their claims to the full enjoyment of the rights of caste, or even have those claims brought in question'. Gough had acceded to the suspension of messing only after he realized that the costs of the popular unrest against it would far outweigh any possible benefits from improvement in prison discipline. Though he found Wilkins's list of various castes that needed to eat separately 'unnecessarily minute',

Gough agreed that it could not have been abbreviated 'to the extent indicated in the Rules of the 9th of July, without recourse to coercion' (IOR F/4/2150/102999: 7–15). The Suddur Nizamat Adalat concluded that 'great consideration for the feelings and prejudices of the prisoners' had been shown in composing the messes, and 'nothing but a dogged determination' on the part of the prisoners 'to oppose the messing system under any form whatever' could have led to such 'open resistance' against the orders of the magistrate. The Adalat expressed the apprehension that any 'indulgence' shown to the Chuprah prisoners would spark off uprisings in hitherto quiescent jails. While it was up to the government of Bengal to decide whether or not to enforce messing, it urged the government to implement uniformly whatever decision it arrived at across all jails (IOR F/4/2150/102999: 5–7).

As the discussion around the Chuprah prisoners' uprising of 1842 travelled upwards in the administrative hierarchy, the lines of enquiry became more general and the debate on messing centred on broader principles. The government of Bengal rejected the argument that messing could only either be enforced rigorously in all jails or be abandoned altogether. Instead, the Bengal authorities insisted that messing could 'still be gradually and cautiously introduced', and it certainly ought to be continued in jails where it was 'already in full and successful operation'. Although it commended Wilkins for his meticulous attention to caste in composing the messes, and the firmness and resolve with which he quashed the uprising, the government also reprimanded him for precipitating the crisis in the first place by flogging the recalcitrant cooks. Magistrates were warned against 'driving their prisoners to extremity on a subject like this' and were enjoined to use suasion rather than force to secure their ends. They were to consult the prisoners about 'the number and constitution of the messes', to 'listen to all not very unreasonable objections', to 'bear with many frivolous seeming scruples', to 'insist only where they . . . (could) surely and safely enforce their views' and to relinquish 'with a good grace', at least temporarily, issues where they foresaw difficulty. In other words, the peaceful imposition of messing was configured not so much as a matter of enunciating proper policy, but more as 'a test of the prudence and ability of the Magistrate', a test in which some would succeed better than others. The government could thus lay the responsibility for preventing bloodshed and uprising at the door of the magistrate, while refusing to renege on policies that were deemed to be provocative by its subjects. This explains how the government of Bengal could, in the same breath, recognize the 'strong repugnance' of the Chuprah prisoners towards messing and berate Wilkins for having underestimated it and yet insist on its implementation without sanctioning the use of 'coercion' which was clearly necessary. Furthermore, the government sent a 'demi-official letter' to all the magistrates of the Behar zillahs, laying the events that had unfolded at Chuprah Jail before them and warning them against any 'resort to undistinguishing force' (IOR F/4/2150/102999: 50–53).

By focusing the discussion about the implementation of messing on the abilities of the magistrate, the government could sidestep a fraught political and intellectual discussion on whether messing caused detriment to caste. Objections based on caste were dismissed as spurious and mere 'pretence', yet magistrates were enjoined to be 'careful' while composing messes so as to not give any grounds for complaint. The same deliberate duality was seen in the government's summation of the response of 'people in general': they reportedly either felt that messing was 'intended to enhance the terrors of punishment or view(ed) it with indifference'. Nonetheless, the Bengal government did suggest to the government of India that all sentences of imprisonment under existing laws be reduced by a period of about one-quarter since messing had 'enhanced the severity of punishment'. It also urged the continuation of the messing system since it was a 'success'. Messing was credited with having brought about a massive improvement in the health of prisoners, as proven by the evidence of the Medical Board. 'Dissatisfaction' with the system had been exhibited in three districts only – Chuprah, Behar and Patna – and in a 'marked manner' at Chuprah alone (IOR F/4/2150/102999: 175–9).

The administrative concerns of the Bengal government about the introduction of messing appear to have been clinical and limited to modalities and logistics: when, how, to what extent, with what degree of success? But this seemingly sanitized and detached register of bureaucratic interest was shot through with a much more human, diffident, even anxious engagement with the 'feelings' of the prisoners and the people in general. These 'feelings' were mostly about caste (though not exhausted by it in range), which in turn was a system that could never be grasped unless through conversation with native actors and, even then, only inadequately so. Hence, in the imposition of messing, caste emerged as a nebulous, volatile and deeply political instrument that could take on various meanings and through which the ruled could find ways of shaping the regimes that sought to exercise control over them. The Chuprah jail uprising, where a moment of sharp contestation of the penal regime being constructed by the company state, provides an entry point into analysing how spatial practices led to the production of jail-scapes in the first half of the nineteenth century. Another set of arguments can be made through the study of a very different moment in history, when messing was imposed with minimal resistance in Bhaugulpore.

V. The 'peaceful' imposition of messing in the Bhaugulpore Jail: 'denying' caste within debates on messing

The messing system had one of its most successful runs in the district of Bhaugulpore. Magistrate H. I. James believed that messing was a system that enhanced the 'terrors' of jail. James argued that cooking was a long-standing amusement of the natives; deprivation of the opportunity to cook, a grievance; and any violation of caste and religious principles acted in the same way as the deprivation of the pleasure of cooking to enhance punishment. In order to implement messing (which he did on 16 October 1841), he divided the different classes of prisoners into messes, allowing one cook to each mess. The labouring and non-labouring prisoners were 'in no way connected by the messing system' (IOR F/4/2150/102999: 78–86). The magistrate contended that scrupulous care was taken during the composition of messes to avoid any infringement of rules and customs necessary for the strict preservation of prisoners' castes, or any injury to their religious feelings. Nevertheless, some prisoners complained initially about being compelled to eat with men of another caste. Magistrate James averred that barring one, most of these complaints were 'frivolous' – they had not much to do with caste, but rather reflected the prisoners' 'great dislike to eat in a mess' and their 'hope' of obtaining 'the indulgence of cooking their food separately'.

And yet, rather than resort to force or coercion, he 'readily settled' these complaints through processes of dialogue and consultation, not just with the prisoners, but also with caste representatives from among native society, whose views he deemed to be widely acceptable. He sent for 'from the Bazaar some six or eight men of the same caste and persuasion as the complainants' and formed them 'on the spot' into a 'punchaite' either in his *cutcherry* or in the jail. Thereafter, he left it to this caste *punchayet* to take decisions. In the one instance where the complaint was proven to be well founded, the concerned prisoner was 'removed into another mess'. James stressed that he had not, even 'in a single instance', enforced messing through 'corporal punishment, extra labour, starvation, or any kind of coercion or severity', even though the measures he adopted were 'not exactly of a sympathising or conciliatory nature'. The example he held out was one where a judicious magistrate could introduce messing without either overt coercion or excessive conciliation – the ideal solution to the problem as the government of Bengal saw it:

> Before passing the orders on the subject, I minutely weighed the propriety and justness of such, for I was well aware of the unpopularity of

> the measures, and knew that if I showed any large amount of consideration for their wishes and feelings or unnecessarily consulted their fancies and prejudices, or displayed any indecision or vacillation on the occasion, I should be overwhelmed with ridiculous excuses and unfounded complaints on the score of caste, and that every obstacle and opposition would be brought forward to prevent the introduction of such salutary measures as I have stated above. I have met with no opposition except on one or two trifling occasions, and I feel certain that I have in no case injured the caste of any one prisoner or forced him to comply with customs or habits opposed to the tenets of his religion.

The appointment of suitable mess cooks was in large part the key to the success of the messing system in Bhaugulpore jail. The magistrate noted that a cook was chosen for each mess and changed every week. There were one or two exceptions to this rule where a Brahmin was selected as cook, since he was 'of that kind of comprehensive caste' which persuaded members of a mess to 'readily agree to eat the food prepared by his hands'. Unlike jails such as that in Gya, the experience in Bhaugulpore appears to have been that Brahmin cooks were acceptable to one and all. The magistrate also insisted that cooking could form only a portion of the labour that prisoner-cooks were required to perform; they had to be given other responsibilities. He thus highlighted the fact that the imposition of messing could compel a re-calibration of punishment not only because of its supposed consequences for caste, but also on account of the redistribution of labour tasks within the jail machinery. The mess cooks were employed in cleaning the jail from sunrise to 10AM, when they commenced cooking after receiving rations from the contractor for their respective messes in the presence of the darogah or *mohurer*. On the arrival of the other prisoners from work, each prisoner's share of the dinner was served out to him from the cooking pots of his mess on a separate leaf or dish. All the food was cooked within the walls of the jail. Each mess was allotted four cooking pots, one for rice, one for *dhall*, one for vegetables and one for fish or meat.

Dietary regimes in jails resisted the standardizing drive behind messing because of the intrinsic complexities in the exercise of enumerating persons for the purposes of eating together. The criminal prisoners ate alone in messes. The civil prisoners were not subject to messing and could purchase their daily food from the maintenance allowance sanctioned and supplied to them by the Civil Court. Those under trial were supplied with a certain quantity of uncooked food, which they cooked for themselves. Messes remained uneven in size and varying in number due to the scrupulous attention given to details of caste and commensality and the fluctuating number of prisoners in jail at any given time. Magistrate James noted that on the day prior to the date of his report, there were 607 prisoners in jail, organized into 26 messes, varying in numbers from 12 to 23 prisoners; with another 14 messes consisting of 4 to 9 members each; while the remainder of the prisoners ate alone or in messes of 1 or 3 each. In contrast, the previous month on 16 July 1842 there had been 599 prisoners in the Bhaugulpore jail, divided into 24 messes with between 12 and 22 members each, and the remainder ate in numbers of 2 or 3 or cooked separately.

As in the composition of messes, the magistrate of Bhaugulpore exercised significant discretion in contouring the jail dietary prescribed by Rule 4 of the messing orders issued by the Nizamat Adalat (dated 9 July 1841). On his own initiative, he added the items of salt, oil, *mussalah* and *julpan* to the prescribed dietary: he felt these items were necessary for the general good health and well-being of the prisoners, and it would be dangerous to deprive them of such 'necessaries'. The 'only change' he had sanctioned was to allow the contractor to supply *urhur dhall* to the Hindu prisoner, and a like quantity of flesh to the Mussulman, in lieu of the prescribed fish (which was impossible to procure at that season of the year. The details of the dietary in force at Bhaugulpore Jail were given as follows:

Jail dietary – 80 *sicca* weight

Sunday – 8 *chittacks* rice, 4 *chittacks julpan*, 4 *chittacks* vegetable, ½ *tola* salt, ½ *tola* oil, 1 *kutcha* tobacco, ½ *seer* wood, ½ *tola mussula*

Monday – 8 *chittacks* rice, 4 *chittacks julpan*, 4 *chittacks* fish or meat, ½ *tola* salt, ½ *tola* oil, 1 *kutcha* tobacco, 1½ *seer* wood, ½ *tola mussula*

Tuesday – 8 *chittacks* rice, 4 *chittacks julpan*, 4 *chittacks* vegetables, ½ *tola* salt, ½ *tola* oil, 1 *kutcha* tobacco, 1½ *seer* wood, ½ *tola mussula*

Wednesday – 10 *chittacks* rice, 4 *chittacks julpan*, 2 *chittacks* dhall, ½ *tola* salt, ½ *tola* oil, 1 *kutcha* tobacco, 1½ *seer* wood, ½ *tola mussula*

Thursday – 8 *chittacks* rice, 4 *chittacks julpan*, 4 *chittacks* fish or meat, ½ *tola* salt, ½ *tola* oil, 1 *kutcha* tobacco, 1½ *seer* wood, ½ *tola mussula*

Friday – 8 *chittacks* rice, 4 *chittacks julpan*, 4 *chittacks* vegetables, ½ *tola* salt, ½ *tola* oil, 1 *kutcha* tobacco, 1½ *seer* wood, ½ *tola mussula*

Saturday – 10 *chittacks* rice, 4 *chittacks julpan*, 2 *chittacks* dhall, ½ *tola* salt, ½ *tola* oil, 1 *kutcha* tobacco, 1½ *seer* wood, ½ *tola mussula*

In exercising such latitude while determining the jail dietary under messing, the magistrate of Bhaugulpore was not an exception. Local officials invariably complained of practical constraints imposed by 'climate, and the habits, feelings, and reasonable prejudices of the people' when following a prescribed dietary (IOR F/4/2150/102999: 88). To give but one other example, of the seventy-three prisoners sentenced to simple imprisonment without labour in the Sylhet jail on 29 July 1842, five had been permitted to cook separately 'on account of their superior caste, and being upcountry men living on attah', and the whole *seer* of rice was not allowed to new convicts (IOR F/4/2150/102999: 91–93). Indeed the absence of a standard diet scale for prisoners was commonly identified as a major hurdle in the implementation of the messing system. As a result, the Medical Board issued a Diet Table dated 17 September 1843, by which an increased scale of rations was adopted, and two cooked meals were allowed daily (Bannerjee 1963: 338–9). In the meantime in the Bhaugulpore jail, copies of the amended dietary in the Hindi and English languages were stuck up at various points for the ready reference of the magistrate, the assistant surgeon and the jail *omlah*. The different conditions comprised in the contract for the daily supply of the prisoners with food were also properly enforced. A laudable attempt was made to correct and even pre-empt any abuse of the messing system.

The magistrate of Bhaugulpore could happily conclude that the messing system had 'very considerable success'. Messing had added to the harshness of the jail sentence and transformed imprisonment into a form of punishment 'much more dreaded by the community'. This was said to be especially true for simple imprisonment without labour, which was otherwise seen as a 'light punishment' (though it did confer some 'moral degradation') by natives who were habituated to taking 'delight in monotonous inactivity'. (In saying so, the magistrate also implicitly identified labour as a significant condition that rendered imprisonment unpalatable to the native population, and therefore added to its punitive and deterrent component.) James argued that prior to messing, the lives of prisoners were replete with material comforts: 'They had a good house over their heads, were supplied with warm blankets, had plenty of companions to converse and smoke with, and amused themselves the greater part of the day by cooking their two meals.' Imprisonment had yielded opportunities for both convivial association and palatable pursuits like cooking, which was, at one and the same time, both 'occupation and luxury'. The magistrate's description of the pleasure that cooking gave to natives and the near-ritualized form it had attained inside jails was lyrical:

> They take pleasure in the sifting and the cleaning of the grain, their eyes sparkle as the wood crackles under their pots, they pride themselves on a savoury and scientific mixture of the salt and the *mussula*, and they glory in the proficiency of their culinary art.

The magistrate of Bhaugulpore was in agreement with most of his contemporaries when he said that messing did add to the 'horrors' of imprisonment.

Where he differed was in arguing that this was not because messing caused injury to caste, but because it deprived prisoners of a dearly culturally valued privilege, hitherto available to them within the jail, and this deprivation rendered imprisonment 'more tedious and irksome'. Therefore, the 'method of having cooked food served out to them' was 'especially disagreeable and hurtful to their taste and feelings'. However, it did not 'infringe(s)' in any way on 'their religious prejudices and doctrines'. The magistrate also differed from most of his counterparts in arguing that the 'people at large' believed that the enhancement of the rigours of imprisonment through the imposition of messing was 'beneficial' because when 'properly conducted', it did not interfere with the 'caste of the inmates'. In other words, Magistrate James re-inscribed messing not as a system that caused injury to caste, or was even primarily about caste, but as one that merely tightened penal conditions within a jail.

Conclusion

Where discussions of caste did take place in relationship to messing, no definitive and universally valid principles could be arrived at. The very axis along which the government was painstakingly trying to order the messes, caste and subcaste was also the site for the subversion of its penal strategy. The organization of everyday socialities on the lines of caste was never a question of doctrine, ancient or otherwise. Practice inscribed caste with meaning and rendered it deeply fluid, contested and above all political – even as the colonial state tried to relegate caste to the realm of the religious. Through such processes a space was produced where the ruled could exercise agency to shape the practices of governance exercised over them by their rulers. Caste within jails was not simply a 'weapon of the weak' used by prisoners to subvert the 'new science of punishment' being imposed by the colonial state (Yang 2004). Caste within jails was itself being constituted through the exercise of colonial power/knowledge, albeit not through a 'simple story of either epistemic domination or of elite collaboration'. Indeed, one can draw on Dirks to argue that British Indian jails were a significant laboratory where the calibration of punishment to caste in penal exercises like the imposition of messing constituted peculiarly colonial (and modern) constructions of caste and led to the rise of the 'ethnographic state' of the nineteenth century (Dirks 2001: 8, 16–17). And yet it is moot whether caste had yet been fully constituted by colonialism as 'the very condition of the Indian social'. What I argue instead, drawing on Henri Lefebvre's work (1991), is that these possibilities were not fully articulated in the company jails of the early 1840s. Messing was about caste, and yet not about caste. In so far as it was about caste, only multiple, polyvalent, conjunctural readings of caste are possible, where it is powerful and also effete, where it stands for one thing and also for another. The ways in which prisoners chose to inhabit messes, the spatial practices of an entire range of actors within jail-scapes, the ways in which messing was 'lived out' gave meaning to system itself. In other words, these distinctive spatial practices produced the space of the jail in the early 1840s.

References

Manuscript

Board's Collections, Volume 102999, BL. IOR F/4/2150.
Board's Collections, Volume 103000, BL. IOR F/4/2150.
Board's Collections, Volume 103001, BL. IOR F/4/2150.
Report of the Prison Discipline Committee. 1838. National Library, Calcutta.

Print

Alam, Muzaffar and Sanjay Subrahmanyam (eds.). 1998. *The Mughal State.* New Delhi: Oxford University Press.

Alavi, Seema. 1995. *The Eighteenth Century in India.* New Delhi: Oxford University Press.

Arnold, David. 2007. 'India, the contested prison', in Frank Dikotter and Ian Brown (eds.), *Cultures of confinement: a history of the prison in Africa, Asia and Latin America*, pp. 147–84. Ithaca, New York: Cornell University Press.

Bannerjee, Tapas Kumar. 1963. *Background to Indian Criminal Law.* Bombay; Calcutta: Orient Longmans.

Bayly, C. A. 1983. *Rulers, Townsmen and Bazaars.* Cambridge: Cambridge University Press.

———. 1996. *Empire and Information: Intelligence Gathering and Social Communication in India, 1780–1870.* Cambridge; New York: Cambridge University Press.

Bayly, Susan. 1999. *Caste, Society and Politics in India from the Eighteenth Century to the Modern Age, The New Cambridge History of India IV.3.* New York: Cambridge University Press.

Cohn, Bernard. 1987. *An Anthropologist among the Historians and Other Essays.* New Delhi: Oxford University Press.

Dirks, Nicholas. 2001. *Castes of Mind: Colonialism and the Making of Modern India.* Princeton, NJ: Princeton University Press.

Fisher, Michael. 1993. *The Politics of British Annexation in India, 1757–1857.* New Delhi; New York: Oxford University Press.

Lefebvre, Henri. 1991. *The Production of Space.* Oxford, UK; Cambridge, MA: Blackwell.

Marshall, P. J. 1976. *East India Fortunes: The British in Bengal in the Eighteenth Century.* Oxford: Clarendon.

———. 1987. *Bengal—the British Bridgehead: Eastern India 1740–182. New Cambridge History of India, II.2.* Cambridge; New York: Cambridge University Press.

Metcalf, Thomas. 1994. *Ideologies of the Raj, New Cambridge History of India, III.4.* Cambridge; New York: Cambridge University Press.

Mouat, F. J. 1862. 'On Prison Statistics and Discipline in Lower Bengal', *Journal of the Statistical Society of London*, 25(2): 175–218.

Sen, Madhurima. 2007. *Prisons in Colonial Bengal, 1838–1919.* Kolkata: Thema.

Singha, Radhika. 1998. *A Despotism of Law: Crime and Justice in Early Colonial India*. New Delhi; New York: Oxford University Press.

Stern, Philip J. 2011. *The Company State: Corporate Sovereignty and the Early Modern Foundations of the British Empire in India*. Oxford: Oxford University Press.

Subrahmanyam, Sanjay, and C. A. Bayly. 1990. 'Portfolio capitalists and the political economy in early modern India', in Sanjay Subrahmanyam (ed.), *Merchants, markets and the state in early modern India*, pp. 242–65. Oxford: Oxford University Press.

Travers, Roberts. 2007. *Ideology and Empire in the Eighteenth Century: The British in Bengal.* New York: Cambridge University Press.

Yang, Anand. 1987. 'Disciplining "Natives": Prisons and Prisoners in early Nineteenth Century India', *South Asia*, 10(2): 29–45.

———. 2004. 'The Lotah Emeutes of 1855: caste, religion and prisons in North India in the Early Nineteenth century', in James H. Mills and Satadru Sen (eds.), *Confronting the body: the politics of physicality in colonial and post-colonial India*, pp. 102–17. London: Anthem Press.

12 A case of multiple existences

The loyal Bombay Purbaiya and his rebellious cousin in Bengal

Sabyasachi Dasgupta

This chapter will consider the divergent religious policies the pre-mutiny Bengal and Bombay armies followed with respect to the native sepoy. It argues that these policies had important consequences for the mutiny. While the native portion of the Bengal army practically disintegrated, the Bombay army held firm despite disturbances in Kolhapur, Karachi, Satara and a few other places. In all, the mutiny affected five out of twenty-nine infantry regiments in the Bombay army (Taylor 1996). This comparison of the Bengal and Bombay armies of the East India Company sheds important light on the mutiny of 1857 and, therefore, the British state's decision to dissolve the East India Company. By the middle of the nineteenth century, when the company's primary function had been managing a vast army, earlier models of Anglo-Indian connection appeared ill-suited to the process of projecting state power. The Bengal army was the primary seed of rebellion against company rule because it was an outmoded collaboration between high-caste Hindus and a company leadership overly subservient to local cultural concerns. The Bombay army, however, remained largely loyal because it was managed like a European army – without Anglo-Indian hybridities that accommodated caste.

One could thus say that the Bombay army remained relatively unaffected, with the bulk of the native soldiers remaining loyal. This was in spite of the presence of a large number of Purbaiya soldiers, who constituted about 30 per cent of the Bombay army. Admittedly they were not in the majority as they were in the Bengal army, whose infantry regiments were marked by the continued predominance of high-caste Purbaiya soldiers. The recruitment policy of the pre-mutiny Bengal army had a pronounced high caste bias; the policymakers of the Bengal army, motivated by beliefs that the high-caste yeoman peasantry or the middle farmer from Awadh and the Bhojpur region of Bihar was brave, honourable and obedient, recruited mainly high-caste men of middle farmer stock from those regions.

This pretty much remained the trend till the mutiny, in spite of challenges to their dominance from the Gurkhas and the Sikhs from the 1830s onwards. The Sikh challenge to Purbaiya domination of the Bengal army infantry regiments sprang up as a consequence of the annexation of Punjab by the British. Nevertheless, Purbaiya domination, albeit on a reduced scale, continued till the fateful events of 1857. To give an example, the Thirty-Fourth Infantry Regiment stationed at Meerut on the eve of 1857 comprised of recruits of whom more than half were upper-caste Purbaiyas.

Recruitment was done through native officers and sepoys who recruited clansmen and neighbours while on furlough to their native places. This had the effect of strongly reinforcing ties of caste, clan and residence. A strong high-caste ethos held the Bengal army in a vice-like grip. Though the recruitment policy of the Bengal army underwent subtle changes over the years, the high caste dominance remained intact until 1857 (Enquiry Committee 1824: 479). A perusal of the role of men of the Thirteenth Regiment, Native Infantry, throws up on a random basis names like Khujan Sing, Sookdeo Sing, Chingun Sing, Madho Singh, Kurm Sing, Hurpaul Misser and Jowahir Sing, with a smattering of Muslim names. Thus, high caste domination of the infantry regiments was a reality till the revolt (Forrest 1893: Appendix 18).

The Purbaiyas were never a majority in the Bombay army, yet they formed a substantial bloc and possessed the potential to play a crucial part in defining the dynamics of the Bombay army. Strangely this powerful bloc remained relatively quiet in the Bombay presidency. They seemed to have no interest in following their rebellious brethren in the Bengal presidency who were spreading havoc across the length and breadth of northern India and central India. Why was it so? Was it because they were foreigners in these parts with no significant local base? Was it because the rumours about the cartridges being sullied with cow and pig fat had lost their zing by the time they travelled to the Bombay presidency? Or did the answer lie in the Bombay army being a much better managed army?

I argue that the answer lay in the contrasting discourses on religion that were in vogue in the two armies. Despite protestations, the Bengal army was as well managed, or ill managed, as the Bombay army. Indeed, if day-to-day disciplinary record of the respective armies were to be the index, the Bengal army had a marginally better record than the Bombay army in the few decades preceding 1857.

The sparing use of the lash in the Bengal army probably reflected this reality. While the high-caste orientation of the Bengal army may have, to some extent, been a determining factor in the lash being sparingly used, the lower incidence of serious crimes (which were officially recorded) among the sepoys of the Bengal army was also a compelling factor behind the sparing use of the lash. If court martials are taken as an index, it seems that in the Bengal army, cases of day-to-day dissent were infrequent, especially when compared to the Madras or Bombay armies, when day-to-day dissent is taken to mean instances where an individual chose to defy authority within everyday practice. Court martial records indicate that day-to-day cases of dissent and murder were rare in the pre-mutiny era and the average was 1.5 cases per year. Compared to that, the average ratio of so-called serious crimes in the Madras and Bombay armies was higher.

Anonymous writers in the *East India United Service Institution Journal* (*EUSIJ*) severely denounced William Bentinck for abolishing flogging. They contradicted the notion that high-caste sepoys felt disgraced on being flogged and ridiculed the idea that flogging had deterred respectable people from entering the service. These writers quoted the duke of Wellington who apparently observed that it was usual practice for the Bengal army to be followed by the relatives of the sepoys and other respectable men on march. In fact, it was always the unpleasant duty of commanding officers or adjutants to turn away respectable men because they did not fulfil some criterion for selection while hundreds of other respectable men in their prime would be taken in.

The impact of the abolition of corporal punishment on the sepoys is difficult to gauge in the absence of independent sepoy voices. If William Sleeman is to be believed, native recruits were happy at the abolition of flogging as they considered flogging a disgrace. However, there were British officers who claimed that native officers had confided that the sepoys had lost all sense of fear after the abolition of corporal punishment. In light of these conflicting voices, court martial records could perhaps be an index of the possible impact of the abolition of corporal punishment on the colonial armies.

Court martial records indicate that the incidence of serious crimes did not increase with the abolition of punishment, nor did cases of day-to-day dissent register any increase with the abolition of corporal punishment in the Indian army. For crimes such as theft, disgraceful conduct and desertion, the average was not beyond that of the preceding decade. For instance, six native soldiers were convicted for mutinous conduct between 1825 and 1833. In 1834 and 1835, only one native soldier was convicted for the same offence. Three native soldiers deserted between 1834 and 1835, whereas the preceding ten years had seen sixteen desertions. The number of convictions for theft during 1834 and 1835 was six, the same rate as that of the years 1834 and 1835. There were, however, eleven instances of murder committed by the sepoys of the Bengal army in 1834 and 1835 in comparison with only ten in the preceding years. Though it is tempting to ascribe the increase in the murder rate to the abolition of corporal punishment in 1834, the fact remains that the average crime rate under the various categories defined by the British in the Bengal army remained low (Hough 1836: 3).

Amiya Barat (1962) argues that the Bengal army failed to address the discontents of the sepoys over declining real wages and the perceived fall in their social prestige. Barat states that slights to the caste sentiments of the sepoys were a recurring cause of disaffection, and dissent often manifested itself over the question of serving overseas and undertaking sea voyages. The lack of status of the Indian commissioned and non-commissioned officers also created problems. Barat affirms that the weaknesses and structural inadequacies of the Bengal army were further compounded by the inability of the colonial authorities to remedy matters. Countless Enquiry Committees set up to enquire into the ills of the Bengal army yielded negligible results. Therefore, according to Barat (1962), 1857 was the logical culmination of long-standing problems within the Bengal army and the inability of the army to address them.

Saul David (2002), like Barat before him, also argues that the Bengal sepoy was discontented over his service conditions. He was concerned with declining wages and allowances, poor housing conditions and the slow rate of promotion. David categorizes the Bengal army as a purely mercenary force commanded by foreign officers. According to him, its loyalty was therefore entirely dependent on the incentives offered to the sepoys. This way, David breaks no new ground since, like Amiya Barat before him, he implies that the mutiny was the inevitable outcome of long-term deterioration in the service conditions of the Bengal army. Though he does not dwell on the various localized mutinies that preceded the mutiny of 1857, it is implicit in his argument that the localized mutinies were a sign of progressive deterioration culminating in the mutiny of 1857. This long-term framework is a tenuous one and is difficult to sustain. Certainly there were some issues affecting the functioning of the company armies, such as the inadequate avenues for, and the slow pace of, the promotion of native soldiers, as well as the transition to a more impersonal mode of command. But the point remains that these were not issues unique to the Bengal armies. Therefore, the framework of long-term decline in the Bengal army culminating in 1857 used by Amiya Barat in the 1960s and Saul David more recently does not hold water.

Votaries of the long-term thesis like Barat and David may yet argue that sepoys in the Bombay and Madras armies were promoted faster. Seniority, if they were to be believed, was only one of the many criteria, and merit was apparently a very important index in determining promotions. These resulted in sepoys enjoying a higher content level in the Bombay and

Madras armies when squared off with the Bengal sepoy. However, this relatively rosy picture for the Bombay and Madras armies gets sullied when we look at the day-to-day records of the Bengal army and also depositions of company officers before the Peel Commission. We find that cases of merit playing an important role in promotions of native recruits in the Bengal army were not rare. While the exact percentage of promotions based on merit overriding seniority is unavailable for the company armies, one needs to revise the erroneous impression of seniority being an ironclad rule determining promotions of native recruits in the Bengal armies (David 2002: 72–73).

The answer therefore must be sought in the contrasting ways the Bengal and Bombay armies dealt with the knotty problem of reconciling the religious sentiments of the high-caste sepoys in both the armies and the sometimes-conflicting demands of military duty. While the Bombay army ensured that religion would not occupy centre stage, religion was central to the ethos of the Bengal army. This, while in no way compromising its quality as a fine and mostly disciplined fighting force, did make Bengal army vulnerable to conflagrations arising out of misunderstandings over religious issues. A perusal of the prevalent discourses in both the armies surrounding religion would further enlighten us.

Very strongly held notions regarding the attachment of the native soldier towards his religious beliefs moulded the company's policy in the Bengal presidency and initially in the Madras armies. It was held that the Oriental was extremely sensitive about issues involving religious customs and sentiments. Colonel Pennington, deposing before the select committee in 1831–1832, had this to say

> Treated kindly one might rest assured of their devoted attachment, but one must not interfere in their religion or in their prejudices regarding caste. Any wrong done to them on these points could not be atoned for by apologies or expressions of regret.
>
> (Select Committee 1831: 11.735v)

Colonial officials were indeed paranoid about treading on the religious sentiments of Indian soldiers. We get an early glimpse of this paranoia by looking into the kind of discourse generated by the Vellore mutiny. In the post-Vellore mutiny phase, a sort of consensus developed that the sepoy's religious sentiments had been hurt and he had to reason to feel aggrieved. In the words of the commander-in-chief of the Madras army:

> Craddock and Bentinck the then governor of Madras Presidency represented a school of view that was firmly convinced of the immutability

> of caste and religious sentiments in general among Indian soldiers of the Madras army. Craddock further commented that while opposition to military and just authority could not be tolerated in a European soldier, exceptions had to made with regard to the Indian soldier. But upon the principles of India, the force of caste, which in its various shape, no European may perfectly comprehend, it is allowable even in a soldiers mind to pause and solicit the advice of the head and his companions in the government.
>
> (Craddock 1806: 8)

Bentinck concurred with Craddock in the belief that the sepoys had genuine reasons to feel that their religious sentiments had been trifled with. Guided by colonial stereotypes regarding the immutability of caste and religious sentiments, in general, Bentinck rescinded the order prohibiting the wearing of caste marks, whiskers and so forth while on parade. However, the rhetoric of caste retained its dominant place in colonial discourse, particularly in the case of the Bengal army. As mentioned earlier, the Bengal army infantry units were of predominantly high-caste Hindus and remained so till 1857. Convinced of the immutability of caste sentiments among high-caste soldiers, the Bengal army followed a policy of placating the caste sentiments of the high-caste sepoys. Until 1856, barring some select regiments, overseas service was voluntary, since high-caste Hindus had inhibitions serving overseas. In 1852, for example overseas service was voluntary for all but six corps of the Bengal army. The Bengal army also recommended special dietary preferences for the high-caste sepoy (Alavi 1991: 74).

This predilection for high-caste soldiers was occasionally tested by disturbances such as the Barrackpore mutiny. Such occurrences prompted an inevitable soul searching on the part of the colonial authorities, though such exercises invariably ended in the status quo remaining fundamentally unaltered. High-caste domination of the infantry regiments was a home truth as far as the Bengal army was concerned. For example, the enquiry committee set up to investigate the Barrackpore mutiny in 1824 commented that the Bengal army had been always predominated by high-caste Hindus. Though the commanding officers made efforts to include low-caste soldiers, the report affirmed that experience had proved that the higher the caste, the better and more respectable the sepoy. This obsession with high-caste soldiers overrode the frustration felt by the colonial state over the multiple challenges high-caste sentiments, practices and ceremonies posed to routine military duties and tasks. As the report commented

> But the nature and character of Hindooism with all its prejudices, forms and ceremonies prove great drawbacks to military efficiency as

> grounded on the European model to which every attempt to fashion him must ever be impolitic and unsuccessful for much time is given up to the routine of religious forms and the very preparation of their daily food is . . . thousand trivial religious formalities from which the European soldier is exempted.
>
> (Enquiry Committee 1824: 479)

While unease about reconciling the religious sentiments of its high-caste soldiers and the needs of military duty as modelled on European notions of discipline is apparent, it was also implicitly conceded that there might be multiple models of military efficiency and there were no universal criteria for judging military discipline and performance. While a high-caste-dominated Bengal army might not pass the test by European standards of military efficiency, the colonial policymakers felt that it could be moulded into a fine army, the rigidity of the soldiers' caste and religious beliefs notwithstanding. The secret lay in not rocking the boat when it came to the question of the religious beliefs of the high-caste soldiers.

However, colonial discourses regarding caste were by no means homogenous. There were different voices that did not believe in the immutability of caste and religious sentiments, particularly in the case of the Bombay army (Peel Committee Report 1859: Appendix 22). In spite of the presence of high-caste men in large numbers, caste sentiments and customs were not allowed to interfere with military duties, and the Bombay sepoy could not refuse to perform any military duty by reason of contravention of his caste beliefs. To cite an instance, all Bombay army regiments were required to go on overseas service and refusal could be construed as disobedience. In the words of Lieutenant Sir W. Collins: 'They have their castes but they never interfere in any way in the army.'

Colonial officials like Martin Gubbins were very appreciative of the ethos of the Bombay army, particularly in the wake of the mutiny of 1857, which was marked by the overwhelming participation of high-caste sepoys of the Bengal army. Gubbins renders an interesting account of his conversation with a retired Bombay army Subedar hailing from Oudh. Reminiscing about his service in the Bombay army, the Subedar said:

> I stood side by side with men of low caste and who dared there say a word? Maratha, Parsee, Brahmin, Chamar, Rajput and many others are there found in the same ranks. But they are all one.
>
> (Gubbins 1894: 103)

Gubbins also mentions an instance of a Bombay army sepoy from Oudh cooking on board ship with his leather belt on. This was supposedly in contravention of his caste beliefs. When questioned about his disregard for his caste rules, the man replied: 'Moolk ka dustoor hai' (Gubbins 1894: 103). These exchanges, if true, perhaps point to the fact that the rigidity of caste sentiments was often not an individual choice but the product of broader social circumstances. The Bombay army had successfully created a milieu where the display of caste rigidity by its high-caste Purbaiya recruits in the public sphere was considered out of tune with the general ethos of the Bombay army. It was quite possibly deemed pragmatic to be viewed as relaxed in issues pertaining to caste.

This is not to say that the Purbaiya soldiers in the Bombay army always concurred readily with the official policy of disregarding their religious sentiments if these were in opposition to the performance of necessary military duties as construed by the colonial state. There were occasions when the Purbaiya soldier sought to evade duties that would necessitate close interaction with low-caste soldiers. Such tendencies were severely criticized by officials of the Bombay school. John Malcolm, for one, was scathing in his criticism of the Hindustani soldiers. He said that while every attention was paid to their religious sentiments, the Hindustani soldiers were occasionally reluctant to perform guard duty with low-caste soldiers and would request their European officers to place them in such a way that they do not have to serve with low-caste soldiers. Malcolm was of the opinion that these soldiers should be told that it was a soldier's responsibility to perform the duties assigned to him or otherwise he could leave the service (Malcolm 1824).

As a consequence of this disregard for caste sentiments in the Bombay army, Bombay army officers often found the preoccupation of the Bengal army with caste strange. Jacobs, a Bombay army officer, was vehement in his denunciation of the Bengal army. According to Jacobs, in the Bombay army,

> The feeble Hindoo became half European and adopted the feelings and ideas of Europeans, as far as his position as a soldier was concerned. In Bengal, on the contrary, the European became half Hindoo and consequently the European officer lost the advantage of superior energy and high moral character.
>
> (Lambrick 1960: 210)

Jacob castigates the European officers of the Bengal army for their excessive regard for the caste beliefs of the sepoys. Consequently the sepoys, instead of looking up to the European officers as superior beings, regarded them as bad Hindus. Jacobs opines that the sepoys believed that their power and value were to be best exhibited by refusing to obey any orders, which they considered inimical to their religious prejudices (Lambrick 1960: 210).

Thus, colonial attitudes to caste and religion were by no means uniform. While caste or religious sentiments were valued in the Bengal and Madras Presidencies, the Bombay army chose to disregard it. The Madras army, after the mutiny at Vellore, chose to get around the problem by recognizing caste and religious sentiments on one hand and changing the recruitment pattern after an initial bias for high castes on the other hand. In the Bengal army, though, recognition of caste sentiments was a sacred policy.

Much of colonial cultural knowledge was based on results and on-field experience. For instance, after an initial dependence on a strong officer–sepoy relationship, the company thought that a very strong officer with arbitrary powers over the sepoy could prove to be counterproductive. Instead of inspiring loyalty on the part of the sepoy, it could provoke open violence. For the company, what mattered in the end was its safe and secure hold over the sepoys and the army, for that was the ultimate guarantee of power in India.

Colonial cultural concepts could be varied, as the differently nuanced policy in the three presidencies showed. Again, the durability or modification of cultural concepts was dictated by results on the ground. For example, the Madras army altered its policy on handling native religious practices and reconciling them with army duties after the Vellore mutiny. It now followed a mean path between the Bengal and Bombay armies. As far as the Bombay and Bengal armies were concerned, they followed diametrically opposite policies in dealing with the religious sensibilities of Indian soldiers. Both the armies had excellent track records. The Bengal army, in spite of occasional problems regarding overseas service, performed excellently on the battleground and won numerous battles for the company. As a result the Bengal army, despite strident criticism of its religious policy, continued pandering to the religious sensibilities of its high-caste recruits. The edifice, however, totally crumbled in 1857, something that the policy-makers of the Bengal army had never visualized.

References

Manuscript

James Craddock. Minute by the Commander-In-Chief: 1806. NAI Foreign (Secret).

John Malcolm. Minute on the Army: 1824. IOR.

Peel Committee Report: 1859. NAI.

Report of the Enquiry Committee of the Barrackpore Mutiny: 1824. NAI Military (Misc.), vol. 11.

Select Committee For Indian Affairs: various years beginning 1831. Teen Murti Library, New Delhi.

Print

Alavi, Seema. 1991. *Sepoys and the Company.* New Delhi: Oxford University Press.

Barat, Amiya. 1962. *Bengal Native Infantry: Its Organisation and Discipline, 1796–1853.* Calcutta: Firma K. L. Mukhopadhyay.

David, Saul. 2002. *The Indian Mutiny, 1857.* London: Penguin.

Forrest, G. W. (ed.) 1893, repr. 2000. *Selections from the Letters, Dispatches and Other State Papers Preserved in the Military Department of the Government of India, 1857–58: vol. 1.* Calcutta: Government Press.

Gubbins, Martin. 1894. *An Account of the Mutinies in Oudh.* London: Richard Bentley.

Hough, William. 1836. *Simplification of Her Majesty and the Honourable East India Company's Mutiny Acts and Articles of War.* Calcutta.

Lambrick, H. T. 1960. *John Jacob of Jacobabad.* London: Cassell.

Taylor, P. J. O. (ed.) 1996. *A Companion to the Indian Mutiny of 1857.* New Delhi: Oxford University Press.

Index